*J*ustice
Not Greed

Edited by Pamela Brubaker and
Rogate Mshana

WCC Publications, Geneva

Published by WCC Publications
PO Box 2100
CH-1211 Geneva 2
Switzerland

oikoumene.org

ISBN 978-2-8254-1548-1

Unless otherwise noted, the Scripture quotations contained herein are from the New Revised Standard Version Bible, copyright ©1989 by the Division of Christian Education of the National Council of the churches of Christ in the U.S.A., and are used by permission. All rights reserved.

Printed in France.

TABLE OF CONTENTS

INTRODUCTION

Dr Rogate R. Mshana,
WCC Director, Justice, Diakonia and Responsibility for Creation

This book is made up of a collection of 14 papers produced by the members of the World Council of Churches' (WCC) Advisory Group on Economic Matters (AGEM), which was reconvened in 2009. The first time such a group was established was in 1979, within the framework of the WCC Commission for Churches Participation in Development (CCPD). It was set up to advise the WCC and its member churches on the global economic issues that affect people and communities around the world. One of the burning issues then was an international financial system that created debt burdens and crises around the world. In 1984, the AGEM produced a document entitled, "The International Financial System: An Ecumenical Critique". As mentioned by Rev. Dr Samuel Kobia[1] in his address to the AGEM09, the world has experienced more than eight major financial crises since 1979, but the current one is comparable to 1929's Great Depression.

The new AGEM09 – which sits within the WCC's Poverty, Wealth and Ecology Project in the context of the Alternative Globalization Addressing People and Earth (AGAPE) process – was called to provide advice to the WCC and its member churches about the way out of the current financial and other related global economic and ecological crises. The concrete results of the meeting include this book and a statement on Just Finance and the Economy of Life, issued by the WCC Central Committee in September 2009 and attached at the end of the book.

The aim of publishing this book is to encourage individuals, students, churches, the wider ecumenical family, secular and non-secular institutions, civil society movements and even other communities of faith to analyze, reflect and act on finding solutions to the current financial and economic systems that have failed to address adequately inequality, poverty and ecological destruction and instead have aggravated these problems.

The views represented in this book are those of the authors, except for the WCC statement on Just Finance and Economy of Life, which calls upon churches, governments and international institutions to respond justly and sustainably to this crisis that has caused suffering for many people, particularly those who are already living in poverty.

---

[1] WCC General Secretary, 2004-2009.

Addressing the global moral and ethical crisis

The main issue emerging from the various papers authored by theologians, ethicists, sociologists and economists composing the AGEM09 attests to the fact that humanity is facing a global moral and ethical crisis to which churches and other faith communities and civil society groups must respond. This moral and ethical crisis has long been the forerunner of the various crises – economic, political and ecological – that continue to ravage the world today. This focus does not, however, rule out nuanced causes of the economic turmoil related to failure of individual countries' systems of accountability.

Why should churches address this problem?

God's mission is to bring good news to the poor and fullness of life to all people and creation. However, the world has embarked on a system – the global economy – that utterly fails to do so. On the contrary, it is hinged on greed instead of on need, and excludes the majority of people while destroying sources of sustenance. Some churches have lost their assets in the current crisis and many people have been deprived of their homes, life savings and livelihoods.

> From the ecumenical movement's perspective, there is no system which cannot be altered, no policy which cannot be changed, no economic system which cannot be reformed or which should be so sacred that it should not be changed if it proved to be unable to adjust to the demands of the poor for justice.[2]

The current system remains hugely unjust and it is imperative for churches to address this problem in the context of God's mission.

Is this book outdated?

The papers in this book were written in 2009, when the crisis was at its most severe. Since then, the world has moved on, but despite the introduction of "stimulus packages" in more than 59 countries amounting to almost 3 trillion US dollars, economic recovery in 2010 is still fragile. It is widely lamented that the crisis was not used as an opportunity for radical change. Dependant on a continued supportive policy stance worldwide, a mild global growth of 2.4 percent is forecast for 2010.[3] But more alarmingly, progress towards the reduction of poverty has slowed considerably. Unemployment rates continue to rise. Particularly poorer countries, but also Portugal, Italy, Ireland, Greece and Spain, are languishing under heavy debts.

---

[2] AGEM, 1984.
[3] See Economic Situation and Prospects 2010, UN, New York.

The problem is that, to date, world leaders have failed both to deal with the root causes of the crisis and to introduce radical changes through the UN, which remains the most democratic forum for the discussion of reforms to international financial architecture. The issues raised in this book remain relevant. This collection provides new material that can be used by churches to reflect on the current crisis and make choices befitting their calling.

The order of papers

These papers were presented at five panels organized during AGEM09 and were followed by intensive exchanges. The first panel raised ethical problems with the present global financial system. The second panel outlined the root causes of the current crisis and the third presented the connection between finance and the real economy. The fourth panel raised possible ethical guidelines for the ecumenical movement while the fifth touched on the role the ecumenical movement could take in advocating proposed ethical principles. Though the AGEM09 discussions were structured in this way, it can be observed that authors were at liberty to write what they each considered important. Subsequently, overlaps are evident as one reads through the various papers.

Contributing authors

Jan Pronk, former minister of environment in the Netherlands and moderator of AGEM09, presented a keynote paper on the "Defaults of Globalization" to set the context of the discussions. In it he sketches a critical historical picture of the genesis of the current global economic, social and political problems, and calls for a "new deal" to construct a "more equitable, more developmental, less lopsided, more universal, more oriented towards social and environmental needs rather than facilitating financial and economic interests" global system.

Pamela K. Brubaker weaves a theo-ethical framework for assessing ethical deficiencies and responding to injustices in her chapter, entitled, "From Apocalypse to Jubilee: Theological Perspectives on Ethical Deficits in the Current Global Financial System". She describes how chronic problems of inequality and poverty have worsened in the wake of the crisis. Towards building alternatives, she concludes with reflections on a Jubilee perspective for just finance.

Musa Filibus examines the ethical deficits of the present global economy from a biblical perspective. He finds that the crisis is a manifestation of moral deficiencies that requires the transformation of hearts and minds, alongside economic transformation to ensure justice for all. He bases his analysis on the premise that economy is a matter of faith, and comes up with proposals for ecumenical principles to help transform the global economic system.

Metropolitan Geevarghes Mor Coorilos raises the fundamental question, "How do/should Christian churches respond to this crisis as a faith-driven community?" He looks at ecumenical and ethical guidelines that could facilitate ongoing attempts to deal with the present global predicament.

Thomas H. Kang opines that in facing the current crisis, churches have not spoken much on an issue they consider to be technical and esoteric. He notes however that the WCC has proposed people-centred development, which has also been emulated by the UN Development Program (UNDP). His chapter, "Christian Ethics, Development and Economic Crisis: An Ecumenical Perspective" deals with suggested ethical guidelines for the ecumenical movement's use in dealing with economic matters.

John Dillon examines two root causes of the current financial crisis, beginning with excessive speculation in the US housing and financial markets. He also links the crisis to global imbalance and the absence of a cooperative international financial order. He discusses how viable proposals for a new international financial system have emerged from the crisis. Implicit in his solution is civil society groups' proposal to end the fundamentalist belief in unfettered markets.

Marie-Aimée Tourres studies the impact of the crisis on the developing world and the proposed global solutions. She also enlightens readers about the disconnection between real and virtual money. She examines the tendency for increasing protectionism and raises the issue of global governance, pointing out that the democratic UN is seriously considered secondary to institutions such as the IMF.

Marcos Arruda introduces the concept of de-growth for the global North and planned growth within the limits of nature and forthcoming generations for the global South. He presents the case for new indicators to measure and plan economic progress by using a gross national happiness (GNH) index. He feels this could be the beginning of a sustainable system that would avoid profiting without producing. He proposes an economy of world solidarity where finance serves the actual economy, rather than having a life of its own.

Xiao Lian focuses on the world financial crisis and the challenges and opportunities for China. Xiao begins with the US sub-prime mortgage crisis and its impact on China. He underscores that unless we deal with the internal conditions of capitalism and with deregulated financial markets, and unless we establish a new financial architecture, not only will we fail to handle the current financial crisis, but we will be unable to avoid its recurrence.

Alexander Cobham describes the economic crisis as a "blood-stained silver lining"; blood-stained because of the unnecessary deaths and undetermined lives of so many women, men and children, but a silver lining because of the rare moment of opportunity it presents. He points out that only a global social movement can build the pressure for change to ultimately deliver the eradication of poverty, social exclusion and economic marginalization. The WCC can play an important role in building and supporting such a movement.

Roel Aalbersberg begins his paper with a narrative, set in rural South India, of an economy based on a different set of values to those that dominate the global financial system. He points at the gap between virtual finance and the real economy. His chapter, "Lift your Lamp above the Bushel" calls on the ecumenical movement to look ahead at this time of the crisis and beyond. "Whatever we try to create in terms of international rules for finance, economy or trade, a guiding principle must be, how does it affect – or better, how does it do justice – to the poor, the widow and the stranger? This is the lamp we are called upon to lift above the bushel."

Mariana Issa Zureikat, another youth economist, approaches the crisis by addressing the dilemma of youth and the need for moral values in consumerism. She analyzes the role of materialism, which led to the financial crisis, and the role the WCC can play in addressing the situation. She examines the flaws of capitalism and proposes the need to introduce the concept of "economorals" – the attempt to understand, develop and apply moral values to the study and elucidation of economic principles. "The purpose of economorals would be to give moral content to economic theories," she concludes.

Kim Yong-Bock, in his chapter entitled "Theological Reflection on the Economic Crisis", calls for a radical questioning of the economic system beyond mere policy adjustments, because people's suffering has reached the stage of ultimate crisis. There is need to deal with the deeper theological problems posed by the myopic and destructive dominant policies and systems. According to him, it is not a matter of normalizing the system, but a matter of life and death requiring deep-seated transformation towards a life-giving economy.

Rienzie Pereira writes on the role of the ecumenical movement in advocating ethical principles. He cautions, however, that although we are quick to blame the "other", be it capitalism or the G20 nations, we cannot escape from the guilt of benefiting from a system that has condemned millions to perish. According to him, "we" refers to the institutionalized religions, Christianity or other, which enjoy the patronage of the principalities and powers. He advocates for a new commitment for change.

Acknowledgments

These authors raise many challenging issues and diverse proposals which could be further reflected upon by churches and the worldwide ecumenical family, including theological colleges. If the issue of reclaiming an economic system that embraces morals, ethics and justice is part of the mission of the ecumenical movement then the authors have certainly provided it with food for thought. The WCC Programme for Justice, Diakonia and Responsibility for Creation will be delighted to receive any feedback on the book.

Sincere thanks go to all the authors listed below, who actively participated in the AGEM09 meeting and contributed their time and knowledge to prepare chapters for this book. The successful moderation of the AGEM09 can be traced to the long experience of Mr Jan Pronk, to whom we are grateful for his readiness and expertise. Special thanks go to Professor Pamela Brubaker, who read and edited the bulk of the papers. We would also like to mention Theodore Gill, who edited the English grammar of some of the papers, and Athena Peralta, WCC consultant on Poverty, Wealth and Ecology, who commented on one of the chapters. This book could not have been published without the assistance of the WCC's Director of Communications, Mark Beach.

Finally, without the financing of AGEM09 by ICCO and Kerk in Actie and Bread for the World during the financial crisis at a time when the WCC was unable to do so, this event would not have been taken place, in which case the WCC could hardly have produced a statement on Just Finance and the Economy of Life. We are thankful for the grant given.

The AGEM09 authors

Mr Jan Pronk, Moderator, AGEM 09.
Prof. Pamela K. Brubaker, California Lutheran University, USA.
Rev. Dr Musa Filibus, Africa Secretary, The Lutheran World Federation, Switzerland.
Metropolitan Geevarghese Mor Coorilos, Syrian Orthodox Church, India; and Moderator, Commission on World Mission and Evangelism (CWME) of the WCC.
Mr Thomas H. Kang, M.A in Economics, University of São Paulo, Brazil.
Mr John Dillon, Program Coordinator, Global Economic Justice, KAIROS Canadian Ecumenical Justice Initiatives.
Dr Marie-Aimée Tourres, Director, Manchester Business School, Sunway University, Malaysia; and Associate Lecturer, CERDI, France.
Dr Marcos Arruda, Director, Institute of Alternative Policies for Southern Cone of Latin America (PACS), Brazil; Member, Jubilee Coordination Committee of the Alliance for

Responsible Plural Solidarity Economy (ALOE); and Fellow, Transnational Institute, the Netherlands.

Prof. Xiao Lian, Director, Centre for American Economic Studies, Institute of World Economics, Chinese Academy of Social Sciences (CASS).

Mr Alexander Cobham, Chief Policy Adviser, Christian Aid, Christian Aid, London,UK.

Mr Roel Aalbersberg, Coordinator, Worldwide Relations desk, ICCO, the Netherlands.

Ms. Mariana Issa Zureikat, B.A. International banking & finance and International Management, Jordan.

Prof. Kim Yong-Bock, Advanced Institute for Integral Study of Life, South Korea.

Rev. Dr Rienzie Perera, Deputy Secretary General, Christian Conference of Asia, Thailand.

Dr Rogate R. Mshana, WCC Director for Justice, Peace and Creation.

ADDRESSING THE GLOBAL FINANCIAL CRISIS:
THE RATIONALE AND THE ROLE OF THE ADVISORY GROUP
ON ECONOMIC MATTERS 2009

Rev. Dr Samuel Kobia,
General Secretary (2004-2009), World Council of Churches

I would like to take this opportunity to extend my sincere gratitude to each member of the Advisory Group on Economic Matters (AGEM). Such a group was first established in 1979 within the framework of the then WCC Commission for Churches Participation in Development (CCPD). The moderator of that first AGEM was Mr Jan Pronk. The then AGEM had organized a series of reflections on various issues of political and economic importance.

One of its four reports was on "The International Financial System: An Ecumenical Critique" which was published in 1984. Since then the world has experienced more than eight financial crises, but the current one is close to the Great Depression of 1930. We therefore felt the need to call for this new AGEM to advise us on how to prepare the churches and the ecumenical movement for their response. I quote from the critique of the international financial system by the 1984 AGEM, which had stated as its principle that,

> [I]t is not the task of the churches to prescribe technical solutions to the world's problems. They wish simply to point at ethically unacceptable consequences of decisions which are made in the world's institutions, leaving it to those institutions to define alternative policies which would not have such consequences. Yet this is all too often *not sufficient*, when advocates of prevailing ideological views on the world's debates all contend that their own particular prescription is the only one possible and that humankind and the poor themselves are those who must adapt to the iron hand of predetermined unquestionable "economic laws".Then the churches must look in more detail into the problems which they have discovered and inform themselves of what is at stake. Then they may insist that technical solutions not only must, but can be found. From the ecumenical movement's perspective there is no system which cannot be altered, no policy which cannot be changed, no economic system which cannot be reformed - or which would be so sacred that it should not be changed, if it proved to be unable to adjust to the demands of the poor for justice.[1]

---

[1] See "Advisory Group on Economic Matters, Reginal Green, ed., WCC/CCPD, The International Financial System: An Ecumenical Critique," WCC 1984.

The working principle for AGEM

The present situation challenges the WCC to analyze the current financial system and to prepare a proposal that would lead to a new global financial architecture embracing ethics and justice. I hope we will work on the basis of the principle already outlined in 1984, which highlights that the ethical perspective of the churches is part of their unique contribution to the world of economics. Christian ethics, from an ecumenical perspective, has stressed social justice as a core component of the Christian message. The God of the Bible is a god of justice, who especially cares for and defends the rights of the most vulnerable, the excluded, and the poor. As we can read in the beginning of the book Isaiah, "learn to do good; seek justice, rescue the oppressed, defend the orphan, plead for the widow" (Is. 1:17). In many biblical texts the triad "widows, orphans and strangers" refers to the poor, the excluded from the society and the most vulnerable who are especially loved by God. "The Lord loves the righteous. The Lord watches over the strangers; he upholds the orphan and the widoe, but the way of the wicked he brings to ruin" (Ps. 146: 8c-9).

Justice is the biblical principle that governs our relationships with creation. To stand for the earth and the people of the earth demands the ability to confront the powerful – as the prophets of the Bible did. Jesus stood in this tradition and challenged his disciples not to shy away from this responsibility. So he calls us to do the same today. The AGEM principle underlines the fundamental biblical and theological understandings of the poor and of justice. It also captures the challenge to the church today – not to retreat from its prophetic role.

The problem of the current financial system

The World Council of Churches and the ecumenical family at large are deeply concerned about the current global financial crisis, which has continued to throw many people into unemployment and poverty. On 15 November 2008 and 2 February 2009, the leaders of 20 nations and the major multilateral financial institutions gathered together in Washington, DC, and London respectively to discuss the future of the global economy. This group included representatives of governments and institutions whose policies are responsible for the current financial meltdown.

The WCC expressed its concern about the effectiveness of a meeting limited to only a few countries. My letter to the chair of the G20 outlined proposals that included calling for the restructuring of the whole financial system by creating a new one under the auspices of the UN. I underlined that what is actually needed today is a new financial architecture in the 21st

century which would include the input of many more voices. Gordon Brown, the chairman of the G20, responded to my letter citing resolutions that referred to our proposals such as the one addressing the problem of tax havens. It was evident that social justice, equity and ethics did not find a place in the G20 statement. This means that a new financial architecture was not fully addressed, since the G20 still makes small adjustments to existing financial systems, which have clearly proved to be the problem.

The crises that accentuated the current global financial system – debt crisis, sub-prime mortgage crisis, currency crisis, banking crisis and capital market crisis – have been particularly severe in industrialized countries, while its effect is spreading rapidly to developing countries. We are witnessing falling commodity prices, the reduction of migrant remittances to home countries and contraction of credits, particularly for small producers. Direct financial investment to developing countries is also on the decline.

This multi-faceted and complex problem has resulted in a variety of inconclusive debates on how best to bring about international financial reform. When such a crisis hit developing countries in the past, such as the Mexican crisis of 1994-1995 or the East Asian crisis beginning in 1997, or when poor countries suffer under debt burdens, industrialized countries continued to define austerity measures as a panacea for poor countries instead of addressing the failure of the whole financial system. Austerity measures for the developing world may have made sense to them when the industrial countries were stable and prosperous. The time has now come to seriously address these problems and to see them as temporary measures that neither help the developed world nor redeem already-struggling developing economies.

Economists differ regarding the causes of the present crisis. However, it is a fact that history is punctuated by financial crises from time to time, while the evolution of the international regulatory framework has not kept pace with the globalization of financial markets. In other words, the security of industrial countries should neither deter efforts for drawing up a global regulatory framework nor give the impression that industrialized countries will regain their prosperity and be secure if merely cosmetic short-term reforms are made while global financial inequality is ignored and left to be solved by markets alone.

Not enough has been done by the financial institutions dealing with financial volatility to reframe guidelines for a just and stable system for all countries and peoples. The WCC calls for a new financial architecture to qualitatively regulate huge and uneven growth. To achieve this change, a solid process that takes on board all global actors and civil society is imperative. Civil society groups and many governments have called for a process much more inclusive of all nations and peoples. Could the United Nations be the forum to design a just global financial and economic system?

The G20 solution is insufficient

The G20 has continued to insist on free markets as the answer. This is a dangerous ideology with regard to financial regulation. Their viewpoint is based on outmoded and discredited ideas.[2] Moreover, the existing financial regulatory institutions, like the Basel Committee on Banking Supervision and the Financial Stability Forum have very limited membership, and cannot issue binding standards and rules. They are heavily influenced by the financial lobby and have proven totally inadequate, both in predicting financial crises and in acting to stem them.

The need for a new international financial architecture under UN auspices

The global financial meltdown – with the U.S economy at its epicentre – has effectively debunked the neoliberal economic myth that deregulated financial markets are "efficient". The 2005 WCC background document, "Alternative Globalization Addressing People and Earth" observed that,

> [n]o international financial institution … is able or willing to control the 1.9 trillion US dollars worth of currencies that are traded everyday. Financial speculation dominates trade in goods and services, diverting resources from long-term productive investments and areas of greatest need. Financial markets are also increasingly unstable, with speculative bubbles and financial crises.

The problems of external debt and capital flight as well as the recent bailout of troubled banks and insurance mainly in institutions in the US and Europe (at 40 times the amount needed to eradicate poverty around the world), makes clear that the international financial system we have today is one that is based on injustice: it is a system wherein the global poor are essentially subsidizing the rich.

According to the UN secretary general, this crisis is threatening the achievement of the millennium development goals, which call for 16 billion US dollars to be set aside for their success. Efforts to avert climate change, mitigation and adaptation measures in poor countries and financing for development are now in danger due to reduced financial flows

---

[2] The press release is available at http://www.londonsummit.gov.uk/en/summit-aims/summit-communique/.

into these sectors. The crisis also imperils existing international pledges of financial support for the food crisis. It is therefore apparent that nothing less than a paradigm shift is needed, and must take place within the framework of the UN, including all countries, civil society and faith-based communities.

Issues for the AGEM09

The AGEM09 was convened by the WCC to look into the following issues:

- How can the churches and church organizations in cooperation with the civil society and religious communities contribute to a new system in which justice can be central in all global financial transactions?
- How can such a system contain ethical principles to deter the abuse of financial systems at the cost of the world's poor?
- How can such a system be linked to the real economy instead of generating bubbles?
- How can the churches play a more active role in calling governments and financial institutions to account for the present debacle?

The AGEM was structured in the form of panels to deal with the following issues:

- Raising ethical deficits of the present global financial system.
- Raising the root causes of the current crisis.
- Connecting finance to real economy.
- Raising possible ecumenical ethical guidelines.
- Stating the role the ecumenical movement could take in advocating for the proposed ethical principles.
- Drafting a statement on the financial crisis for the central committee.

Terms of reference

The AGEM09 had the following terms of reference:

- To discern what is at stake in the current financial architecture.
- To propose a process that could lead to a new financial architecture.
- To outline the theological and ethical basis for such a new architecture.

The AGEM09 gathered information and put in places strategies to be shared with the churches and the ecumenical movement, to promote a better understanding of the root causes of the present crisis and the way out, based on ethical principles and on social justice. Our proposed answers are what follows.

ADDRESSING THE DEFAULTS OF GLOBALIZATION

Jan Pronk

I was born just before the beginning of World War II. It was the final stage in a period of globalization characterized by catastrophes: two world wars, mass genocide, fascism, communist dictatorship, a world economic crisis and the colonization of nearly half of the world.

Globalization is not a new or recent phenomenon. Globalization started right at the beginning of the history of mankind, as soon as people began to communicate and trade with each other, to visit places beyond the horizons of their own livelihoods and to migrate to areas that promised better chances for survival and economic progress. So globalization is eternal, despite developing new dimensions in the first half of the twentieth century.

The previous century

There had been many wars in Europe before, but never before had wars starting in Europe spread throughout the world. There had been genocide before, but the scale of the Holocaust made it a catastrophe, shaking the very foundations of human civilization. For centuries, nations had been ruled by violent authoritarian regimes oppressing the people. However, populist movements and notions of freedom and democracy had gradually developed into countervailing forces, suppressing the powers of the rulers and elites who were serving their own interests while disregarding those of the weaker and poorer. However, the rise of communist, fascist and Nazi ideologies resulted in regimes with absolute power and ruthlessness towards their subjects. Together these regimes dominated an unprecedentedly large part of the world's population. This resulted in millions and millions of victims.

There had been economic crises before. However, the world economic crisis of the 1930s was unique. The crisis, which began in the financial system of an economically advanced country, spread from there to many other sectors of the world economy and resulted in economic hardship everywhere.

Colonization had given a decisive shape to globalization. Colonization was not a new phenomenon, but in the first half of the twentieth century a relatively small number of Western countries, together comprising a relatively small part of the world's population, had brought under supervision a larger part of the other continents than ever before.

This is my reading of the first half of the previous century. Of course there were also other developments: scientific and technological findings, breakthroughs in communication, cultural renewal, all of which meant progress. However, these developments mainly emanated from the West, the centre of globalization, and resulted in Western countries taking a stronger hold on the then-periphery of the world economy and polity. They even facilitated the spread of the catastrophic breakdowns, which also started in the West, to the rest of the world.

A new world order

All this changed after the end of the Second World War. A new international order was created on the basis of a new value system and principles of international law. Such principles had been studied and proposed before, but they never had been generally accepted and applied by all countries. From 1945 onwards, a body of rules of international law prevailed, based on consensus and as a result of international talks. The international body the United Nations was created as the embodiment of international law. International law itself became the embodiment of globally shared values.

Sovereignty of the nation-state was one of those shared values. This was new, a revolution in international power systems. In the centuries before, a country with economic, political or military power could easily invade or oppress the people in another country. There was no institution or legal principle to stop any individual nation from overwhelming another. This was brought to an end after 1945. For the first time in world history the principle of sovereignty of the nation-state was generally accepted, together with institutions – international law, the UN Charter with its chapters on peacekeeping, the UN Security Council and its rules and procedures – that could oversee its implementation. These institutions were not strong by themselves, but their strength was enhanced by the fact that the country with the largest surplus of power in the world was willing to protect the new system. The United States of America, the main victor of the Second World War, was willing to share its power with other countries to render authority to the new institutions. That was new. Without that willingness the world would never have seen a new international order emerging with any degree of sustainability.

The new order was based on generally accepted principles beyond the sovereignty of the nation-state. Amongst those were the well-known tenets of human rights. But the new concept of the development of nations and their people was a value in itself, as was the principle of cooperation. These values implied some sort of common commitment to live up to such principles and to meet objectives based upon them. The same applied to ideals such as international monetary stability and free trade, and that of preferential treatment for weak countries and infant economies. As a matter of fact, during the decades following its establishment, the United Nations has become the main global platform for discussion and agreement on new concepts, values, principles and rules.

These new concepts were the result of scientific studies, expert meetings and stakeholder symposia, followed by international talks and negotiations, and lead to declarations, resolutions, charters and treaties, and to more-or-less consensus decisions from world bodies such as the General Assembly of the United Nations, the Security Council and the Boards of the Bretton Woods institutions. This cooperation has gone on until today. New principles such as human development, sustainable development, human security, humanitarian law, the responsibility to protect, the precautionary principle and the common but differentiated responsibility to combat climate change are the result of recent negotiations against the background of new political, economic, technological and ecological developments on our planet. The breakthrough in international civilization was that for the first time in world history, an international community emerged, choosing to build a system that would help the world as a whole to overcome the catastrophic consequences of globalization.

Was it successful? Yes, to a certain extent. The greatest success the end of colonial rule under the new consensus that no country was allowed to oppress any other. The independence of India and Pakistan was the beginning of the end of colonization. The end actually came with the independence of the former Portuguese colonies in Africa, such as Angola and Mozambique. It took only 30 years to achieve this objective. At the end of the 1970s a few small countries were not yet fully independent, but this did not substantially impact world political relations anymore.

Decolonization was a success. Globalization got a new face. The new nation-states represented a very large part of the world population and could now deal with the traditionally powerful countries on a more-or-less equal footing. However, it was only a partial success. The new states, and other developing countries, did not get a fair deal. Their economic perspective was less rosy. A country's political independence should have a strong and sustained economic basis. However, the international financial and monetary system and export markets for developing countries, in particular commodities markets, were tilted in favour of the countries of the North. Developing countries came to the conclusion that legal autonomy as a nation-state was not enough. It should be complemented by economic self-reliance. In their, view meeting this objective required the establishment of a new international economic order.

The new international economic order (NEIO)

For a full decade talks were held in the framework of UNCTAD, the new UN organization which, in 1964, had been established to further the economic development of the new countries. In 1975, during the Seventh Special Session of the General Assembly of the United Nations, a consensus text was agreed upon that outlined principles of a new international economic order. However, these were not put into practice. There was not enough political will on the side of the North, despite the shock of the oil crisis of 1973, which had resulted from a deliberate joint action of oil-exporting developing countries to raise the price of oil. Cheap oil had fuelled the economic recovery and growth in the North after the Second World War. A substantial price increase would have had a serious impact on the economic perspective of the industrialized countries, which could no longer neglect the demands of the South. That is what many of us foresaw. However, oil-importing rich countries reacted by exploring their own oil resources and by resorting to nuclear energy. Before the oil-price increase, neither alternative had been cost effective. The result was not only a further widening of the gap between richer and poorer countries, but also a world economic slump, which was soon aggravated by debt defaults of quite a few developing countries.

The world economic crisis of 2008, resulting from debt default in the rich world, is being addressed with aggressive policies to prevent a breakdown of the financial system and to stimulate economic activity. The answer to the crisis in the 1980s was quite different, however. It consisted of a general prescription to adjust to a downward trend on the markets, rather than to stimulate demand. Government expenditures were cut, which resulted in major decreases in public services, for instance in health and education. Agricultural investments were brought down. World commodity prices decreased. Poverty increased, as did income inequality.

Another new world order

In retrospect, during the 1980–90s a new world order was indeed established, but it was quite different from what had been intended during the preceding two decades. This new order was not based on a common political consensus reached by all nation-states working together. Politics was not in the lead. The new order was based on technology and economics, on unprecedented breakthroughs in communication and information technology, and on the emergence of a truly global market no longer hindered by geographical distances or time differences. A real-time world economy emerged, with a 24/7 character and complete information about everything, everywhere and anytime, facilitating massive, speedy reactions to any new market development anywhere.

Politics was not in the lead, barring one major exception. The end of the Cold War in 1989 was the result of political decisions in the East and the West. Economic forces did play a role, as the economic perspective of the Soviet Union and the Eastern Bloc turned out to be bleak, but it was political decisions on both sides of the divide that made the difference. Those decisions were not only taken by the respective regimes; they also resulted from an unstoppable change in the aspirations of people living in formerly communist nations. They resulted in a new worldwide hope that from now on, the focus could be shifted away from security, ideological conflict and the prevention of war, towards sustainability, worldwide integration and the preservation of peace. Resources that had hitherto been invested in an arms race should in the future be spent on poverty reduction, food security, the preservation of the world's natural environment and its biodiversity and the prevention of climate change.

This could have been possible. The end of the Cold War provided an opportunity for real and sustainable globalization. However, this would have required additional political decisions concerning the setting of priorities, the allocation of resources and the reduction of inequalities. Left to market forces alone, these three categories of decision would result in less sustainability, more poverty and greater inequality. However, politics did not steer development, growth, welfare, poverty reduction or the protection of the environment. Politics followed the market and aimed at improving the mechanics of the market by creating a level playing field for market forces, ensuring the worldwide mobility of information, technology, capital, money and goods.

Technological breakthroughs had given a major boost to worldwide information and communication. For the first time in world history, the world economy became a true world market. Transnational financial and economic corporations became bigger and bigger, entered into mergers and became conglomerates with activities in many different economic sectors, whereby the distinction between the financial sector and the real economy became less significant. Decisions concerning investment, production, marketing and trade in the real economy were taken by the same people who decided about money and finance, buying and selling shares and companies, transferring short-term and long-term capital all around the globe, taking and assessing risks.

This resulted in the creation of world economic giants, powerful oligopolies, and less and less transparent networks of financial institutions, production enterprises and trading houses. Products could be sold easily, because of the increasing purchasing power of an emerging global middle class. This power was easily tapped because this middle class could be globally bombarded with advertising, through all media, preaching the gospel of quick, easy and greedy consumer satisfaction. We got a new world economic order indeed, but one very different from that which had been advocated in the 1970s.

Globalization got another new face. In the 1990s it was discussed by the United Nations, in the Bretton Woods institutions and the WTO. These negotiations resulted in a further facilitation of globalization. The aim was to create a level playing field worldwide for production, finance, insurance, trade and capital movements. It was held that the world market should work as efficiently as possible, so international bureaucrats and politicians were following the guidance provided by the market and facilitating the workings of the market mechanism. In that respect we did quite well. International procedures, rules, regulations and institutions were established, which helped to implement the newly prevailing views on the primordial significance of the free flow of capital and goods, high levels of material consumption and the fast realization of profits. These objectives, if and when attained, would lead to high economic growth, which in turn was expected to result in higher employment and less poverty and, thus, in greater welfare. This was the neoliberal view on the workings of the world market.

Globalization: lopsided, Western, capitalist

The political facilitation of the market mechanism did not take more than a decade. It was successful because the growth rates of world production, trade and finance increased substantially. However, it too was only a partial success. Many other problems were not addressed. This was partly due to the view that problems such as poverty and unemployment would be indirectly solved by higher economic growth. This was not the case, as could have been apparent from the experiences of the 1960s and 1970s. Other issues were put on the international agenda, such as safeguarding the environment, but without the same motivation as the endeavours to liberalize finance and trade. Climate change, the pollution of the atmosphere, deforestation, the reduction of bio-diversity, the loss of soil fertility, the growing scarcity of water, all these issues were discussed but to no effect. It was not possible to reach worldwide political agreement on measures to tackle these worldwide problems. Politicians were aware that these problems had to be dealt with globally, because the underlying forces did not respect the frontiers of nation-states. However, because these forces mostly came from the historically rich countries – together comprising no more than a quarter of the world's population – and because many populous and poor countries claimed a right to development, it was very difficult to reach agreement on the burden of adjustment. Some new principles were agreed upon, such as the precautionary principle and the principle of equal but different responsibilities of nation-states. However, no new effective structures were built to address these threats. Recourse was sought to voluntary measures only, without obligations and sanctions, in contrast to compulsory measures taken in the areas of trade and finance. Meanwhile pollution and depletion went so fast that we were running behind the facts. The facts changed very quickly. We lost control.

Other issues were neglected as well. We did not build international institutions to deal adequately with social problems such as the social consequences of capitalist economic growth. These included unemployment due to technological progress, resulting in a substitution of labour by capital; child labour and labour during long hours under harsh circumstances, often with wages below the subsistence level; a growing informalization of labour; indebtedness of small farmers; migration due to a loss of perspective in the homeland area; mass poverty in megacities; decreasing food security due to a lack of investment in agriculture; decreasing access for poor people to primary education and health care; increasing prices of medication for AIDS and tropical diseases. This is a long but not exhaustive list of neglected areas. Of course these issues have been widely reported and discussed. Targets were set, promises were made. However, no adequate decisions were made concerning implementation of the targets. No institutions were established with authority to steer policies towards these objectives. Resources were set aside but not spent and, after some time, reallocated in order to serve the interests of the middle class.

So globalization was lopsided in quite a few respects. Issues other than the workings of the world market were left to individual nations. This choice could be defended by pointing to each nation-state's responsibility for the welfare of its citizens. However, much of the social deficit within nations is due to global forces: global climate change, global preferences for foreign and capital-intensive technologies and land use patterns, the emergence of a global middle class dictating priorities for resources utilization. These global forces were supported by global institutions. Leaving international social consequences to individual nations will at best result in a mitigation of these consequences, not in an effective tackling of root causes.

Globalization was not only incomplete and one-sided, it was Western as well. It had started in the West. Technology came from the West; innovations were copied elsewhere, but they originated in the West. Foreign investment capital came from the West. Global communication and information passed along Western channels. The new approaches to markets and policies were Western-value driven.

This is not to say that such Western values were wrong, but they were Western, not Asian, or African or Arab. When in international talks a confrontation took place between Western and other values – for instance, concerning governance issues or principles of property and the rule of law – the Western values always prevailed. Mostly these values reflected modernity. The new notions were a faint shadow of values that had been cherished in Western countries after the French Revolution (e.g., equality and fraternity) or after the 1930s (e.g., solidarity, public responsibility and social welfare). Instead they strongly reflected the neoliberal principles that, in the 1980s, had become popular as guidelines for adjustment to an economic downturn and, in the 1990s, as symbols of a victory in an ideological battle between East and West.

At the turn of the millennium the prevailing character of globalization was not only lopsided and Western, but also capitalist. Companies and shareholders were aiming to maximize profit by means of fast and massive capital accumulation. Private earnings skyrocketed, which was facilitated by a blurring of the dividing line between personal interests and what is good for the company. Risk was shifted on to others and from there to others again, until a complete lack of transparency clouded economic and social cost-benefit relations. Social and environmental concerns were neglected. Inequalities widened. The poor population strata were excluded from the economy rather than integrated into society. Emissions of greenhouse gasses and other chemical substances threatening the health of third parties and future generations multiplied. An overriding drive to make money with money ousted feelings of social responsibility. Capitalism helped globalization to blossom. In turn, globalization facilitated the evolution of the capitalist system into its purest form ever.

Global apartheid

Globalization has done a lot of good for many people in many countries, India included. Many have benefited from sustained economic growth, high material welfare, broad communication possibilities and cost reductions due to technological innovation. Globalization has opened a world of options for people not only in the West, but also in Asia, Africa, Latin America and the Middle East. People can communicate with everyone else in the world, provided that they belong to the same global middle class and have access to the market in general, and to capital and knowledge and to modern means of communication in particular. This is unprecedented. But at the same time, globalization has strengthened an economic system in which many people don't have any of this access. They are excluded from the system, which does not seem to want them any more. In the present world economic system there is not much need for many people's contributions. Both the labour power and the purchasing power of the world's underclass seem to be dispensable. Since 1980–1990 inequality has increased at a very high rate. Presently all domestic and international statistical indices of inequality are much higher than before the beginning of 1989. From that year until the world economic crisis of 2008–2009, the world went through a period of high growth. However, the proceeds were not used to reduce poverty, lessen inequality or sustain the ecology. This is what world leaders promised the world's population in 1992 at the United Nations World Conference on Sustainable Development in Rio de Janeiro. The promise was not kept. On the contrary, inequality has widened.

One might argue that in any economy there has always been inequality and that there always will be. Poverty and inequality seem to be unavoidable. Poverty, it is argued, has always been with us and not much can be done about it. It is true that complete eradication of absolute poverty is very difficult. However, that is not the issue. The issue is not whether poverty and inequality still exist, but whether in a certain period there is more or less poverty than before, and whether inequality is rising or declining. The trend matters more than the facts measured at one specific moment. This is also true politically, because an upward trend to access and welfare for more people would boost hope and expectations, while a downward trend would feed feelings of frustration.

What matters are the reactions to poverty and inequality. Trends are manmade. For instance, towards the end of the 19th century, people confronted with absolute poverty and huge inequality fought back. They formed labour unions and used their power as the production mechanism of the goods enabling capitalist entrepreneurs to increase earnings and profits and further accumulate their capital. Labourers concluded that they were providing an essential function in the process and went on strike. They didn't accept exploitation and impoverishment. In response to this, entrepreneurs and elites who aspired for sustained profits and increasing incomes came to the conclusion that too much poverty and too much inequality was counterproductive. The wages of the labourers had to be increased, in order to enable the underclass to buy more products. It was understood that sound conditions in industrial markets would depend on healthy labour relations. Towards the end of the great industrial revolution of that century, within individual nation-states it was the economic and socially enlightened self-interest of entrepreneurs and other upper-classes, next to possible ethical values, that played an important role in reducing the poverty of people belonging to the underclass. So it was the resistance by victims of exploitation together with rational considerations amongst capitalists that pointed to a deal. The same considerations laid the basis for Keynesian economic policies during a downturn in the business cycle and for the American New Deal and Western European social welfare policies after the Second World War. Feelings of solidarity and other ethical values always went hand in hand with economic and political rationality. Both considerations had one thing in common: the desire to strengthen the sustainability of the society concerned.

Towards the end of the 1970s, efforts were made in favour of a similar approach for the world economy as a whole. This was proposed in the so-called Brandt Report published under the title, "Our Common Future". The report argued that developing countries should be supported, not only for moral reasons, but also because it would benefit the world as a whole. No society, neither national nor global, can afford too much inequality. Too much poverty and inequality within a society endangers its stability. The answer is to boost the world underclass, the indebted developing countries with a low national income and meagre export earnings, and the poor people within those countries. Within UNCTAD, the United Nations Conference for Trade and Development, we tried the same approach. Secretary General Gamani Corea distanced himself from the paradigm advocated by his predecessor Raul Prebish, who had pointed at a structural divide between the economies in the centre and those in the periphery of the world. Corea pleaded for international economic policies based on an awareness of mutual interest between rich and poor nations. It didn't work out. Both the Brandt Report and UNCTAD were shifted aside. Nobody accepted the underlying concepts and ideas. Talks between developed and developing nations failed completely.

And why wouldn't they fail? I have come to the conclusion that to a high degree this is due to globalization itself. As I indicated earlier, sooner or later within any economy people realize that there is a limit to poverty and inequality that cannot be overstepped without risking the stability of that economy and the sustainability of the society and polity concerned. The awareness grows: the poor are needed. However, as long as products and services can easily be sold to a middle class living far away, sales being facilitated by modern means of communication, you don't need the poor around your corner. And the global middle class is huge, it is several billions of people and costs of communication are low. Because globalization means steadily decreasing costs of communication, members of the global middle class, commanding a certain degree of purchasing power, do not live far away from each other. In today's world markets, neither geographical distances nor time differences play a role any more. Internet, email, TV commercials, financial trading arrangements, sea containers and civil aviation transportation enable 24/7 communication amongst all members of that class, wherever they live. Globalization enhances the feeling of mutual connectivity amongst educated people, industrial workers, employees working in financial enterprises and service-providing companies, students, consumers, internet users, holders of bank accounts and credit cards, people watching TV, people buying air tickets and consumers in general all around the world. People belonging to one's own class, though living on the other side of the globe, seem to be closer than poor people around the corner in your own society. Globalization also means that the world's underclass does not exist in the minds of the world's middle class. Even if they live around the corner, they look far away and dispensable.

Of course, such an explanation holds for a certain period only. At a certain moment, in any market in any society, the same mechanism will work as it has in any other nation. But because of globalization, which did away with national frontiers and has annihilated the importance of geographic and time distances, much time will pass before the mechanism will work in world society as a whole. The world's middle class of today – those people with a reasonable level of living, earning a decent income which enables them not only to survive but also to enter the market, to buy and to save – amounts to about four billion people, two thirds of the world's population. For quite some time these four billion do not seem to need the economic participation of the other two billion, neither their labour, nor their demand as consumers. So these people are forgotten, or even seen as a hindrance to accumulation of further welfare by the middle class itself, because enabling the poor to participate might require investment, an effort to enhance their productive capacity, which would demand a redistribution of resources, which would be seen as cost without benefit. In a global society, much more so and for much longer than in a national society, the poor are seen as a burden on those who live on the bright side of the divide.

So, there is a two thirds–one third divide in the world as a whole and it will take many decades before the mechanism will work correctly again. One of consequences of globalization is that moral and rational reasons to address inequality and poverty are fading away. Greed ("I want it all and I want it now") breeds selfishness and greed excludes; other people are not seen as human beings, but as cost factors.

In the past, in nation-states with capitalist economies, poverty was the collateral damage of economic growth. There was poverty, substantive but accidental, but it had to be cured and, if possible, prevented. However, in the global capitalist system of today, poverty seems to be created and maintained, because any effort to remedy the poverty of people in the underclass would be detrimental to the middle class. So, poverty is no longer collateral damage within the system, but a calculated default of the system itself. Efforts to avert, contain and reduce poverty are half-hearted; resources for relief, abatement and defrayal are shallow. At the same time, the greed of the middle class incites a material consumption pattern with disastrous consequences for the world's environment, biodiversity and climate. It seems as if today's global middle-class consumers feel certain that technological progress will enable future generations to cope with the problems they are creating for them. This is nothing other than a careless discounting of the interests and welfare of people yet unborn.

This is a worldwide phenomenon. It is taking place everywhere. There is not only collateral damage within the system, without adequate remedial action; there are calculated defaults inherent to the system and a careless discounting of the future. The system seems to be heading for a crisis. Globalization cannot be halted. But the present character of globalization can be changed. Currently globalization is good for many, not only for an elite but for more or less two thirds of the world's population. At the same time it is bad for many others, the remaining one third, partly because they are being neglected, partly because they are being exploited and deprived of their resources. The living spaces of poor people, homelands of indigenous people, livelihoods of small farmers and pastoralists are being taken by others with economic and political power. The settlements of the poor, often no more than a shelter or a shanty, are being demolished in order to make room for the urban middle class. The poorest people are living in the worst places in the world. The most vulnerable amongst them run the risk that the land upon which they used to live will be occupied and that they will be driven away from their livelihoods. In the words of Jan Breman, a Dutch development researcher who studied, amongst others, the lives of poor people in Gujarat, these people are "down and out". Indeed, in many countries, for instance in India, Sudan, South Africa and the Netherlands, the most vulnerable people are being told, "You don't belong here, we need the living space for ourselves, get out, stay away and never come back."

All this is global apartheid, in the words of former President Mbeki of South Africa in his address to the United Nations Conference on Sustainable Development in Johannesburg, in 2002, ten years after the preceding meeting in Rio de Janeiro. Globalization cannot be stopped. Global apartheid, however, can be stopped. Globalization can be made less lopsided, less Western and less capitalist. It can be made developmental.

Development is conflict

Without an effort to change, the world is bound to go through many more conflicts. By its very nature, development is change. In any society there are always people with a vested interest in maintaining the status quo next to people who would benefit from change. Development means that those who already benefit from the status quo – bigger landowners or powerful elites within a nation, or traditional rich countries in the world economy – will have to stand back and make room for others. That means that conflict is inherent to development. This conflict may be purely economic, but they can also be political or religious, or tribal or ethnic, or everything at the same time. Development means a struggle for progress for ever more people and requires a change in the existing power relations in a society. Such intended change breeds conflict. Conflict is inherent to development. Conflict cannot be wished away, they cannot be prevented, only managed and contained, in order to prevent further escalation, for instance from a more-or-less economic conflict into something also political and cultural. Escalation towards other regions or across borders can be prevented, but not the conflict itself. Development goes hand in hand with conflict. We should aim not at the suppression of conflicts, but of the violence caused by them.

Development thinkers and policy makers have learned this the hard way. That includes me. We thought that development required stability before change. We have learned, however, that this is not possible, at least not if such a process of change is supposed to benefit more and different people. However, there is no alternative. A lack of development also means conflict. A situation in which people are being exploited, impoverished and excluded is no less conflict-ridden than a process of rectification and reform. If people feel that there are no prospects, they will resist. If they conclude that the others do not see them as human beings but as people who shouldn't exist, they will fight back. They will fight the values of those who rule the system. If they understand that those who belong to the middle class consider them a threat, a potential enemy, for the sole reason that they belong to a specific group – a religion, an ethnic minority, a race, a tribe – they will turn their backs on the system and build a new one for themselves. Not everybody will resort to resistance and revolt. Poverty and deprivation do not necessarily lead to violence. Most poor people have to expend all their energy on daily survival. But amongst them there will be always opinion leaders and activists who take a stand. Others will agree. Youth will follow, in particular those who are unemployed. At present, many young people are unemployed all around the world.

A New Deal

So what should be done? Two things. Firstly, we need a new world system. The system we have is not good enough. It ought to be more equitable, more developmental, less lopsided, more universal, more oriented towards social and environmental needs, rather than facilitating financial and economic interests. The system that has emerged since the Second World War has done a lot of good, but further development has stagnated and it has become deficient in many respects. During the first decade of the new millennium, it has led to a number of crises: a food crisis, with many people not able to feed themselves daily, while others have more than enough; an energy crisis, the overexploitation of scarce fossil fuels, inadequate investment in sustainable energy; an environmental crisis, comprising climate change, loss of biodiversity; a welfare crisis made up of too much blatant poverty, overconsumption by the well-to-do, ever growing inequalities; and, recently, a financial and economic crisis, a breakdown of the international financial system and a world depression.

These crises are related to each other in many respects. They originate in different causes, but they have three elements in common. Firstly, huge inequality between people on all markets concerned. Secondly, greed and the short-term horizons of middle class people with access to these markets. Thirdly, deficient policy institutions with a mandate to address consequences of market failure. This third element is the most alarming of all. There are major threats to the future welfare and security of the world's population. This phenomenon is not new. Institutions have been established to deal with threats: international law, the United Nations, international agencies with a mandate in fields such as trade, finance, development, energy and agriculture. All of these have been eroded. None of them functions adequately. Even more alarming than the threats themselves is the fact that we seem to have lost the capacity to address them. That is the main reason why a reform of the international architecture is so urgently needed.

The second priority concerns all individual nation-states: the fight against poverty, the reversal of inequality and the securing of sustainability. A reform of international systems will be needed not only for the reasons mentioned above, but also in order to help individual nations to meet these objectives. However, no government should hide behind delays in international reform. Many causes of poverty can be dealt with at home, in particular political causes: tilted priorities, bad governance, undemocratic processes of decision-making, unequal access to domestic resources and assets, deficient institutions dealing with human rights violations. If domestic defaults are not addressed, people will lose not only their perspective on future progress, but also their faith in the functioning of society and its institutions.

This is a call for a two-track approach, worldwide and at home. The call is not new. It also rang in the mid 20th century. At the time it was answered by the establishment of a new world order with arrangements based on international law, peace agreements, reconstruction, decolonization, development, social welfare policies and human rights charters. It was a New Deal for the world. It has been eroded. Presently the world is facing new challenges, different but no less threatening than those of a hundred years ago. The challenges are highly complicated because of the course of globalization and the conflicts that are universally inherent to the inescapable processes of development. We need another New Deal, a new world compact for sustainable development. The welfare and security of future generations is at stake.

FROM APOCALYPSE TO JUBILEE: THEOLOGICAL PERSPECTIVES ON ETHICAL DEFICITS IN THE CURRENT GLOBAL FINANCIAL SYSTEM

Pamela K. Brubaker

> God's gift of life is a comprehensive gift, encompassing the multitude of creation and creatures. Made in the image of God, individual human beings recognize the human dignity of the other; they affirm their mutual vulnerability and dependence on others, the earth, and God. They all belong to God's household of life (*oikos* - the earth community) which is marked by God's solidarity with those pushed to the margins of the networks of life and God's compassionate desire for a life that overcomes the various faces of violence and death.[1]

Endless accumulation of possessions and pursuit of wealth can become our god as we yearn for a life without limits. "Ah, you who join house to house, who add field to field, until there is room for no one but you" (Is. 5:8). Many look to material possessions and money as the means for participating in the "fullness of life", and thus become ever more dependent on economic transactions. But Jesus asks, "What does it profit them if they gain the whole world, but lose or forfeit themselves?" (Luke 9:25)[2]

The ethical deficits of the present global financial system are clearest during periods of crisis, although its failure to meet the needs of justice for the poor and for creation is persistent. While we more often hear about financial deficits, the first definition for the word deficit in the dictionary is "deficiency in amount or quality, or a lack or impairment in a functional capacity." (The second is "an excess of expenditure over revenue".)[3] This definition implies a standard of judgment and system of accounting – what is of value? Justice for the poor and for creation is our standard, according to the AGEM concept paper.

Christian ethicist Karen Lebacqz has shown that in our contemporary world there is no single agreed standard for justice. In *Justice in an Unjust World: Foundations for a Christian Approach to Justice,* Lebacqz insists that injustice should be the starting point of a Christian approach. She develops a twofold approach of historical consciousness and biblical

---

[1] Theology and Globalization Consultation, "Moved in God's Spirit," World Council of Churches, 6 September, 2004.
[2] Evangelical Lutheran Church in America, "A Social Statement on: Sufficient, Sustainable Livelihood for All," 1999 p. 13. www.elca.org/socialstatements
[3] http://www.merriam-webster.com/dictionary/deficitww

remembrance. "Historical consciousness requires that we name and claim the injustices in the world. ... biblical remembrance then requires that we search for biblical stories that illumine the proper response to such injustices."[4] Adapting her approach, I begin with a naming of injustices carried out by the present system, interpreted through a biblical lens. The heart of the chapter presents theo-ethical frameworks for assessing ethical deficiencies and responding to injustices. I conclude with reflections on a jubilee perspective for just finance.

Apocalyptic perspectives on the financial crisis

Globally, the gap between the richest 20 percent of the world's population and the poorest 20 percent has grown from 30–1 in 1960 to 74–1 in 1994 to, 100–1 today. The income of the richest one percent of the global population is equal to that of the poorest 57 percent. The richest two percent own more than half of all household wealth, the poorest half barely one percent. At least 26,000 children die every day from poverty and malnutrition. Although there have been gains in health, education, and poverty reduction among the world's people, 18 countries with a total population of 460 million people had lower scores on the human development index in 2003 than in 1990 – "an unprecedented reversal". Simply put, "global markets are far from equitable", reported the *World Development Report 2006,* "and the rules governing their functioning have a disproportionate negative impact on developing countries" who have less voice in negotiating these rules.[5]

Furthermore, the gains that have been made – the 200 million people brought above the poverty line of 2.50 US dollars per day since 1999 – are disappearing. According to the World Bank, between 73 and 105 million people have already been pushed into poverty by the food crisis. They estimate that if the financial crisis persists, as many as 53 million additional people will fall below the poverty line. Mayra Buvinic, World Bank Gender Equality and Development spokesperson, states that gender-specific impacts of the crisis – "such as the expected drop in women's income and girls' school enrolment and the rise in mortality rates among infant girls" – will increase poverty and jeopardize future development. An additional 200,000 to 400,000 infants will die each year, the majority of whom are girls. Evidence from developing countries shows that when economies grew, the wellbeing of both girls and boys improved. However, during crises, infant deaths were predominantly among girls.[6]

---

[4] *Justice in an Unjust World: Foundations for a Christian Approach to Justice,* Minneapolis: Augsburg Publishing House, 1987, p. 148.

[5] *World Development Report 2006: Equity and Development,* World Bank Group, 2005, p. 16.

[6] Commission on the Status of Women (CSW), Press Release: "Governments must focus on women as economic agents during global financial crisis if their disproportionate suffering is to be averted", 5 March 2009, pp.1, 8. http://www.un.org/News/Press/docs/2009/wom1721.doc.htm,

This reality contrasts with the image of God's household of life with which this paper began. Interestingly, protestors at the April 2009 G20 meeting on the financial crisis drew on biblical imagery to "protest against a system they said had robbed the poor to benefit the rich."[7] Large figures portraying the four horsemen of the apocalypse (Rev. 6) were near the beginning of the march and were shown repeatedly in news coverage of the event. The four horses represented financial crimes, war, climate change and homelessness. In reflecting on these images, one may think of financial crimes such as usury, or outrageous bonuses to bailed-out AIG management, or the innumerable odious and illegitimate debts imposed on the global South; of a hundred thousand or more civilian casualties, some five thousand military casualties, and the exorbitant cost – up to 3 trillion US dollars – of US and NATO wars in Iraq and Afghanistan; of climate change exacerbating drought, fire and crop failures in southern California, Australia and countries in Africa; or the loss of hundreds of species of flora and fauna in the Amazon, or polar bears floating forlornly on tiny ice floes in the Arctic; of tent cities of middle-class families who lost their homes through foreclosure in Sacramento, the capital of California; or the millions of homeless or poorly sheltered people in slums around the world.

How, though, is this reality related to the global financial system? Rogate Mshana offered a helpful description in a 2004 talk:

> In simple terms, a financial system is the group of institutions in the economy that help to match one person's savings with another person's investment. Financial markets which are part of the financial system are financial institutions through which savers can directly provide funds to borrowers.

There are also institutions through which savers can indirectly provide funds to borrowers. He rightfully asserts, though, that the global financial system is more complex than this. It must be viewed from the perspective of the political economy, within which financial capital at the global level is "managed from the centre ... while the periphery falls deep into crises." Mshana identifies the major global financial actors as private institutions such as large transnational banks, national governments and international financial institutions – particularly the IMF, the World Bank and regional development banks. "Through financial transactions, these three sets of institutions are responsible for most domestic and global movement of financial capital."[8]

---

[7] William Maclean and Michael Holden, "G20 protestors smash windows, clash with police", Reuters.com, 1 April 2009.

[8] Rogate Mshana, "The current financial system is one of the main causes of inequality in the global economy", WCC, January 9, 2004. http://www.oikoumene.org/en/resources/documents/wcc-programmes/public-witness-addressing-power-affirming-peace/poverty-wealth-and-ecology/finance-speculation-debt/r-mshana-on-current-financial-system.html.

Drawing on this description, one might assert that the purpose of the global financial system is to provide credit for the real economy and for development. However, a careful analysis of its functioning might lead one to conclude that it actually serves to enrich the wealthy elite (in both developed and developing countries) and to enable the US and its allies to dominate and control developing countries. For instance, the IMF is requiring contractionary policies as conditions for loans made since the global recession began. Robert Weissman points out that, "the logic of providing assistance to developing countries is to help them adopt expansionary policies in time of economic downturn." Yet the loan conditionalities imposed by the IMF forces countries in financial distress to pursue contractionary policies. Most tellingly, these are the opposite of the stimulation policies adopted by rich countries, which the IMF supports for them (rich countries).[9] In other words, rich countries are increasing government spending to stimulate demand, and cutting interest rates and lowering taxes. In contrast, the IMF has required El Salvador, Pakistan and countries in Eastern Europe to cut spending, and in some cases to cut wages and/or raise interest rates, policies which tend to contract economies.

The US government, in conjunction with the other countries in the G7 (Canada, Germany, France, Great Britain, Italy and Japan), plays a crucial role in setting trade and finance policy in these global institutions. Both the World Bank and the IMF have a voting system based mainly on the value of the shares held by its member countries. The US effectively has veto power in both institutions. It often uses this power to protect US interests, particularly corporate interests.[10] For instance, in 2003 the US blocked an IMF proposal to establish a sovereign debt restructuring mechanism that would have permitted debtor countries to make a case for the reduction or cancellation of their debts.

Joseph Stiglitz, former senior economist at the World Bank and Nobel laureate in economics, has pointed out that some economic prescriptions – such as the IMF encouraged developing countries to open their capital markets – were not based on empirical evidence as claimed, but on "ideology". The ideology Stiglitz refers to is neoliberalism, the prevailing political-economic paradigm of the last three decades. Neoliberalism looks to private capital and "free markets" to allocate resources and promote growth. It advocates policies of liberalization, privatization and deregulation and was imposed in the 1980s on about 100 countries as

---

[9] Robert Weissman, "No Blank Check for the IMF", April 13 2009. http://www.multinationalmonitor.org/editorsblog. See also Kevin P. Gallagher, "The G20's failing grade", guardian.co.uk, April 6, 2009, and "Global Crisis in Need of Global Solutions", NEXOS 7, http://www.ase.tufts.edu/gdae/Pubs/rp/LATNG20Mar09.pdf ; and Mark Wesibrot, "IMF Shouldn't Get Money Without Reform", NYTimes.com, April 24, 2009.

[10] For further discussion of US policy, see my chapter, "Reforming Global Policies", in *Justice in a Global Economy: Policies for Home, Community, and World,* ed. Pamela K. Brubaker, Rebecca Todd Peters, and Laura Stivers, Westminster John Knox, 2006.

conditions for IMF-imposed structural adjustment policies.[11] Most of these countries are still subject to these policies as their debts have not been cancelled or paid off. Stiglitz charges that the 1997 Asian financial crisis showed that capital market liberalization led to unnecessary instability and a slowdown in economic growth. The policies were also anti-democratic. Although there was a consensus at the time that, "fundamental reform of the global financial architecture" was needed, it has not happened. Stiglitz charges that, "while the current system may lead to unnecessary instability, it serves some interests well – those of Wall Street."[12]

Brazilian theologian Jung Mo Sung poignantly describes how this process plays out. He discusses Paul Samuelson's description of the nature of the market, which states that, "commodities should go to where there is a greater number of votes or dollars." According to this logic, the only one deemed viable, "'J.D. Rockefeller's dog can receive the milk that a poor child needs to prevent rickets.'" Samuelson acknowledges that from an ethical perspective this is wrong, but he claims that the market is the only mechanism in modern societies able to coordinate economic processes. Sung concludes that, "the sufferings and deaths of the poor, to the extent that they are considered the other side of the coin of 'redeeming progress', are interpreted as necessary sacrifices." This means that, "the sacrifices are always imposed on the poorer populations, while the richer sectors benefit from the life sacrifice of the poor which results in the increasing of their wealth." Sung analyzes the grounding of "necessary sacrifices" in Christianity's interpretation of the death of Jesus as a necessary sacrifice. For example, Michael Novak advocates what he calls democratic capitalism and asks, "If God so willed his beloved Son to suffer, why would He spare us?" For too many, this logic provides a "sacred canopy", legitimizing the sacrifice of the poor. (Sung reminds us, though, that Jesus tells us that God wants mercy – not sacrifice.)[13]

Neoliberalism – free market capitalism – becomes "a beast" which first devours the poor and then itself. Michael Parenti uses the beast imagery in his article, "Capitalism's Self-Inflicted

---

[11] "The Peace Research Institute in Oslo found that most of the civil wars of the past decade have taken place in countries with high poverty levels, little fresh water, land degradation, high external debts, and a history of vigorous IMF intervention." Cited in Heather Eaton, "Can Ecofeminism Withstand Corporate Globalization?" in *Ecofeminism and Globalization: Exploring Culture, Context, and Religion*, ed. Heather Eaton and Lois Ann Lorentzen, Rowman and Littlefield, 2003, p. 28.

[12] Joseph Stiglitz, Globalization and its Discontents, New York: W.W. Norton, 2002, pp. xiv, 33-88; "Financial Hypocrisy," Project Syndicate, 2007, www.project-syndicate.org.

[13] Jung Mo Sung, *Desire, Market and Religion,* Reclaiming Liberation Theology Series, SCM Press, 2007, pp. 18, 61, 90-94. Sung cites Mario H. Simonsen of Brazil, who used the term "the necessary sacrifice to progress" in arguing that although one hopes to minimize it, accelerated growth usually demands sacrifice which naturally includes a certain increase in income concentration. I am grateful to Kelly Denton-Borhaug for introducing me to Sung's work and for her insights into its relevance to my chapter.

Apocalypse", describing capitalism as a "self-devouring beast". He states that, "an economy dedicated to speedups and wage cuts, to making workers produce more and more for less and less is always in danger of a crash." A frequently overlooked process of self-destruction is when unsupervised moneyed players, "the more active command component of the financial system begins to devour less organized sources of wealth" within the real economy. One role of the capitalist state is to prevent "the capitalist system from devouring itself", a role that it has not played well recently.[14]

Former Federal Reserve Chair Alan Greenspan's testimony before a Congressional hearing in October 2008 indicates the role free market ideology played in the financial crisis. Greenspan confessed that he had been mistaken in presuming that financial actors' self-interests "were such that they were best capable of protecting their own shareholders and their equity in the firms." He admitted under questioning that the crisis exposed a "flaw" in his ideology, which held "that free, competitive markets are by far the unrivalled way to organize economies."[15]

Parenti points to another crucial factor: the "immense inequality in economic power … translates into a formidable inequality of political power, which makes it all the more difficult to impose democratic regulations."[16] One could extend Parenti's analysis to the failure of the US, until recently, to seriously engage the challenge of climate change. The United Nations Environmental Programme warns that, "the current level of atmospheric $CO2$ concentration is already at an ecological threshold if no drastic actions are taken immediately." They warn that, "the world's poor are especially vulnerable to climate-induced rising sea levels, coastal erosion, and frequent storms."[17] The poor in New Orleans still suffering displacement almost three years after Hurricane Katrina can testify to this.

Stiglitz recently stated that the current global recession bears a "made-in-America label". Since the 1960s and the war in Vietnam, some US religious progressives speak of living in

---

[14] Michael Parenti, "Capitalism's Self-Inflicted Apocalypse", CommonDreams.org, January 21, 2009.

[15] Greenspan added that this ideology – "the model that I perceived is the critical functioning structure that defines how the world works" – had "very considerable evidence that it was working exceptionally well" for 40 years or more. http://www.pbs.org/newshour/bb/business/july-dec08/crisishearing_10-23.html. Some might characterize Greenspan's position as idolization of the market, but Greenspan makes clear that he thought that this model was based on evidence.

[16] Parenti, op. cit.

[17] IPCC, Summary for Policymakers. In: *Climate Change 2007: Impacts, Adaptation and Vulnerability. Contribution of Working Group II to the Fourth Assessment Report of the Intergovernmental Panel on Climate Change*, M.L. Parry, O.F. Canziani, J.P. Palutikof, P.J. van der Linden and C.E. Hanson, Eds., Cambridge University Press, pp. 7-22,http://www.ipcc.ch/publications_and_data/ar4/wg2/en/contents.html; see especially p. 18. Some critics question whether the approach of the Obama administration adequately engages this crisis.

"the belly of the beast". Barbara Rossing's study of the book of Revelation is very helpful in understanding this imagery, which is popular among US Christian evangelicals and dispensationalists who interpret the US not as the beast, but as on the side of a conquering "warrior", Jesus. Rossing persuasively argues that Jesus conquers not through violence and holy war, but through "Lamb power" – the power of nonviolent love to change the world. She concludes that, "in every time and place, Revelation calls on us to 'come out' of the beast's realm of violence and injustice so that we can participate in the beloved city of God."[18]

Some in the US were hopeful that the 2008 election would indicate a turning point – a coming out of the realm of violence and injustice. Although there has been a welcome change in tone and a change in direction on some important domestic and foreign policies (especially climate change), it is not yet clear that the Obama administration has turned away from a neoliberal approach to the global economy. The inequality in economic and political power mentioned by Parenti continues to be a concern. *Multinational Monitor* found that,

> … the financial sector spent more than five billion US dollars on federal campaign contributions and lobbying in the US over the last decade. Political candidates received more than 1.725 billion US dollars in federal elections from 1998–2008 from finance, insurance and real estate corporations. During that 10-year period, about 55 percent went to Republicans and 45 percent to Democrats. But in the 2008 election cycle, Democrats took just more than half of the financial sector's contributions.[19]

Some Democrats are opposing more progressive elements of Obama's budget and economic proposals, raising questions about whose interests they serve. A crucial element of the policy debate is the proper role of government and markets.

Frameworks for ethical analysis of markets and economic life

Daniel Finn's *The Moral Ecology of Markets* is particularly useful for exploring this topic. Finn is both a Christian ethicist and an economist, who has written broadly on economic matters. Although he does not specifically discuss financial markets in this book, his approach is applicable. Finn contends that, "an adequate analysis of markets, whether a

---

[18] Barbara Rossing, *The Rapture Exposed: The Message of Hope in the Book of* Revelation, Westview Press, 2004, p. 170.

[19] Robert Weissman, "By the Numbers: Throwing Money at the Political Process", Multinational Monitor, January/February 2009, p. 12. See the full report, Sold Out: How Wall Street and Washington Betrayed America, March 2009, http://www.wallstreetwatch.org/reports/sold_out.pdf which documents the regulatory steps passed by Congress during this 10 year period, all of which contributed significantly to the financial crisis.

defence or a critique, must include an articulation of their moral underpinnings, including the moral significance of the other institutional elements that form the context for markets."

As a theologian and ethicist, he does not reject the claim of economists that self-interest can lead to just outcomes. He gives this claim "a conditional moral approval ... if markets have been properly defined by law, if essential goods and services are provided, if the morality of individuals and groups is apparent, and if there exists a vibrant civil society."

Finn notes that there will be disagreement and debate about what legal restraints are needed, "what goods and services are essential, which morality is appropriate, and how to understand the institutions of civil society."[20] He does not resolve these questions; rather he offers a framework for engaging in those debates to encourage dialogue among competing views. Theo-ethical stances can be drawn upon to take a position on the questions Finn raises. I examine three: Roman Catholic social teaching (Finn's tradition), Lutheran social ethics, and human rights.

Roman Catholic social teaching

The US Catholic Bishops' *Economic Justice for All: Pastoral Letter on Catholic Social Teaching and the US Economy* presents ethical norms for economic life: love and solidarity, justice and participation, and overcoming marginalization and powerlessness. It begins with its theological grounding:

> The life and words of Jesus and the teaching of his Church call us to serve those in need and to work actively for social and economic justice. As a community of believers, we know that our faith is tested by the quality of justice among us, that we can best measure our life together by how the poor and the vulnerable are treated. This is not a new concern for us. It is as old as the Hebrew prophets, as compelling as the Sermon on the Mount, and as current as the powerful voice of Pope John Paul II defending the dignity of the human person.[21]

The bishops distinguish three dimensions of basic justice, which Catholic social teaching shares with "much philosophical reflection: commutative, distributive and social justice."

> Commutative justice calls for fundamental fairness in all agreements and exchanges between individuals or private social groups. ... Distributive justice requires that

---

[20] Daniel Finn, *The Moral Ecology of Markets,* Cambridge University Press, 2006, pp. 33, 145. Although he disagrees with some of the claims of market critics, Finn does agree that economic theories are not "value-free."
[21] Para. 8.

the allocation of income, wealth, and power in society be evaluated in light of its effects on persons whose basic material needs are unmet. ... Social justice implies

that persons have an obligation to be active and productive participants in the life of society and that society has a duty to enable them to participate in this way.[22]

These three types of basic justice (with the addition of ecological sustainability) are useful principles for economic life and a moral analysis of markets. Using these principles to evaluate the ethical deficits of the present financial system broadens an analytic framework to include those not steeped in biblical narratives and traditions. They are widely accepted and can be useful in developing awareness of injustices and building political will to correct them.

Lutheran social ethics

The ethical criterion advocated by the Evangelical Lutheran Church in America is also useful and can be supported by both religious and secular people. This principle is "sufficient, sustainable livelihood for all" and is the title of the Social Statement on Economic Life, adopted in 1999. Its theo-ethical basis is primarily the Great Commandment:

If the economic arena becomes a reigning power for us, the question arises: in what or whom shall we place our trust and hope? The First Commandment is clear: "You shall have no other gods before me" (Ex. 20:3). Or as Jesus said, "You cannot serve God and wealth" (Matt. 6:24c, Luke 16:13). ... Through the cross of Christ, God forgives our sin and frees us from bondage to false gods. Faith in Christ fulfills the First Commandment. We are called to love the neighbour and be stewards in economic life, which, distorted by sin, is still God's good creation.

The ELCA asserts that, "Our faith in God provides a vantage point for critiquing any and every system of this world, all of which fall short of what God intends." It then points to particular conditions that are not compatible with the reign of God: "human impoverishment, excessive accumulation and consumerism driven by greed, gross economic disparities, and the degradation of nature." Thus, based on this faith stance,

---

[22] US Catholic Bishops, Economic Justice for All: Pastoral Letter on Catholic Social Teaching and the US Economy, Washington, DC, 1986, http://www.usccb.org/sdwp/international/EconomicJusticeforAll.pdf Paragraphs 69, 70, and 71. Pope Benedict XVI also asserts that the market is subject to these three principles of justice in his recent Encyclical, Caritas In Veritate, paragraph 35. I use the Pastoral Letter of the US Catholic Bishops and the Social Statement of the Evangelical Lutheran Church in America to lift up US voices critiquing the current economic system, which is dominated by our government and corporations.

"sufficient, sustainable livelihood for all" is a benchmark for affirming, opposing, and seeking changes in economic life.[23]

Summing up, it seems that financial markets – and by extension, the current global financial system – do not meet Finn's criteria for assessing their morality. A strong case can be made that these markets have not been properly defined by law (commutative justice), do not provide essential goods and services (distributive justice), and the morality of individuals and groups is not apparent (social justice). Nor do they meet the criterion of "sufficient, sustainable livelihood for all", as the current crisis shows so starkly.

Human rights

Theologian and ethicist Larry Rasmussen contends that the church's universal vision and conviction is of "the necessary, full inclusion of the excluded, on egalitarian terms." Universalism and egalitarianism are both "assertions of faith itself, whether or not they also have secular grounds." These assertions are "the converging Christian ground for one of the lasting moral achievements of modernity itself – universal human rights."[24] Roman Catholic social teaching, Lutheran social ethics and other religious traditions endorse human rights, both first-generation political and civil rights and second-generation social, economic and cultural rights.

The discourse of human rights is needed, along with the discourse of social ethics, to more fully assess ethical deficits in the current financial system. A human rights framework is particularly useful since the Universal Declaration of Human Rights (UDHR) has been adopted by all member states of the United Nations. Thus it is more representative of the aspirations and commitments of diverse human communities than are particular religious documents. It also provides useful grounds for advocating for international policies that move the financial system in a more just direction.

The current financial and economic system shifted the burden of global financial risks to poor countries and households, Sakiko Fukuda-Parr contended during a recent panel at the UN Commission on the Status of Women (CSW). She rightly insists that neither economic stability nor human security can be assured by national policies alone; they must be supported by international efforts. She points to article 28 of the UDHR, which states that everyone is entitled to a social international order in which rights and freedoms could be fully realized. Human rights define "the essential conditions of dignity and freedom to which everyone is

---

[23] "A Social Statement on: Sufficient, Sustainable Livelihood for All," op.cit, pp. 2-3.

[24] Larry R. Rasmussen, *Moral Fragments & Moral Community: A Proposal for Church in Society*, Fortress Press, 1993, pp. 148-9.

entitled," and carry obligations, "including to adequate subsistence, as outlined in article 25." She draws on the work of philosopher Thomas Pogge to charge that, "the international community had a duty to not only assist, but to reform, the global social arrangements that contributed to the non-fulfilment of basic subsistence rights."[25] Her analysis clarifies ways the current financial system is deficient in adhering to human rights obligations and powerfully calls for reform of current arrangements.

The United Nations Environment Programme cautions, though, that, "as governments devise a new international financial architecture to prevent future crises of this scale and find ways to jump-start economic recovery, they need also to recognize and address the risks from another brewing crisis with sweeping impact – climate change."[26]

The Greenhouse Development Rights Framework addresses the right to development in a climate-constrained world. It contends that it is unacceptable and unrealistic to expect people who are poor to focus valuable resources on the climate change crisis. The framework is based on the necessary conclusion that, "others who are wealthier and have enjoyed higher levels of emissions already, must take on their fair share of the effort." Countries in which poor people live should be required to reduce their emissions, but it is "the global consuming class – both within these countries and especially in the industrialized countries" – that must pay.[27] This framework advocates justice for both the poor and creation. It recognizes distinct responsibilities for different groups, as does the jubilee tradition.

A jubilee perspective on just finance

In her discussion of a Christian approach to justice, Lebacqz draws on the biblical jubilee tradition to make an important qualification to how we understand a biblical response to

---

[25] Sakiko Fukuda-Parr, "Human Impact of the Financial Crisis: Gender and Human Rights Perspectives", Commission on the Status of Women, United Nations, March 2009.

[26] United Nations Environment Programme, Global Green New Deal – A Policy Brief, March 2009. http://www.unep. ch/etb/publications/Green%20Economy/UNEP%20Policy%20Brief%20Eng.pdf.

[27] Paul Baer, Tom Athanasiou, Sivan Kartha, and Eric Kemp-Benedict, *The Greenhouse Development Rights Framework: The right to development in a climate constrained world,* Publication Series on Ecology – Volume 1, Published by the Heinrich Böll Foundation, Christian Aid, EcoEquity and the Stockholm Environment Institute; Revised second edition Berlin, November 2008. The Greenhouse Development Rights framework (GDRs) is, accordingly, designed to protect the right to sustainable human development, even as it drives rapid global emission reductions. It proceeds in the only possible way, by operationalizing the official principles of the UN's Framework Convention on Climate Change, according to which states commit themselves to "protect the climate system … on the basis of equity and in accordance with their common but differentiated responsibilities and respective capabilities," p. 16. This approach resonates with the "Proposed statement on eco-justice and ecological debt," World Council of Churches, 2008, www.oikumene.org.

injustice. It has two aspects: on one side is God's response to injustice and on the other is the human response. Human response, though, must be divided, "for injustice has the effect of dividing the world into oppressed and oppressors." More recent work in theology and ethics nuances these categories of oppressed and oppressors, thinking about oppression as a complex multi-faceted system with some advantaged in one category – such as gender or class – and disadvantaged in another – such as race or ethnicity. Keeping this in mind, there is still truth in Lebacqz' claim that, "for the oppressed, God's response to injustice is characterized both by rescue/liberation and by reticence/invitation to encounter. Both invite the oppressed to cry out, to protest, and to resist injustice." Sometimes crying out is life-threatening, and others may cry out on behalf of the oppressed. The WCC has spoken of being a voice for the voiceless; this is an act of solidarity. "For the oppressor God's response to injustice takes the form of rebuke and requisition. Both require redress – the setting right of things gone wrong."[28]

These two sides of justice come together "in the jubilee image of new beginnings. Liberation joins with redress to provide for political emancipation and economic restructuring." Lebacqz insists that this image "implies a justice not determined by nor limited to past possibilities." Rather, "it is an explosion into the new." She also refers to these new beginnings as restorative: "What is restored is new socio-political beginnings (jubilee), new attitudes of community (jubilation), and new life (the logic is that the people may live)."[29]

Lebacqz's approach resonates with the WCC concept of transformation justice (which may more accurately describe her vision). The WCC developed the concept of transformative justice in their work on overcoming racism, acknowledging in part that in some situations there may not have been a just state to be restored. The WCC AGAPE (Alternative Globalization Addressing People and Earth) document states that, "transformative justice emphasizes the constructive task of building just, participatory and sustainable communities wherever human beings have to bear the consequences of inequality and exclusion in the economic and political system." It insists that, "the jubilee tradition advocates access to resources in favour of just relationships with other humans, animals, and the land. Justice calls for deep transformation of relationships within society and with the earth." It rightly claims that, "the present level of accelerated resource extraction and energy consumption cannot be sustained in the longer term." Thus, "[a]ny viable alternative for the future must fulfil the criteria of social and ecological justice, enabling life in dignity in just and sustainable communities for generations to come."[30] These criteria must apply to alternatives to the current global financial system.

---

[28] Lebacqz, *Justice in an Unjust World,* pp. 148-49.

[29] Ibid., p. 153.

[30] *AGAPE: A Background Document*, World Council of Churches, 2005, p. 40.

The AGAPE document also draws on the jubilee tradition to assert that it "fully restores the access by the poor to the resources of production and wellbeing." It rightly notes that this goes "far beyond distributive justice to restitution of people's capacity and means to provide for life."[31] This is a crucial point because it makes clear that provision of a social safety net, although essential within neoliberal capitalism, is not adequate to our vision of a more just and sustainable world. Feminist theologians and economists charge that economic systems and policies must place paramount value on caring and provisioning for human life if they are to be just and sustainable. Athena Peralta points out that, "what is typically considered economically 'efficient' may actually represent a transfer of costs from the market to the household and ecological realms such that women's work and the environment are effectively subsidizing economic production."[32]

A crucial deficit of the current financial system is its own system of accounting, which ascribes value only to goods and services traded in the market (including illegal ones). However, much care work (social reproduction) is non-market and thus not included in national accounts, which influence public policy. This can have insidious results. Economist Diane Elson points out that the assumption that social reproduction will accommodate itself to economic policy decisions can only be taken for granted, "if people can live on fresh air or women's unpaid work is available in unlimited supplies."[33] Since we know that neither of these things is true, malnutrition and hunger likely increase, as do infant deaths.

The impact of the current financial crisis on the domain of non-market work and social reproduction has not received much analysis, although this impact is also gendered. Parliamentarians at the recent CSW meeting charged that the issue of unpaid work needs much more attention.[34] Economist Lourdes Beneria has asserted that since "unpaid work represents roughly 25 to 50 percent of economic activity, depending on the country and methods of estimation, its exclusion from national accounts is difficult to justify." We need, she suggests, "to ask the fundamental questions – what is value, what is of value to society, how to measure and evaluate human wellbeing and how to identify who

---

[31] Ibid., p.31. This booklet lists several examples of alternative programs., such as the Christian Economy of Communion of the Focolari movement, http://www.edc-online.org/.

[32] Athena Peralta, *Á Caring Economy: A Feminist Contribution to the Agape Process,* World Council of Churches, 2005, p.3.

[33] Diane Elson, "Talking to the Boys: Gender and Economic Growth Models", *Feminist Visions of Development*, Routledge, 1998, p. 164. In addition, if policies do not take account of ecological costs (seen only as "externalities") they assume that natural resources and "sink" capacity for pollutants are unlimited - which is also not the case. Eco-feminist theology analyzes the links between the exploitation of women and nature. See Aruna Gnanadason, *Listen to the Women! Listen to the Earth!* Geneva: WCC Publications, 2005.

[34] CSW, Press Release, op cit.

contributes to it?"[35] This task is also crucial to a jubilee, which returns the unpaid work of caregiving to its rightful place and includes both women and men as caregivers of children, vulnerable people, and the earth itself. I envision an *oikos* filled with multi-generational, just, sustainable, caring and participatory communities.

Conclusion

Apocalyptic perspectives dramatically illumine the human and ecological costs of the current financial system. Frameworks grounded in theological and philosophical ethical perspectives are useful in clarifying the ethical deficits of this system and offering criteria for a more just financial architecture. Political will is needed to make certain that the financial crisis is addressed in ways that meet the requirement of justice for the poor and creation and to ensure that alternatives are just, caring and sustainable. The ecumenical movement can play a crucial role in generating this will. May our vision of and commitment to the flourishing of God's household of life empower us to speak and act on behalf of all peoples and creation.

---

[35] Lourdes Beneria, *Gender, Development, and Globalization,* Routledge, 2003, p. 151.

JUSTICE NOT GREED: BIBLICAL PERSPECTIVES ON ETHICAL DEFICITS OF THE PRESENT GLOBAL FINANCIAL SYSTEM

Musa Panti Filibus

Addressing the Finnish Parliament during his visit, the UN Secretary General Ban Ki-moon remarked that the global financial crisis,

> ... has shaken the foundations of the global economy – its rules, its credibility, its values. And it has been a sobering lesson in global interdependence. I fear that if we do not act boldly to confront this crisis, it could lead to social unrest and political instability in many parts of the world. In fact, we have already seen governments fall as a result.[1]

This remark points to the fundamental reality that the global economic crisis is not only financial, but has a human dimension. The crisis inflicts pain both on those who benefited from the system and those who have been in bondage to it. Ongoing debates indicate that the crisis is not an accident, but something that has been eating away inside the system, a manifestation of moral deficiencies that required earlier attention. While governments try to to salvage the ship from further wreckage, the crisis points to the need for economic transformation to ensure justice for all. This in turn requires the transformation of human hearts and the culture of greed.

The task is to raise ethical deficits of the present global financial system, from biblical and theological perspectives, based on the premise that economy is a matter of faith for a number of reasons. The market controls productivity and the use of resources and thus affects all human beings and creation. The way the market is managed today has consequences for future generations. The market also relates to political power, raising questions of social justice. Those with more political power have more control over the earth's resources and those who do not are excluded and marginalized. Whatever way the economy is structured, it has deep implications for humanity and the creation. For millions around the world, the economy is a matter of life and death, causing a daily struggle. The global economy also affects relationships between human beings and with God. Therefore, an ecumenical contribution to debates on an alternative economic future is rooted in the church's biblical and Christian heritage and faith values.

---

[1] Ban Ki-moon, "All should do their part", UN Secretary-General Ban Ki-moon's Speech to the Finnish Parliament on Tuesday 26 May. *Helsinki Times*, Issue 22 (101), 28 May – 3 June 2009, p. 2

The system and the current situation

Economic globalization and the financial crisis

It is common knowledge that globalization has been an engine of many positive developments. The capitalist system is supposed to provide new opportunities and increase the welfare of all peoples.[2] It is even argued that economic globalization has brought more wealth to more people than any other system in history: "It rewards investment, labour and thrift, and rises on innovation. Better ideas and better products push out inferior ideas and inferior products."[3] According to market ethics, better productivity is seen as the healthiest development. Economic globalization has also brought people and countries closer through new technology, communication and transport systems.

Conversely, economic globalization has increased the unequal distribution of wealth, the debts of developing countries and human suffering. It increases people's sense of hopelessness.[4] In many parts of the world, rural populations who depend largely on agriculture are devastated by impacts of climatic changes such as draughts and floods due to overexploitation of the earth's resources. In the words of the Apostle Paul, "the whole creation is groaning in labour pains" for deliverance (Rom. 8:22-23). Already, in 1999, the UNDP Human Development report showed that economic globalization had furthered the gap between the extremely wealthy and those who have nothing except their lives to cling unto. It has also widened the gap between industrialized and developing nations, instead of what was supposed to be a "steady increase and fair distribution of wealth."[5] Despite an improved system of communication, human beings find themselves more isolated from each other. The traditional sense of community is increasingly giving way to the "I" or "me". Thus, we all live in one world, but not necessarily as a community of people.

The current economic crisis has deep systemic consequences. It exacerbates the pain of those already in abject poverty, the viability of less developed states and environmental injustice. Many families have lost their savings and pensions and are unable to cover essential needs such as education and social security. The shame and embarrassment for individuals – and their families – found to be linked to the crisis is unimaginable. For developing countries,

---

[2] The Lutheran World Federation. "For the Healing of the World: Official Report LWF Tenth Assembly, Winnipeg, Canada, 21-31 July 2003", Geneva, Switzerland, 2004, pp 60-62.

[3] R. Albert Mohler., Jr. "A Christian View of the Economic Crisis", Christian Post, Sep. 2008. http://www.christianpost.com/Opinion/Columns/2008/09/a-christian-view-of-the-economic-crisis-25/page3.html.

[4] LWF. "For the Healing of the World." op cit. pp. 60-62.

[5] UNDP Human Development Report, 1999. http://hdr.undp.org/en/media/HDR_1999_EN.pdf

the economic crisis is a "full-blown development crisis".[6] It has negative consequences for people's livelihoods, in terms of firms, jobs, revenue and reduction in capital inflows from trade and remittances. These consequences heighten the possibility of conflict around resource control. It is not unlikely that some African countries will not record significant growth per capita for some time due to the worsening of the debt burden.

The crisis reveals a serious lack of balance in the world's economy, built on the principle of rapid increase, financial growth and gains, which have become the universal goal in life. Those who succeed in the game are acclaimed as heroes. But what this free, successful market has brought is chaos. The crisis has not only shaken the foundations of the global economy, as the UN Secretary General Ban Ki-Moon points out, but in fact questions our belief in endless economic growth. From a faith perspective, the crisis points us beyond a trust and dependence on the work of human hands.

Human greed and the culture of "more"

Human greed has been widely identified as a key force behind the current global economic and financial system and a *de facto* cause of its collapse[7] that merits attention. A brief overview of the Old and New Testaments reveal different illustrations of the term "greed". [8] Greed is desire for more with the risk that the neighbour is seen as the object of exploitation,(2 Pet. 2:3, 14), or "unjust gain (Prov. 15:27; Jer. 6.13). The Hebrew text in Prov. 15:27 uses a play on words, implying "being greedy with greed". Elsewhere, it is suggested that the original Hebrew idea of "being greedy with greed" was also used to denote "cutting off someone's profit". This has the sense not only of competing to earn more than others, but also of creating cunning ways to deny those others the chance to increase their interest. This finds its contemporary expression in the so-called "dumping" of goods, especially by mega companies from developed countries. While advocates of the free market would have us believe that dumping of cheaper products is good for the poor, it is clear that it stifles local growth and innovation. Actually, there is no such thing as a "free market", because the market is not a living being with hands and legs. It is just a system driven by some powerful people who want to run the world unbridled. The idea of a "free market" is deceit and hypocrisy.

---

[6] "Impact of the Crisis on African Economics – Sustaining Growth and Poverty Reduction: An African Perspective and Recommendations to the G20," a report from the Committee of African Finance Ministers and Central Bank Governors established to monitor the Crisis, March 21, 2009. p. 1.

[7] See Ulrich Duchrow, "The Financial Crisis in Biblical and Theological Perspectives", University of Heidelberg, Germany. http://www.jubilee4justice.org/Financial_Crisis_in_Christian_Perspective.pdf; Walter Brueggemann, "From Anxiety to Milk and Honey", Sojourners Magazine, Feb 2009. http://findarticles.com/p/articles/mi_qa4010/is_200902/ai_n31426890/; Roelf Haan. The Economics of Honor: Biblical Reflections on Money and Property. Trans Bert Hielema. W.B. Eerdmans, Grand Rapids, Michigan, 2009.

[8] See Geoffrey W. Bromiley, Ed. *The International Standard Bible Encyclopedia,* vol. 2. (Wm. B. Eerdmans, 1988) pp. 567 - 568.

Using a pictorial language, Job speaks of the greedy having insatiable appetites – "nothing [is] left after they [have] eaten" – and even in sufficiency they are in "distress" (Job 20:20). While Psalm 57:4 likens greed to a lion devouring people, Proverbs likens those engulfed by greed for wealth to death: "They never have enough. They gather all nations for themselves and collect all peoples as their own" (Hab. 2:5b). Greed pushes people to regard other human beings as property. Peter compares the greedy to false teachers who eagerly use deception in order to exploit the religiously naïve, and goes further to accuse the false teachers of having "hearts trained in greed" (2 Pet. 2:3, 14). Wisdom literature points out that greed leads to hostile strife (C.f., Prov. 28:25, James 4:2). The world is learning that what was considered a successful market was simply deception upon deception. Global social stability is under threat if this cycle of deceit is allowed to continue.

Both the New Testament and Old Testament condemn greed as a vice among the wicked or "fools". For they trust their possessions, saying that God will neither see nor seek them out (Ps. 10:3; 1 Cor. 5.10, Prov. 28:26). The Apostle Paul warns the Corinthians to be aware that greed will not permit a person to inherit the kingdom of God (1 Cor. 10:11). But greed is not a disease exclusive to the wealthy. As some biblical texts indicate, greed is a disease of the human heart (Mark 7:21). It is a problem for those with enormous wealth, those relatively well-to-do (the middle class) and the poor. It has an element of excessive self-concern and -aggrandizement, not necessarily related to the amount of goods or wealth. Therefore it is a mindset that prevents a person from seeing beyond the self, and everything else is valued and evaluated only in terms of possession. A biblical response to greed is the message of God who calls us out of selfish interest towards each other, to the service of the neighbour.

Opinions vary regarding what constitutes human greed in the current system. As far I understand from some key biblical texts, greed is not just about making profit. By its nature, the market can only be sustained by profit and interest. Thus, making an income and satisfying one's own or one's neighbour's needs for material possession do not in themselves constitute greed. Elsewhere, the scripture values honest labour, dedicated workers and investment that lead to interest or growth. In one of his parables, Jesus spoke positively of servants who invested and profited from the resources entrusted to them. Someone who fears risks and buries the talent may be proud that he did not squander his talent; nonetheless, his master reprimands him for not putting the talent to use.

> You wicked and lazy slave! You knew, did you, that I reap where I did not sow, and gather where I did not scatter? Then you ought to have invested my money with the bankers, and on my return I would have received what was my own with interest (Matt. 25:26-27).

In light of this parable, the crucial question about the current financial system is how gains are made. There is also the question of how much gain should be made. Thus, the unlawful and deceitful pursuit of wealth warrants criticism, not wealth by itself. There are a number of elements in the current system that relate to the question of human greed.

Greed fuels the temptation that drives the human desire for unlimited or unrealistic gain. This includes using illegitimate means to gain, at the expense of one's neighbour.[9] Undoubtedly, markets can provide incentives for increased productivity. However, markets, like the people that drive them, are not perfect systems. Moreover, since by its ethics the market focuses on monetary rewards and more profit, it can lure people into greed. Rebecca M. Blank argues that when markets focus on monetary rewards and profits, they can provide the incentives and opportunities for unhealthy, abusive economic behaviour. A system that overemphasizes more sales, profits and greater wealth as the only definition of economic success can dislodge "an individual's moral compass towards defrauding customers and shady bookkeeping, whether at the lowest grassroots or highest corporative level." [10] Greed can lead to the exploitation of the weak, and can deprive the poor of their rights. It entices persons to deceive business partners and pushes investors to irrational risks, the consequences of which they are not prepared to bear. But since profit has no conscience, deception and lies are not considered amoral as long as they lead to profit.

The feeling of financial insecurity and anxiety about the future makes people more vulnerable to greed. It creates fertile ground for the temptation to amass wealth by any means to guarantee the future. On the other hand, self-sufficiency and confidence leads to preoccupation with tearing down old barns for new ones as the purpose of life.[11] In their self confidence, fools conclude that, "there is no God" (Ps. 14:1). Jesus once spoke in parables about a rich man who, when his farm yielded much harvest, felt so secure about his future he decided,

> I will pull down my barns and build larger ones, and there I will store all my grain and my goods. And I will say to my soul, Soul, you have ample goods laid up for many years; relax, eat, drink, be merry (Luke 12:18-19).

But in the later part of the parable, just when the man was sure of his economic future, the hour came unexpectedly, like a thief. "God said to him, 'You fool! This very night your life

---

[9] Mohler, "A Christian View of the Economic Crisis,", op.cit..

[10] Rebecca M. Blank, Panelist, "Is the Market Moral? A Dialogue on Religion, Economics & Justice", The Pew Forum on Religion and Public Life, Wednesday, May 19, 2004. http://pewforum.org/events/?EventID=57

[11] Brueggemann, "From Anxiety to Milk and Honey", op. cit.

I shall judge between sheep and sheep, between rams and goats. Is it not enough for you to feed on the good pasture, but you must tread down with your feet the rest of your pasture? When you drink of clear water, must you foul the rest with your feet? And must my sheep eat what you have trodden with your feet, and drink what you have fouled with your feet? (Ezek. 34: 17-19)

The shepherds symbolize rich landowners who claim the most fertile land and turn the needy into subjects of charity. Economic exploitation today is not only forced labour and low wages, but the abusive use of economic power resulting in massive social, political and economic exclusion.

A culture of accumulation distorts the meaning of life. The glorification of money and material possessions is idolatry, like the story of the golden calf in the book of Exodus. Just as the golden calf symbolized a new system of worship, replacing the worship of God, today there is a risk that human life centres on money. Human beings have been fooled into believing that material accumulation guarantees joy, which has been challenged. A Christian response affirms that life is not just about profit and accumulation; materialism is a false measure of a person's value. In the gospel of Luke, Jesus questions what profit a person gains if he or she acquires the whole world and loses his or her life (Luke 9:25). Similarly, 1 Timothy 6:10 shows that those preoccupied with eagerness for wealth, "pierced themselves" with many pains. True joy is not found in accumulation alone but in the love of the creator and our relation to God and our neighbours. To have wealth is to be entrusted with stewardship so that the wealth serves humanity and creation, not the other way round.

Some proposals for ecumenical principles towards transforming the global economic system

The current economic crisis hurts. But it also creates an opportunity for transformation. The international community, through the United Nations, has an opportunity to take responsibility for balancing power in the global economy and to put in place a mechanism to control and monitor the market. Those who have supported and benefited from the current system should have the courage to accept that their rules are imperfect, like any human system. It is also crucial that the inhabitants of this one earth have the moral courage to listen to each other and work together to find a universal solution. Corruption – often seen as a problem exclusive to developing nations – knows no boundaries, as the financial crisis has at least revealed and must be addressed in developed as well as developing countries.

The crisis challenges the churches to think critically about their participation in a system of which the goal is virtual wealth that harms many people. It also challenges the ecumenical movement to insist on economic justice and policies to guarantee the sustainability of creation. We can identify a number of principles which should be applied in the future.

A principle of enough

Transformation of the economy requires the nurturing of a culture and ethics of "enough for all". One theological starting point is to affirm that the God we serve is a God of abundance and not scarcity. God has graciously created enough to go round, "sufficient for everyone's need but not for everyone's greed."[16] Moses clearly expressed this when he spoke to the children of Israel.

> This is what the Lord has commanded: "Gather as much of it as each of you needs, an omer to a person according to the number of persons, all providing for those in their own tents." The Israelites did so, some gathering more, some less. But when they measured it with an omer, those who gathered much had nothing over, and those who gathered little had no shortage; they gathered as much as each of them needed. And Moses said to them, "Let no one leave any of it over until morning." But they did not listen to Moses; some left part of it until morning, and it bred worms and became foul. And Moses was angry with them. Morning by morning they gathered it, each as much as each needed; but when the sun grew hot, it melted (Ex. 16:16-21).

This text again makes plain the folly of gathering, hoarding and having too much confidence in wealth as guarantee of security. It can get "foul". An economy based on the ethical principle of enough makes us all question how much wealth each person really needs. How determined are we to leave the earth in better shape for its future inhabitants? Moses warns the children of Israel to gather only as much as they need for the day. Likewise, Jesus teaches his disciples to pray, "give us today our daily bread". These words not only urge us against gluttony but point beyond ourselves to God, who cares for all including sparrows.

The principle of enough is "sufficiency".[17] It addresses the range of equitable consumption for each person. It is also about being content, a secret Paul learnt through self-discipline.

---

[16] "KAIROS Calls for a Moral Response to the Economic Crisis". http://www.kairoscanada.org/fileadmin/fe/files/PDF/Letters/2009/aMoralResponse2FinancialCrisis.pdf
See also Duchrow, 2009, on Exodus 16 as the "Magna Carta" of economy of enough for all.
[17] KAIROS, op. cit.

> I know what it is to have little, and I know what it is to have plenty. In any and all circumstances I have learned the secret of being well fed and of going hungry, of having plenty and of being in need. I can do all things through him who strengthens me. In any case, it was kind of you to share my distress. I have been paid in full and have more than enough (Phil. 4:12-14, 18a).

Contentment is a virtue that cannot be imposed on an individual or a people. Although a community can nurture contentment, it must first take root in the hearts of individuals. Nurturing contentment requires fine lines to be drawn between the extremely wealthy and the extremely poor. It also calls attention to the capacity of both extreme wealth and extreme poverty to enslave. The book of Proverbs poignantly expresses the dangers of overwhelming wealth and excruciating poverty.

> [G]ive me neither poverty nor riches; feed me with the food that I need, or I shall be full, and deny you, and say, "Who is the Lord?" or I shall be poor, and steal, and profane the name of my God (Prov. 30:8b-9).

Further buttressing the point, Roelf Haan in his book, *The Economics of Honor*, explains that while riches stifle knowledge, poverty endangers the honouring of God.[18] It is for these reasons that the church prays with the author of Proverbs to be spared from extreme wealth and extreme poverty.

An economy built on the principle of enough urges us to shape our thinking differently, to recognize that the earth is not just a place for unrestrained growth but also a place of stewardship and responsibility towards each other, a place where human beings can live in peace and justice and, together with all creation, can relax and share God's gifts of nature.

For the service of the neighbour

Love of one's neighbour is a fundamental principle of both human existence and the economy. This places upon the wealthy and powerful a strong spiritual calling to be in solidarity with and protect the lives and integrity of those in vulnerable conditions. According to Haan, the wealthy have a high spiritual calling, "to bring a fragrant and pleasing sacrifice out of solidarity" with those who need someone to share in their distress.[19] This principle reveals that those who share their possessions with their neighbours are those who gain the most.

---

[18] Haan, 74.
[19] Haan, 74.

A daily devotional on 1 John 3:11 by Malcolm Guite of Girton College, UK, drew my attention in a very interesting way to what it means to share: "The next beggar who holds out a hand to you is not asking, but giving, giving you the chance to participate, become part of God's life-giving generosity."[20] In other words, we strip money and wealth of its power to enslave when we share without expecting something in return and when we treat our neighbours as human beings, not objects of charity. Generosity is the way of God. As a giver, God teaches those who believe in the Son to counter the temptation to accumulate money; "Let each of you look not to your own interest, but to the interests of others."[21]

Equity and justice for all

The principles of equity and justice for all are crucial for transforming the global economic system, and building peace and peaceful coexistence. Recent political turmoil around the world proves that there will be no peace without justice. In his 2003 report the Director-General of the International Labour Office supports this viewpoint.

> ...political and social stability is hard to envision if a large proportion of the world's people are excluded from the increasingly visible concentration of wealth and see little or no opportunity of ever participating in the benefits of global economic integration. Increasing expenditure on preserving law and order nationally and internationally, without investing in tackling the roots of the tensions caused by inequality and lack of opportunity, is not a sufficient answer to growing security concerns. It will not work and – in many ways it is already failing.[22]

According to the ILO report, economic and social injustice act as an incubator for social unrest. Expressly, the book of Deuteronomy urges Israelite officials to ensure just decisions for the people and warns against partiality and corruption. Social relationships, including the economy, must be based on justice alone: "Justice, and only justice, you shall pursue ..."[23] The principle of equity ensures fair decision-making and participation in sustaining the world for the common good. God's economy pays special attention to the weak and poor; so must we.

Equally important is regulation of the excessive interests so costly to humans and the creation. An economy based on the principle of justice for all pays attention to the deep

---

[20] Malcolm Guite, *Reflections for Daily Prayer: Next Before Lent to Pentecost*, 23 February – 30 May 2009. Church House Publishing, London, 2009, p. 82.

[21] Phil 2:4, in Haan, 74.

[22] *Working Out of Poverty*, Report of the Director-General, International Labour Conference 91st Session, 2003, The International Labor Office, Geneva, Switzerland, p. 12.

[23] Deut. 16: 20. See also Micah 6:8, who insists the Lord requires justice, to love kindness, and to walk humbly with God.

ecological crisis confronting the world. It insists that humans are part of God's creation, and must not treat the earth as though they are its only inhabitants. A balance is needed between social and environmental justice to ensure the protection and promotion of human dignity and access to the basic human rights to life and livelihood.

A sustainable and just economy must address the debt crisis that stifles growth in developing countries. Despite years of promises, stronger nations and their institutions have failed to deal with the debt burden squarely. It is also well known that many of the so-called debtor nations have repaid their debts many times. Indeed, what wealthy nations are doing is extracting wealth from the poor, making it extremely difficult for them to escape poverty. It turns out that it is the wealthy who are indebted to the poor. Using debts as means of attaining gains is usury. It denies the poor their rights (Job 8, Isa 10). The prophet Nehemiah gives a clear response, "Let us stop this taking of interest" (Neh. 5:10).

Churches must act with a common voice to address the debt question, alongside governments and civil societies. The International Symposium on Illegitimate External Debt in Oslo, Norway, in October 2008 – jointly convened by Norwegian Church Aid, the Lutheran World Federation and the Church of Sweden – affirmed the church's role in exercising moral guidance in relation to matters of economic governance.[24] The ecumenical response is a call for an international mechanism equivalent to the UN Security Council, mandated to monitor, arbitrate and ensure accountability and justice regarding international and national debt. For their part, African nations must intensify campaigns to repatriate stolen wealth. They must also take more seriously accountability in governance, and the building of democratic structures to harnesses their citizens' skills rather than exporting labour to richer nations.

Democratic and distributive power

It is time that the dictatorial policies of the global economy were challenged. It is ironical that proponents of political democracy are suddenly undemocratic when it comes to economic matters. Interestingly, G8 finance ministers meeting in the heat of the crisis still portrayed themselves as speaking on behalf of the whole world; "We discussed regulatory reform in our countries and at the *international level.*"[25] It appears they have failed to learn a lesson, and remain determined to discuss the fates of other nations in their absence. This

---

[24] "International Symposium on Illegitimate External Debt Oslo, Norway, 20-23 October 2008 Outcome document". http://www.erlassjahr.de/dev/cms/upload/aktionen/2008/publikationen/20081024_Symposium_message_FINAL.pdf.

[25] "Statement of the G8 Finance Ministers", Lecce, Italy, 13 June, 2009, emphasis author's. http://www.minfin.ru/common/img/uploaded/library/2009/07/G8_Finance_eng_(4).pdf

is what happened in the 1800s, when European countries shared the continent of Africa among themselves like piece of meat, without the Africans at the table. In the 21st century, a few nations should not be allowed to make unilateral decisions affecting the economy of the entire world. God has not relinquished to a specific group of people the power to decide over global resources. The psalmist says, "The earth is the Lord's and all that is in it, the world, and those who live in it; for he has founded it ..." (Ps. 24:1-2). The earth is habitation for all. Similarly, it is the responsibility of all the earth's occupants to shape the use of its resources.

Re-visioning development

The global financial crisis points to a significant failure of the development agenda and calls for a fresh approach to understanding human development. Development measured by capital increase only, is self-deception. For example, in recent years a positive growth in national gross domestic product (GDP) has been reported in many African countries as sign of "development". This does not necessarily mean more people have access to food. It does not increase the number of people living without fear of war and oppression, and does not necessarily mean improved access to basic healthcare and decent employment. If anything, many of the newly employed have been forced to become the so-called "working poor". Instead of working their way out of systemic poverty, many will hand it on to their children. Driving through the cities of Lagos, Nairobi or Windhoek, for instance, reveals the contrasting conditions of three groups of people living side by side: Most visible is the sharp contrast between the extremely wealthy who are a tiny minority. The group fairly able to manage their livelihoods is a little larger than the first group. The vast majority are struggling daily for survival. Many of these people are professionally qualified, yet, like the labourers in Jesus' parable, stand by the roadside or streets with their tools, "idle" all day because no one has hired them (Matt. 20:1-7). Most, including children, survive on hard-earned pennies, if they survive at all. Then there are those who are compelled to stretch out their hands and beg. From almost all the major cities in Africa come stories of professionals who have to engage in supplementary self-employment after working hours, such as driving taxis, to make ends meet. The GDP growth has not reached them.

In addition to GDP, the number and quality of people in decent work should be used to measure economic success. Development should invest in people's basic needs such as education and health. How much this investment benefits the lowest socio-economic levels of society, families and communities is an important yardstick for development. In the words of the Roman Catholic Archbishop Migliore, meeting these needs would significantly contribute to the "harmonious functioning of society",[26] a moral responsibility for all world leaders To assume this responsibility requires political will on the part of both economically strong nations and those still developing their economies. It also requires the power of collective stories respecting the voices of those suffering the most.[27] Equally important is dialogue between governments, religious communities, business communities and other civil society organizations. A purely top-down approach to development will remain at the top if no attention is given to those whose lives are deeply affected.[28]

Development needs to be approached holistically. The question of the human person must be at its heart. It should meet the needs of the present generation without compromising the ability of future generations to meet their needs. A booklet titled *Guiding Principles for Sustainable Development* – published by the LWF in 2002 – defines sustainable development as, "… a process of change by which the basic needs and human rights of individuals and communities in any given society are realized while at the same time protecting the basic needs and human rights of other communities and future generations." Here, development is to be understood not merely in technical language but from social, cultural and religious perspectives.[29] For this reason the financial crisis should not be addressed in isolation from other crises: food, energy, climate and ecology. In Africa, it must include crises of governance, peace and social instability, social services, economic colonialism and new forms of slavery such as human trafficking and forced labour.

Looking forward

As we look ahead it becomes apparent that the determination of the ecumenical movement to advocate a different global financial system is in opposition to the forces that claim to

---

[26] Statement by Archbishop Celestino Migliore Apostolic Nuncio, Permanent Observer of the Holy See International Conference on Financing for Development Doha, Qatar, 1 December 2008. http://www.holyseemission. org/1Dec2008.html.

[27] Archbishop Migliore has noted "… The recent financial crisis demonstrates that when political will is combined with concern for the common good we are able to generate, within months, substantial funds for financial markets which are far greater than the total amount of ODA expended since Monterrey. Surely, it goes without saying that the same political will and concern for the common good of the financial systems applies to the poorest and most vulnerable. The international community must also give greater respect for the voices of those countries and individuals most in need of financial assistance an economy that gives greater respect for the voices of those suffering." Ibid.

[28] Karen L. Bloomquist and Musa Panti Filibus, eds., *"So the Poor have hope, and injustice shuts its mouth": Poverty and the Mission of the church in Africa,* The Lutheran World Federation, 2007. Several of the conference papers make clear that top-down approach to development that does not take the person and environment seriously is a "whole" myth, hanging up there. See particularly Flora Madame Muscoda "Myths and Realities of Poverty in Africa: the Impact of Debt and Global Policies on Local Economies", pp. 45-64; and Zephaniah Kameeta, "The Church and poverty in Africa", pp 65-70.

[29] The Lutheran World Federation. *Guiding Principles for Sustainable Development,* 2002, p. 3.

hold the keys to the world's economies. We also know that transforming power is not a cheap venture. While the market is a place where greed and injustice operate, it can also promote justice, lift people out of poverty and care for the environment. The response is neither fright nor escape, but a balanced interaction with the economy achieved by engaging governments, other civil organizations and the private sector. The body of Christ is called to live and serve God in a world where the forces of sin operate. The church must live with the firm conviction that the world is also a place where God's gospel of grace is preached and love abounds.

At the heart of the struggle for economic transformation is the struggle for the transformation of human hearts and cultures. These are crucial for establishing justice in the world. In the words of Pope Benedict XVI, the world must realize that, "justice cannot be created only with economic reforms, which are necessary, but it also requires the presence of just people." [30] This means that necessary corrective measures must be taken to curtail the blatant trampling of the rights of the poor. At the same time, we must persist in faith and prayer for change in human hearts within both the church and society.

---

[30] Catholic News Service, "Global financial crisis contributes to delay of encyclical, pope says", February 26, 2009. http://www.catholicnews.com/data/stories/cns/0900901.htm

THE CURRENT GLOBAL FINANCIAL CRISIS: SOME ECUMENICAL AND ETHICAL GUIDELINES FOR AN ALTERNATIVE ECONOMIC ARCHITECTURE

Metropolitan Geevarghese Mor Coorilos

> The greatest tactical problem with modern Christianity is to reconcile its dependence upon the rich with its natural devotion to the poor.
> Will Durant

> Money has hypertrophied. The instrument that symbolized the real wealth created by humankind has itself been transformed, virtually into real wealth. From being a symbol of goods to be exchanged on the market, it has become merchandise itself. This is a fiction, an illusion. Like the Anti-Christ, who presents himself as the real Christ but is just hollow pretence, to day's globalized capitalism has made a farce of money. It no longer represents real wealth, and this may be a fatal disease for globalized capitalism.[1]

The views expressed in the above quotations appear to capture the spirit of the crisis that the present world, both secular and sacred, is facing at the global level. The secular world, although shocked at the current financial tsunami, is yet to show any convincing indication that it has recognized the inherent lacunae of market capitalism. The Christian churches, too, are struggling to maintain a balance between the theological and ethical content of their faith and the actual application of it in the highly globalized and money-oriented world of today. Obviously there is great deal of mismatch between the two. How do/should Christian churches respond to this crisis as a faith-driven community? This chapter strives to look at the ecumenical and ethical guidelines that can facilitate our ongoing attempts to deal with the present global predicament, particularly in the economic sector.

Some features of the contemporary global crisis

On 15 September 2008, leading international bank Lehman Brothers admitted that it had gone bankrupt. Within a few days, several other financial giants followed suit. Bear Stearns, AIG, Fannie Mae and Freddie Mac, Merrill Lynch, Washington Mutual ... All of them collapsed like a pack of cards – an unprecedented development in the history of modern capitalism.

---

[1] Marcos Arruda,"NeoLiberal Financial Globalization: Capitalism, A Grave Illness" in *Echoes*, 15/1999, p.20.

In terms of magnitude and depth, there is little doubt that the contemporary global catastrophe is by far the worst financial fiasco so far. It has even outmatched the Great Depression of the 1930s. Global capitalism has undergone drastic changes ever since. As C. Rangarajan, former governor of the Reserve Bank of India suggests,[2] the Great Depression of the 1930s forced countries worldwide to recognize yet again the significant role of the state in the financial management of a nation. As a consequence, nation-states introduced several safety-net measures such as social security schemes and also brought the financial systems, banking in particular, under state regulations. However, since the 1980s we have seen a reversal of economic policies, with an expanded role of the free market reaching its zenith in the recent past. Another facet of this marketization of the economy has been the deregulation process, applied in virtually every segment of economic activity.

It is perhaps not incorrect to suggest that the current crisis occurred when the housing bubble in the US suddenly collapsed. A mortgage crisis broke out there in 2007. With the central bank consistently increasing interest rates in order to pay off government debts, millions of small-business owners found themselves unable to repay their loans. The US immediately saw a collapse in the real estate market. Major banks had to simply write off huge amounts of loan debt because they were not covered by real collateral. To date, major banks all over the world have lost money to the tune of 1.4 trillion US dollars exclusively due to outstanding loans.[3] This was termed "the sub-prime crisis" by economic analysts as it was caused by financial institutions lending or investing money to purchase financial assets that are below (sub) prime level, thereby carrying higher risks of default. The housing market – which Sasidharan describes as a hugely speculative bubble[4] – collapsed due to huge loan amounts that had to be written off. According to Srivatsa Krishna, prime loans accounted for some 16 percent of the US mortgage market as against a much lower two percent in 2002. The arrears rate of sub prime mortgages was close to 21 percent in 2008. These provided the initial spark for the financial devastation that followed soon after. A key factor in causing the crisis were credit default swaps (CDS), insurance cover for mortgage derivatives, which proved to be anything but insurance cover. One must note that before the housing market crumbled, CDS accounted for some 60 trillion dollars nominal value, which in actual terms was four times the national debt of the US.[5]

---

[2] See C. Rangarajan, "Capitalism and the Economic Crisis" in *The Hindu*, 11, 2009, p.10.

[3] Stefan Engel, "The International Financial Crisis 2008 Manifests a New Phenomenon in the Imperialist World System" in *Red Star*, Vol. 9, December 2008, issue 12, p. 8.

[4] Sasidharan, "Crisis of Finance Capital" in ibid, p. 13.

[5] See Srivatsa Krishna, "The logic of casino capitalism" in *Cultural and Banking Solidarity*, vol.13, No.1, p. 27.

The crisis: the larger picture

Although the crisis occurred very recently, it has been in the making for quite some time. In fact, what is at stake is the ideology of economic globalization, the modern face of unfettered market capitalism. Thanks to the liberalization that began in the early 1990s, economic activities were left almost entirely to the open market system. Those who could compete in the market could profit. All barriers were lifted so that capital could flow freely across nations. The role of the state was minimized – if not completely removed – in most countries and governments left important policy decisions to the boardrooms where CEOs of global financial systems made decisions. This phase of global capitalism, called economic globalization, paid little attention to history. In their insatiable pursuit of profit, their attention was focussed entirely on the Wall Streets where the rich and the elite traded to make instant, big money, ignoring in the process the Main Streets, where the poor and the marginalized struggle to survive. In other words, any aspects of justice (social, economic and ecological) were by and large bypassed by the proponents of modern capitalism. In their mad quest for profit and economic growth, they ignored the social and ecological costs associated with their projects. The eradication of poverty, an increase in job opportunities, ensured food security, the welfare of the poor and vulnerable sections of society such as women have not been the stated objectives of these new policies.

According to the UNDP's 2005 report, the world today has one billion people (of whom 70 percent are women) with a daily income of less than a dollar. Whilst globalization promotes the internationalization of capital, it does not globalize labour. In fact, it loathes labour, leading to "casualization" and "feminization" of labour. The kind of pressure that globalization and its model of development exerts on the environment is huge, causing problems such as global warming, the desertification of forests and so on. Structural adjustment policies imposed on Third World countries in the form of scrapping agricultural subsidies have resulted in a drastic escalation of death due to poverty and hunger in several parts of the world. All these facts have been convincingly established by scholars and social activists.

What is of greater importance, however, is to look at the latest phase of global capitalism and its impact on the world, especially the lives of the poor and marginalized. This phase of global capitalism is known by different names such as "casino capitalism", "corporate-turbo capitalism", "megabyte capitalism" and so on. It is called "casino capitalism" because it referred to a situation where excessive financial capital is expended on speculative business instead of harnessing real capital goods for production.[6] As in casinos, the dice are

---

[6] See Sasidharan, op.cit, p.17

heavily loaded here. Money hitherto used for the production of goods has virtually lost this function. The world economic system is now largely dominated by "speculative financial capital". Money has taken electronic form. One cannot touch it, only follow its shadow . It is displayed on computer screens linked to financial hubs like Tokyo, London, Frankfurt, Chicago, New York, Hong Kong, Singapore and Mumbai. It is not located in any one place. It keeps moving. It is managed and manipulated by investors, traders, stockbrokers, policy makers and corporate managers. About one trillion US dollars travel around the world every day. Comparing it with the total world GDP, which is about 45 trillion US dollars, one can imagine the intensity and volume of business that takes place in speculative money markets.

All this trade revolves around the relentlessly fluctuating rates of foreign exchange, interest rates and profit odds, and hence involves huge risks. Bank deposits, insurance and pension funds are all traded in these markets with no guarantee of profitable returns. The maxim seems to be "maximum profit for maximum amount of risk". What is interesting is that the same investors, the global corporate firms, participate in all major stock markets. What happens in one place affects the other centres of speculative business almost immediately. As Mohan Razu illustrates,[7] 1980s Japan's speculative bubbles in stocks and real estate eventually had an impact on the US economy. Defaults in Argentina, which was already struck by recession, led to hikes in interest rates in Brazil, Mexico and South Africa. The ramifications of speculative business disasters are felt almost simultaneously across nations, with serious implications not just for the economy of a particular nation, but for the global economy as well. In summary, the global capitalism that we experience today in its electronic form is highly speculative, risk-ridden and greed-oriented. It is not organic, as it alienates human beings from others and also from the actual fields of production of goods. It is not oriented towards communities and is therefore devoid of any dimension of social and economic justice. From a faith perspective, especially from a Christian viewpoint, it amounts to absolutization of money in human lives and raises several theological and ethical issues for our reflection.

Faith and economy: towards ethical economics

The word "economy" is derived from the Greek *oikonomia*, itself a combination of the two words *oikos* and *nomos* meaning "house" or "household" and "law" respectively. "Economy", therefore, terminologically denotes management or administration of the household (earth). In fact, "economy", "ecology" and "ecumenism" share a common root word, *oikos*, suggesting that they are interrelated. Economics, therefore, is about the way the

---

[7] I. John Mohan Razu, *Global Capitalism as Hydra*, Build/ISPCK, New Delhi, 2006.

resources of the earth are managed. However, it is not to be understood as an exclusively secular concept. It is also a theologically loaded category. In fact, in the Patristic period, theology was perceived in two ways, firstly and foremost as *theologia*, which was systematic articulation of faith in the triune God, and secondly as *oikonomia*, which dealt with the divine economy of salvation brought about in, through and by Jesus Christ. The Christ event, from the divine incarnation to the eschatological *parousia* was perceived as *oikonomia*. The divine economy of the Christ event provides us with a key criterion to evaluate the various forms of economic system. Justice characterises the divine economy, expressed in solidarity with the victims of oppressive systems. The trinitarian God is present in history in a special way through the person of Jesus Christ, who represents the divine economy on earth. Justice is the hallmark of this economy and therefore any economic system that is not justice-oriented needs to be approached with suspicion as far as the faith community is concerned.

According to Theogenis, "Justice is a virtue in which all other virtues are subsumed." Put differently, justice is an ethical category and a moral imperative at the heart of the divine economy of salvation. The Bible interprets justice as seeking what is due for the disadvantaged and the less privileged. The bottom line is that all human beings are entitled to enjoy a holistic life. The Hebrew terms *mispat* and *sedek* are related. Both justice and righteousness are part of the very essence (*ontos*) of God. The biblical notion of justice is not value-neutral, nor does it represent a passive state of being. It is a verbal noun, not without praxis. Justice demands a responsive action from the believer. As we read in Micah 6:8, "What does the Lord require of you but to do justice and love kindness?" And as Jeremiah puts it, to know the Lord is to do justice (Jer. 22:15-16). Viewed from this perspective, economic systems that are detached from social justice and not biased towards the poor and marginalized are deemed flawed and therefore irreconcilable with the fundamental tenets of the Christian vision of divine economy.

Biblical justice is grounded in relationships and therefore communitarian. This is best expressed in the commandment, "Love your neighbour as yourself." Justice is concretely manifested in just relationships with our neighbours, the poor and the needy. In this sense, justice is distributive. Divine justice, an important dimension of the divine economy, is concretely expressed in the divine "option for the poor" – "There will, however, be no one in need among you" (Deut. 15:4). is not simply a utopian ideal of justice but very much a realistic vision of justice. Hence the missionary call to do justice, articulated most mightily in the Nazareth Manifesto by Jesus Christ (Luke. 4:18-19)

According to Stephen Mott, a fundamental precept of biblical justice is the principle of redress – inequalities need to be redressed and the rights of the poor restored. It is this vision of justice that underpins the institution of jubilee year (Lev. 25). The theological principle that underpins this tradition is that earth and its resources belong to God and to God alone and that they are meant for the wellbeing of all. God the Economist, as Douglas Meeks puts it, is a God of justice. It is an undeniable fact that the present, market-oriented economic system benefits only a tiny minority and further worsens the plight of the poor. The entire Christ event (*oikonomia*) was an expression of God's intervention in history on behalf of the vulnerable and the poor, the victims of injustice. This has to be the ethical and ecumenical guideline for any economic system – an economic system that is geared towards social justice. Dibeela calls it the "Eucharistic model" of economy.[8] This model is one of sharing resources with everyone, irrespective of their ability to compete.

This is unlike the present economic system, which is bent on privatising capital for the rich and the powerful. Divine economy is by nature incarnational, pitching tents among the homeless, identifying with the oppressed. The current patterns of capitalist economic engineering seem to lack a human face. They tend to push the poor, the working class, the Dalits, women and other marginalized sections of society into further penury, starvation, and psychological trauma. An ethical economy would be antithetical to these economies focussed on maximising profit and concentrating capital in the hands of a few rich people. Ethical economics is not guided by the principle that wants are unlimited because such an economy cannot be ecologically sustainable. Meeting unrestrained wants would require unrestricted production, which in turn would put infinite pressure on the earth's resources. An alternative system that is not an eco-just economy (environmentally sustainable and socially just) cannot be a credible alternative. As M. A. Oommen[9] suggests, an ethical economics must recognize nature as the common resource of all. The Christ-event, the divine economy, *oikonomia*, was God becoming a human being, an earthling, thus identifying not only with human beings but with the earth, the whole of creation, as well. This calls for an alternative economy that has a human and an earthly face.

It is an irrefutable fact that global capitalism has been instrumental in contributing towards global warming and other environmental problems. Yet, the rich and industrialized nations that account for the major chunk of pollution today have shown no willingness to pay for what they have caused. An alternative economy must be a green economy. Coincidence though it may well be, the immediate catalyst of the global economic crisis came from the housing market. An ethical

---

[8] Moiseraele Prince Dibeela, "Conversion, Evangelism and Market" in *International Review of Mission*, vol. 97, no. 386/387, July/October, 2008, pp. 194-196.

[9] M.A. Oommen (Ed), *Globalization: Its Meaning and Magnitude* (Malayalam), Kerala Bhasha Institute, Trivandrum, 2000, p.13.

...ure must naturally start by rebuilding the house, the household, the *oikos*, ...od. It must, first of all, set the house (ecology) in order. "To till and keep ...divine call and therefore the mandate of faith communities. Environmental justi... , an important aspect of the task and content of an ethical economics.

God or Mammon?

Also at stake in all this crisis is the issue of the sovereignty of God. As Mohan Razu succinctly puts it, market capitalism has effectively reversed some fundamental theological paradigms in that it has mammonised the divine and divinised Mammon.[10] In today's world of financial or casino capitalism, money has assumed absolute power. All *via eminatiae* postulates that classical theology used to refer to God such as *omnipotent, omniscient*, etc., are now applied to the new god, Mammon. Money-theism, as Rogate Mshana[11] terms it, has come to stay.

The sovereignty of God has been supplanted by that of Mammon (capital). Maximum profit, even at the cost of maximum risk, appears to be the guiding principle of economic engineering today. Money has become the pivotal point around which everything else, including interpersonal relationships, seems to revolve. One is reminded of the famous words of Shaw in *Major Barbara*, "I am a millionaire and that is my religion." Money and market are no more a means but an end in itself.

Mammon has assumed the role of a demi-god who advocates a spirituality of consumerism. God and Mammon are kept as two sides of the same coin. Yet the gospel call could not be clearer, "You cannot serve God and wealth[Mammon]" (Luke 16:13). In the context of the globalized economy, this reminds us of Jesus' command to the rich young ruler to "sell all that you own and distribute the money to the poor" (Luke 18:18-22). It implies that undue wealth and the accumulation of capital involves crime and hence is unethical. Paradoxically enough, luxury and spirituality seem to coexist today. This occurs in the economy of salvation, in the new *ecclesia* of the market where salvation (prosperity) is accomplished for a few of the rich and elite.

Christians need to look at capital, in today's context of excessive and speculative capital, against the backdrop of Jesus' teachings on wealth and property. He said, "Blessed are you to you who are rich, for you have received your consolation" (Luke 6:20,24). The divine economy of salvation is in contradistinction to the

---

[10] I. John Mohan Razu, op.cit., pp. 244 ff.

[11] Rogate R. Mshana, "The AGAPE Process: A Challenge for Transformative Mission and Ecumenism in the 21st Century" in *International Review of Mission*, op.cit., pp. 220-232.

market economy of prosperity and profit making. The divine economy of salvation, which is also eschatological in nature, is offered to the poor, and the rich find no place there. As Samuel Rayan interprets, "they (the rich) finish in the now and their present is a dead thing because their wealth, splendour and power is death to numberless children, men, women, physically, psychically and socially."[12]

God the Economist in Jesus Christ also expressed in no uncertain terms his attitude towards a market economy with his triumphant entry to the Jerusalem temple. His purging the temple off all corrupt and unethical economic activities (Matt. 21). was a clear denunciation of the irrational logic and unethical practice of free market enterprise. He challenged the "stock market" inside the temple and thus challenged marketization of temple (church). What we need today is a temple (church) that practises ethical economy and a just and inclusive economy. As a faith community, we need to examine critically the ideology of capital to which even the churches have become subservient. To quote Mshana, "Regrettably, money-theism has infiltrated some churches and made them forget that it is God's justice that is at the heart of the Christian faith."[13]

Initiatives such as the AGAPE Process and its Call for Action, the ACCRA Confession on Covenanting on Justice Movement and the recent Oikotree initiative are some hopeful and tangible expressions of the global Christian church trying to reaffirm its faith in the divine economy of salvation, an economy that respects justice, fairness and the integrity of the whole creation. In this sense, the UNDP calls for a global environmental agency and for an international court for human rights are indeed deemed welcome initiatives. Unfortunately though – and a concern shared with Mshana – some of our churches have not shown a willingness to take a strong stance against the discredited, profit-driven capitalist economic systems that are fundamentalist in their market determinism. Theological positions against economic globalization and unencumbered free market system are often, albeit wrongly, interpreted by such churches as "ideologically driven" and as attempts to go back to the outdated (Marxist) socialist path of economics.

This concern is unfounded, in my view, as there is little choice between Marxist socialism and market capitalism, as both systems stand discredited and thoroughly exposed. Both are essentially materialistic, exploitative, and ecologically insensitive and unsustainable. The divine economy as exemplified by Christ and explicated in the Bible does not have much in common with either of these systems. It is oriented towards the wellbeing of all. It is an "economy in the service of

---

[12] Samuel Rayan, "Early Christianity as Counter-Culture" in Philip Mathew and Ajit Muricken (Eds); *Religion, Ideology and Culture* Culture Horizon, Bangalore, 1987, p. 130.
[13] Rogate R. Mshana, op. cit, p. 223.

life", as Duchrow and Gueck would call it.[14] They argue that the divine economy is inclusive and does not exclude those who do not have the resources to compete in the free market. The divine economy is protective of the poor, whereas the neoliberal economy is oriented towards the welfare of the rich and the privileged. One must note that even in the present crisis, the US government and other Western nations have pumped in tax payers' money in huge volumes, to "save" the economy; which is to say, to save the rich financial institutions. The economic index in the divine economy is the welfare of the poor, whereas the index of the market economy is the profit of the rich and the elite. The former is based on solidarity with victims of injustice whilst the latter is based on competition among the powerful.

In sum, the divine economy is primarily located in Main Streets, hamlets and workplaces where the poor toil hard to eke out a living, whereas the crumbling economic system of casino capitalism is exclusively located in Wall Streets. Alternative financial architectures must be built on the basis of social justice, fairness and the integrity of creation. It should call for an alternative ethic, an ethic that challenges all kinds of fundamentalism in economics, be it fundamentalism of capital or of labour; of capitalism or Marxism, of corporatism or statism, of ideological determinism or "end of ideology" syndrome. It must be an economics that puts the sovereignty of God above that of Mammon, communities above markets, the basic needs of the majority poor above the consumerist greed of the minority elite, and justice above profit motive.

Today's churches can actually take lessons from the early church's response to the then globalized context of imperialism. The early church went beyond challenging the empire. The book of Revelation speaks to the contemporary situation meaningfully where the Caesar worship of biblical times is supplanted by Mammon worship (Rev. 17). It depicts the Roman Empire as a harlot living in luxury. In verse 10, the author of Revelation speaks of seven kings who have fallen. This must have been a clear reference to certain emperors who had persecuted Christians. One can see parallels with the new empire of capitalism and think of the fall of kings and emperors in our own recent history: Lehman Brothers, AIG, Fannie Mae and Freddie Mac, Merrill Lynch and Washington Mutual, to name just a few.

Revelation 18 is a prophetic passage on the fall of the empire.[15] The intensity and authority of this utterance indicates the optimism of John about the fall of the empire. He speaks of the fall as if it had already fallen fully, that is to say prophetically.

---

[14] Quoted in Mohan Razu, op.cit, p. 263.

[15] "He cried with a loud voice saying: Fallen, fallen is Babylon the great. It has become a dwelling place of demons, and a haunt of every foul spirit …from the power of her luxury." Rev.18:2-3.

Conclusion

As a faith-driven community, a moral community, the church is supposed to influence the wider world towards the ideals of the divine economy of salvation. Our task is not to offer the salvation of the market – that is, material prosperity for a few – but to make available the divine economy of salvation in Jesus Christ to all, that is justice for all, life in all its fullness (John 10:10). The divine economy is ethically grounded, whereas the neoliberal capitalist economy is a "free" market economy, an economy without limits or moral regulations. Regulation, in its theological sense, can be understood as an affirmative category. It must be perceived as a moral insurance against injustice and corruption. Faith communities are governed by ethical principles. The God-given Decalogue for the people of Israel is a classic example. Jesus Christ himself upheld the importance of moral guidelines for organising life and summed up the Decalogue in two commandments, that is, to love God and to love one's neighbour as oneself.

Neoliberal economy does not want to be guided by ethical principles and it has in effect replaced these principles with its own unwritten principles that are quite contrary to the biblical ones. The commandments of the market are to love money with all your heart mind and soul; and to love oneself at the cost of the basic needs of one's neighbour. In an economy devoid of these two cardinal precepts – the love of God and faith in His sovereignty (that God is the owner of all that was, is, and will be) and the love of neighbour – commitment to social justice would fall short of the ideals of Jesus Christ and of the vision of God's reign on earth. In fact, from a Christian theological perspective, it could be said that sin originated when humanity refused to be governed by certain divine regulations, even in its barest minimum.

The church will be able to claim the status of a moral community only if it allows itself to be governed by moral principles and criteria such as justice, peace and the integrity of creation. The current economic crisis appears to present us with a good example of a sinful scenario where human beings, albeit the rich and the powerful, try to organize life, especially economic engineering, without any moral and ethical principles or guidelines. For the faith communities everywhere, however, the present economic crisis also offers the opportunity to repent of their own sins of either reconciling with or even participating – directly or otherwise – in unjust and unethical economic systems. It is also a challenge to try and persuade the global financial giants to go through this process of metanoia themselves by bringing ethics and morality back to economics.

some kind of equality of resources. The main difference between these two positions concerns the *equalisandum* of the theories of justice that underlie their positions.[5] While Christian neoliberalism is concerned with liberty as the most important evaluative space, Christian socialism is primarily concerned with equal distributions of resources (assets, income, etc.). Christian neoliberals could be identified by the theory of justice defended by the libertarian tradition represented for example by Robert Nozick in contemporary political theory.[6] In their turn, Christian socialists are identified with Marxian and neo-Marxian theories.

Both of these views have some advantages – even the neoliberal one – and many shortcomings. With respect to neoliberals or libertarians, we need to consider the fact that individual liberties are important and a prerequisite to democratic society. Political freedom is almost consensually considered as one of the most important human rights. This is common ground between classical liberal and libertarian traditions of political thought. The problem here is that individual liberty is regarded as the unique evaluative space, which is a very radical normative view. This is different from viewing liberty as one amongst the most important issues. Few Christian theologians and laypeople would argue that individual liberty is the only important thing to be considered. If individual liberty is considered an overriding principle, it becomes an iron law that totally disregards both consequences and circumstances. It is hard to find a biblical endorsement of such a radical point of view.

Furthermore, many neoliberals (both Christian and non-Christian) also mention efficiency as the most important criterion of evaluation. Efficient results could only be achieved through free markets without intervention, according to the economic theory in their most simplistic models.[7] However, efficiency need not be considered as the ultimate goal. Although efficiency can be considered an important aspect, as well as individual liberty, few Christians could justify efficiency as an overriding principle that must be pursued to the detriment of other aspects such as equality. In the next section I will argue that efficiency also causes problems as the norm in welfare economics and the way it is used in economic theory, making it easier to understand why efficiency need not take priority over all issues. If there are so many criticisms of neoliberalism within Christian circles, Christian neoliberalism

---

[5] G. A. Cohen, "On the Currency of Egalitarian Justice", *Ethics*, Vol. 99, No. 4, July 1989, p. 908. defines *equalisandum* in the following way: "An *equalisandum* claim specifies that which ought to be equalized, what, that is, people should be rendered equal in."

[6] R. Nozick, *Anarchy, State and Utopia*, New York: Basic Books, 1974.

[7] Some restrictive assumptions are needed in order to achieve efficient results. We are not questioning here if the theory is correct. Even if it is correct, choosing efficiency (also called optimality) as the most important criterion needs further justification in ethical terms. This justification would not be supported by Christian ethics according to many theological streams.

represents a small part of Christian thought on these matters and hence is not very useful for an organization such as the WCC, which seeks to represent several Christian traditions.

In its turn, Christian socialism also has some contributions to make. Christian socialism is not synonymous with the theology of liberation but it is strongly associated with that stream. This theology had the virtue of having pointed to the preference for the poor, which is clearly rooted in the Bible. Evidently, it does not mean that the gospel has come only to the poor, but that God has often preferred to be associated with those who appear least in the Bible. Rather than being born into a rich family, Jesus was born into poverty. Liberation theologians can collect numerous biblical examples of the same idea. Although many Christians accept some of the ideas of liberation theology, an ecumenical perspective cannot base itself in any one specific theology. However, it is true that this theology is one of the most active in speaking out on issues concerning economics and politics and, therefore, good contributions can be found therein.

On the other hand, another important aspect is the systemic criticisms by Christian socialism of capitalism or market economies. Christian socialism usually condemns the whole market system and used to suggest (and still suggests) that capitalism should be replaced by socialism. According to this view, socialism would be clearly more coherent with Christian ethics. This is definitely a polemical issue and clearly has no unanimity among Christians. An ecumenical perspective must criticize some clear problems generated by unregulated markets. Few would deny that the market is an imperfect mechanism and that these imperfections must somehow be addressed by states. However, scholars have already been contemplating market imperfections in economic theory. Moreover, the experience of some capitalist countries shows that the market can function in a more egalitarian way, as happens in the Nordic countries, the most prominent examples of welfare-state economies with low income inequality. Despite recognizing several problems with respect to markets, advocating the replacement of the whole system is definitely not, at least nowadays, representative of the views within the whole ecumenical movement.

Another difficulty concerning these two radical positions is related to history. Libertarians would say that their theories have never been completely applied, despite what happened during the 1980s and the 1990s. So-called neoliberal ideas are strongly criticized by many Christians because of their consequences to many populations who suffered enormously with the increase of poverty and destitution. The IMF and World Bank programmes, such as structural adjustments programmes, failed in many areas, which led these institutions to review some of their ideas. On the other hand, socialists would argue that socialism as they conceive it has never been implemented. Most communist countries exemplified persecution, a lack of respect of basic liberties, religious intolerance and so on. Moreover, economic inefficiency and poverty were also very common. Indeed, it is hard to maintain that these are the way forward, despite their claims. In addition, many member churches of the WCC, mainly Orthodox churches, have terrible recollections of communist times in which they were persecuted.

There are two remaining views that must now be considered. There is what Grenholm calls "Christian social conservatism", which understands that the capitalist system should be maintained due to its efficiency properties, despite an excessive individualism that requires regulation. However, the goal of this view is not the egalitarian distribution of power and resources, because equal distribution does not respect individual differences. This view is, therefore, clearly based on the doctrine of creation and relates strongly with the idea of an order created by God. If we want to locate this view in political philosophy, we could say that this is a non-egalitarian view. It requires neither equality of resources or/and welfare, nor even equality of rights (as some argue that libertarians do). Notwithstanding, it does not claim the superiority of an economy based on the *laissez-faire*.

Christian social liberalism is an attempt to find a middle way between the virtues of ideal capitalism and ideal socialism. It recognizes that markets generate growth and are relatively efficient allocators of resources. At the same time, according to Grenholm,

> ...the state has also got an economic responsibility, in order to promote social welfare and justice. A political regulation of the market is desirable, as a means to promote democratic participation in economic decisions.[8]

Therefore, Christian social liberalism states that markets and state must participate in the economy, complementing each other. One of the most important authors to defend this view among Christian theologians is Ronald Preston, who recognizes the problems of the extreme positions reviewed earlier. In contemporary theories of justice, Christian social liberalism takes a view relatively similar to the works of John Rawls and his liberal-egalitarian position[9]. Approaches based on capabilities, such as the ones defended by Amartya Sen and Martha Nussbaum, can also be associated with this view.

These two positions are less radical and, in my personal opinion, can be more appropriate to an ecumenical point of view. However, as mentioned before, the Bible does not clearly

---

[8] Op.cit. pp 50-51.
[9] J. Rawls, *A Theory of Justice*, Cambridge, MA: Harvard University Press, 1971.

indicate what would constitute a Christian economic system or a Christian state. The Bible only gives us hints about these issues. We recognize that material life matters, as well as spiritual life. If so, in order to obey Jesus' command about loving our neighbour, the church must say something when a crisis harms the poorest. Nevertheless, the church cannot be naïve or make simple, superficial statements. This requires that before speaking, churches need to understand thoroughly how economics and politics work, which requires a good knowledge of, for example, economic theory. Before publicly assessing an economic policy, churches must understand the possible consequences of that policy. This would enable churches to critically evaluate economic measures, since they would be able to justify their criticisms of those measures according to Christian ethics. This also means that churches would be able to discuss the ethical presumptions underlying this economic theory, since they would guide policymakers' goals (usually unconsciously).

Churches can improve their analyses and gain credibility by clearly expressing the ethical values that ground our thinking and by showing a good knowledge of the ethical assumptions held by policy-makers. Moreover, an open ethical debate stimulates people to opine, increasing legitimacy and giving room to democratic dissent within churches.[10] Only after a thorough evaluation of what economists and policymakers think about people's wellbeing and development will they listen to us.

The emergence of a new development ethics

The WCC has been calling for a new ethics of development for a long time. According to van Drimmelen,[11] at its inception the WCC – which was created in 1948 – had a view of development very similar to the one traditionally espoused by economists. However, as soon as it became clear that the trickle-down effect was not happening, the WCC started to question whether economic growth was sufficient for real development. Van Drimmelen shows that the WCC then moved to propose people-centred ideas of development, mainly after input from its growing constituency of churches from developing countries.

Despite some excesses, the input from these theologians was important to show that there was something really wrong with the ideas of development prevalent among economists at

---

[10] We are not here praising the division, but different opinions and dissentions are unavoidable within the ecumenical family. They are even necessary to find a view that respects all traditions. Thus, we need to search for minimal consensus, uniting our voices as churches and persons who recognize Christ as Lord and Savior. Similar argument can be found in C. Schwambach, "On political ethics at the basis of a global evangelical consensus", *Evangelical Review of Theology*, 32, 2008, pp. 118-135.

[11] R. Van Drimmelen, "Historical Overview of Ecumenical Debate about Development", in Mshana, R. *Wealth Creation and Justice*, Geneva: WCC Publications, 2002.

the time. We do not need to summarize what is already written on the topic. It is important to highlight the fact that long before the current spread of ideas on human development and pro-poor policies, the WCC was already advocating for a people-centred approach to development. The narrow focus on economic growth was correctly considered insufficient to raise the living standards of the poorest.

Nonetheless, the change has been slower among economists and policy-makers. But it has happened, as we can see in the popularization of the Human Development Reports, published by the UN Development Programme (UNDP). The UNDP also publishes the Human Development Index (HDI), which comprises not only measures of income such as the GDP, but also includes measures of educational and health achievements. It reflects a continuous and slow change towards more open concepts of development.

The changing view of development

In economics, development used to be synonymous with per-capita GDP growth. This concept was accepted because it assumed the existence of a Kuznets curve (which states that economic growth tends to concentrate income in the beginning, but leads to a further fall in inequality) and a trickle-down idea: the benefits would eventually reach the poorest. This idea proved misleading, at least to some extent. Countries like Brazil and Mexico presented high rates of economic growth with increasing inequality. Unfortunately, there was no later decrease in inequality.

GDP per capita was mistakenly seen as an accurate measure of the development of a nation. GDP per capita is an average and, therefore, does not take into account distribution of wealth. It also does not directly measure important aspects of wellbeing, such as education and health achievements, as HDI does. Another shortcoming of per capita GDP as a measure of development is that it disregards political considerations. The existence or absence of political rights is completely dismissed. Even the HDI does not take this into account.

These three shortcomings reflect the utilitarian assumptions that implicitly underlie welfare economics. Classical utilitarianism, a very well known ethical theory, has the following defining characteristics: (a) sum-ranking, which means that the sum (or the average) is what matters; (b) welfarism, which considers utilities as the only evaluative space; and (c) consequentialism, which states that a state of affairs can only be evaluated through its consequences. GDP per capita is a measure that relatively satisfies all these utilitarian requirements.[12] A systematization and criticism of utilitarianism and welfare economics can

---

[12] Resources are means to fulfil people's desires. Since utility functions are subjective and always maximized, a higher budget almost always means higher utilities in standard microeconomic theory.

be found elsewhere.[13] The important message here is that welfare economics is implicitly supported by some kind of utilitarianism, and that Christian ethics needs not to endorse such an ethical position.

The kind of utilitarianism used by standard welfare economics has several problems. One of the most important is related to the impossibility of making interpersonal comparisons of utility. Since utility is the only evaluative space in a welfarist approach, and utility is considered completely subjective, there is no way to make an interpersonal comparison. One cannot say that a rich person eating caviar is better off than a poor person eating bread, since utility is subjective. If we asserted that, we would be comparing non-comparable things. Utility has no objective character. Objectivism when evaluating people's welfare was considered normative and, hence, non-scientific. This had two important consequences: if utility is subjective and we cannot say if one individual is better off than another, distribution and poverty are left out of the analysis. The only thing we could say is that one is better off than previously condition. The other consequence is that there was no room for ethical considerations. Why then would we need to hear what Christian ethics has to say?

However, what we have seen up until now is that economics' claim to be a positive science without normative propositions does not hold. The utilitarian assumptions underlying economics are normative and need to be scrutinized. Such a perspective is clearly limited when it is the objective of research concern poverty and destitution, since these have strong ties with distributional issues. These theoretical and ethical problems generated the reaction against old development theories. The capability approach is a result of this reaction.

The Capability Approach

The approach to development that has been raising attention lately is the so-called Capability Approach, whose main intellectual leaders are Amartya Sen and Martha Nussbaum. Sen has argued that development must be seen as expansion of substantive freedoms, that can be defined as follows:

> Expansion of freedom is viewed, in this approach, both as the primary end and as the principal means of development. Development consists of the removal of various types of unfreedoms that leave people with little choice and little opportunity of

---

[13] A. Sen, *On Ethics and Economics,* London: Basic Blackwell, 1989. Sen criticizes utilitarianism mainly because of the first two assumptions. He is not against consequentialism as such, but defends a broader idea of consequentialism that also encompasses some principles. Thus, Sen is not defending an ethics based solely on principles either. The capability approach looks for informational pluralism rather than idolizing a criterion such as efficiency or liberty. I thank Sabina Alkire for asking me to explain about informational pluralism, which is an important aspect of the capability approach.

exercising their reasoned agency. The removal of substantial unfreedoms, it is argued here, is *constitutive* of development.[14]

According to Sen, among the substantive freedoms, we can include

> elementary capabilities like being able to avoid such deprivations as starvation, undernourishment, escapable morbidity and premature mortality, as well as the freedoms that are associated with being literate and numerate, enjoying political participation and uncensored speech and so on.[15]

One of the main points is that variables such as income and wealth are considered means rather than ends of the development process. Income is one of the means that allows people to live the type of life they want to live. There are, however, other means that improve people's wellbeing and substantive freedoms. If public health and educational services are adequate, income and wealth are not good variables to measure people's real wellbeing. These achievements must count and, therefore, we need to measure them directly. On the other hand, if a country is very unequal, per capita income will be a very imperfect proxy of wellbeing.

Furthermore, as noted in the quotation above, this approach focuses on people's real deprivations. Consequently, issues such as poverty are addressed in a more proper way. One of the findings of this approach is that poverty is multidimensional – it cannot be reduced merely to lack of income. Carefully studying aspects of poverty is crucial if we really want to decrease people's suffering. The academic production of this line of thought, which brought back ethical and justice issues to economics, is strongly linked to the surge of the human development reports.

This approach also allows us to escape from the radical old views that always put the market on one side and state on the other. Neither the market, nor the state, is a god (Exodus 20:3). Markets and growth are important because they are means to achieve wellbeing. If our approach must be people-centred, markets are therefore only important because of the benefits they can bring. The market must not be treated as a god; it cannot be idealized. We also cannot believe that the state will solve all problems; the state cannot be treated as a god either. States and markets may bring benefits or losses, depending on how they are used. Sen shows how markets can be powerful instruments to combat poverty, but he also shows the importance of public policies in order to raise wellbeing levels.[16]

---

[14] A. Sen, *Development as Freedom,* New York: Anchor Books, 1999, p. xii.
[15] Ibid., p. 36.
[16] 1999, op.cit.

The ethical content of this approach has attracted the attention of Christians, as well as other religious groups. The Human Development and Capability Association,[17] which is an organization intended to promote the Capability Approach, has a thematic group on human development and religion. There are several Christian participants in this group – including ministers, theologians and highly ranked economists and social scientists.[18]

A possible role of the WCC in the current economic crisis

During the current crisis, churches have not spoken much about very technical issues – and churches must reflect carefully before saying anything on the matter. For example, although an ethical approach to capital flight may be interesting, churches must take care because the evidence on free or controlled capital movement is not clear. It is still hard to say whether capital controls are good or bad for economies. The empirical evidence is very ambiguous and there is a lot of variation in the results, depending on the kind of controls that are adopted.[19] However, scholars such as Joseph Stiglitz have convincingly argued that rapid capital liberalization can bring instability to developing countries.[20]

Fortunately, we have seen that churches have promptly used their prophetic voices on issues directly concerning poverty. Rather than focusing on abstract, non-consensual theories, churches have spoken directly about those who are most affected. Churches have also coherently addressed some issues regarding political power. Due to the London Summit, the Roman Catholic Church, through Pope Benedict XVI, released an open letter to the British Prime Minister with the following declaration,

---

[17] http://www.capabilityapproach.org/

[18] Among scholars interested in the relations between Christian ethics and the capability approach, there are economists such as Sabina Alkire (Dept. of International Development – University of Oxford and also an Anglican priest) and Severine Deneulin (Dept. of Economics, University of Bath), just to give some examples, besides some theologians. On possible ethical extensions of the capability approach, see S. Alkire and R. Black, "A Practical Reason Theory of Development Ethics: Furthering the Capabilities Approach" *Journal of International Development,* 9 (2), (1997), pp 263-279, who see the framework proposed by the well-known philosopher John Finnis as a good way forward (which does not mean that they necessarily supports some of Finnis' conservative ideas). See also T. Ogletree, "Corporate Capitalism and the Common Good – A Framework for Addressing the Challenges of a Global Economy", *Journal of Religious Ethics,* 30 (1) (2002), pp. 79-106, and Grenholm (op.cit.) for more information about capabilities and Christian ethics.

[19] According to B. Eichengreen, "Capital account liberalization: what do cross-country studies tell us?" *The World Bank Economic Review,* 15 (3), 2002, pp. 341-365, liberalization of capital movements is a very controversial issue, since the empirical analysis is inconclusive. The same opinion is endorsed by E. Prasad *et al., Effects of financial globalization on developing countries: some empirical evidence,* Washington: International Monetary Fund, 2003.

[20] J. Stiglitz, *Making Globalization Work,* London: Penguin UK, 2007.

The London Summit, just like the one in Washington in 2008, for practical and pressing reasons is limited to the convocation of those states who represent 90 percent of the world's gross production and 80 percent of world trade. In this framework, sub-Saharan Africa is represented by just one state and some regional organizations. This situation must prompt a profound reflection among the summit participants, since those whose voice has least force in the political scene are precisely the ones who suffer most from the harmful effects of a crisis for which they do not bear responsibility.[21]

The Archbishop of Canterbury stated that, "Ethics [...] is about negotiating conditions in which the most vulnerable are not abandoned," among many other considerations concerning the crisis. He continued, saying that,

> ... [a] goal of growth simply as an indefinite expansion of purchasing power is either vacuous or malign – malign to the extent that it inevitably implies the diminution of the capacity of others in a world of limited resource. Remember the significance of scarcity and vulnerability in shaping a sense of what ethical behaviour looks like.[22]

Several religious leaders in the United Kingdom, including Anglicans, Catholics, Evangelicals, Orthodox and also Buddhists, Hindus, Jews and Muslims, wrote a document together, stating that,

> ... [w]e need to be properly conscious that all communities include, and must pay special attention to the needs of poor, marginalized and vulnerable people. To forget their needs would be to compound regrettable past failures with needless future injustices [...] The international community has made important commitments to the developing world. The Millennium Development Goals are of fundamental importance and cannot now be forgotten. Even in these difficult times we strongly urge the leaders of the G20 to hold fast to the commitments they have made to the world's poorest people. We still need to find ways to enable poorer countries to trade their way to prosperity. We hold that promises made to the poor are especially sacred.[23]

The ethical foundations of these statements clearly show that the WCC must also endorse them. Human dignity issues must be addressed by churches. The more we unite our voices, the more likely we will be heard. As an ecumenical organization that bases its convictions in Christian faith and ethics, the WCC must join all those who agree with this position.

---

[21] Pope Benedict XVI, "Letter from His Holiness Pope Benedict XVI to Prime Minister Gordon Brown", 2009.
[22] Lambeth Palace press release, "Ethics, Economics and Global Justice", March 7, 2009.
[23] "Religious Leaders Communiqué to the G20", 2009.

These positions are clearly similar to the social liberal ethical standpoint. They all refer to the necessity of protecting the poorest against the deleterious effects of the current crisis. In accordance to this, other points should be considered such as (a) transparency in financial markets, (b) democratic governance in a globalized world, (c) economic recovery that benefit the poor, and (d) equity.

Transparency in financial markets

Further studies are needed on the necessity of more transparency in financial markets. The new instruments created by financial markets are to a large degree the causes of the current crisis. The creation of the modern market system was only possible because some business morality was developed, alongside the enforcement of laws that were necessary for exchanges to take place. Ethical behaviour and legal obligations were crucial to make the system work. However, the new instruments created problems.

The moral and legal obligations associated with financial transactions have in recent years become much harder to trace, thanks to the rapid development of secondary markets involving derivatives and other financial instruments. A sub-prime lender who misleads a borrower into taking unwise risks can now pass off the financial assets to third parties who are remote from the original transaction. Accountability has been badly undermined, and the need for supervision and regulation has become much stronger.[24]

The claim for transparency in financial markets is not a suggestion that markets are evil, but it is a plea for more honesty in transactions, i.e., for not stealing from our neighbour by trying to hide information just to satisfy greedy desires (Jer. 16:13). Luther's insights in the Large Catechism can be particularly interesting.

> "To steal" can include "taking advantage of our neighbour in any sort of dealing that results in loss to him [or her] … wherever business is transacted and money is exchanged for goods or labour." "You shall not covet" means "God does not wish you to deprive your neighbour of anything that is [theirs], letting [them] suffer loss while you gratify your greed."[25]

Calling for people not to be greedy is far from sufficient. Because we live in a sinful world, churches must ask for the creation of institutions to ensure transparency in transactions, including financial market transactions. Since authorities and governments are also sinful, churches must use their prophetic voices to ensure that governments enforce accountability laws.

---

[24] A. Sen, "Capitalism Beyond the Crisis", *The New York Review of Books* 56 (5), March 26, 2009.
[25] Evangelical Lutheran Church in America (ELCA), "A Social Statement on: Sufficient, Sustainable Livelihood for All", 1999.

The church must clearly state the importance of ethics within the economy and society. Churches cannot just condemn the world through the application of the law, but must also spread the gospel. As part of the sinful society that generates such crises, Christians must repent of their sins and announce Christ's grace. Ethics are important because, for Christians, Jesus' commandment about loving one's neighbour has ethical considerations. Ethical claims cannot be simply condemnations, but must also contain something deeper that might help us move towards a more just world.

Democratic Governance

As already noted in the declaration of the Roman Catholic Church quoted above, the participation of the voiceless (i.e. the poorest countries) in major economic decisions is a matter to be considered. Although some of the troubles of poor countries are also due to the local political leaders and elites, the main economies cannot forget that they are also responsible for the situations in the poorer countries – through institutional persistence due to colonial history or through unjust trade barriers. How democratic are the international financial institutions? How democratic are decisions taken by the big economies only? Although change in these matters is hard, the church must be the voice of the voiceless. And of course, change is not impossible, as history shows.

Documents such as the AGAPE Process and the interesting response to it by the Church of Norway are good examples of studies that defend the participation of poorer countries in important economic decisions.[26] Much has already been written on the topic by the WCC and its member churches, concerning the role of the poorest in decisions taken by the international financial institutions. It certainly deserves further technical scrutiny.

Economic recovery that benefits the poor

It is expected that many actions will be taken in order to ensure a rapid economic recovery. It is likely that in a few months the most important economies will start to present positive growth rates again. Keynesian ideas that were considered almost dead in the last few decades are back in the debate. I will not here address the technicalities of fiscal and monetary stimuli to demand. Economists will certainly find ways of making financial markets work again and growth will return. However, as I have argued before, growth is not enough and, therefore, Keynesian or non-Keynesian recipes may be necessary to recovery, but they remain insufficient. As Amartya Sen points out,

---

[26] Church of Norway, op.cit. and World Council of Churches, *Alternative Globalization Addressing Peoples and Earth (AGAPE)*, Geneva: WCC, 2005.

Since the suffering of the most deprived people in each economy – and in the world – demands the most urgent attention, the role of supportive cooperation between business and government cannot stop at the mutually coordinated expansion of an economy. There is a critical need to pay special attention to the underdogs of society in planning a response to the current crisis, and in going beyond measures to produce general economic expansion. *Families threatened with unemployment, with lack of medical care, and with social as well as economic deprivation have been hit particularly hard. The limitations of Keynesian economics to address their problems demand much greater recognition.*[27]

In all these matters, churches need to coherently link what they say to a people-centred concept of development. Clearly, initiatives such as the Capability Approach and those promoted by the UNDP (HDR and HDI) – as well as the commission recently organized by the French president in order to find measures other than GDP – can be supported, although not necessarily fully, by churches. Since these initiatives are people-centred, respecting issues such as human dignity, churches can certainly make valuable contributions.

Equity

Equity is another important aspect that tends to be forgotten in times of crisis. As during the Great Depression in 1929, this economic crisis seems to be affecting the poor people more than the rich, despite the huge losses in capital markets. The rise of poverty and inequality is an important issue. Churches should be concerned about increasing inequality, not only as a matter of principle, but also due to the possible harmful consequences to people's lives of rising inequality.

Crisis and subsequent income inequality mean that poor people lose more than rich people. Obviously, they also lead to an increase in absolute poverty and destitution. Moreover, social stability is threatened when poverty increases. The spread of violence and suffering is a real risk and, in this case, even the richest should be worried about it. Avoiding this eventuality may be difficult, but churches are called upon to raise their voices against it, calling for measures to protect the poor from suffering major losses.

Final remarks

In order to critically evaluate development initiatives, churches need to understand the debate. Which one of the possible Christian ethical approaches to economic justice do our churches endorse? Based upon the answer to the first question, what kind of development ethics can

---

[27] Sen, 2009, op.cit.

THE ROOT CAUSES OF THE CURRENT FINANCIAL CRISIS

John Dillon

> The crisis is unprecedented in the truly global reach of both its origins and its effects. Surpluses in emerging countries powered western bubbles. When they burst, the crisis struck the core of the global system, leaving no country sheltered from its consequences. We have learnt at great cost the need to manage the global economy better, global financial markets in particular.
>
> "Lessons learnt for capitalism's future", *Financial Times*, 13 April 2009

While the current financial crisis can be traced to a multitude of factors, three interrelated causes stand out: globalized markets, speculative bubbles made possible by financial innovation and the absence of a cooperative international monetary system. None of these phenomena is new. Although this crisis has its own unique features, it has followed the sequence aptly described by the title of Charles Kindleberger's historical study, *Manias, Panics and Crashes*. Kindleberger explains how speculative manias are fed by an expansion of credit that is often abetted by the development of new financial instruments. He describes how,

> At a late stage, speculation tends to detach itself from really valuable objects and turn to delusive ones. A larger group of people seeks to become rich without a real understanding of the process involved. Not surprisingly swindlers and catchpenny schemes flourish.[1]

The immediate precipitating cause of the current crisis, the collapse of the US housing market, fits into the classic pattern described by Kindleberger. In the mania stage an 8 trillion-dollar housing bubble was financed by cheap credit made possible by the globalization of financial markets, as will be explained below. Homebuyers were seduced by so called "teaser loans" offering low interest rates for an initial period. These purchasers, who were disproportionately members of the black and Latino communities, were not always informed of the fine print in their contracts regarding future interest rate increases. Those who did know that their payments would rise were reassured that they could always refinance or sell their properties for a profit as housing prices seemed destined to rise endlessly.

---

[1] Charles P. Kindleberger, *Manias, Panics, and Crashes: A History of Financial Crises*, Toronto: John Wiley and Sons, 1996, p. 14.

Paul Krugman reports that at its peak in the summer of 2006 US housing was,

> [...] probably overvalued by more than 50 percent, which meant that to eliminate the overvaluation, prices would have to fall by a third. In some metropolitan areas, the overvaluation was much worse. In Miami, for example, home prices appeared to be at least twice as high as the fundamentals would justify.[2]

What made this housing bubble different from earlier speculative manias was the dramatic growth in the use of innovative financial derivatives that encouraged excessive risk-taking. One innovation, devised by bond traders at Salomon Brothers in New York in 1983, allowed mortgage lenders to repackage loans of dubious quality for sale as collateralized debt obligations (CDOs) to investors such as banks, hedge funds or pension funds located anywhere in the world. Bundled consumer loans and home mortgages became "the biggest US export business of the 21st century. More than 27 trillion US dollars of these securities" were sold between 2001 and October 2008.[3] As lenders sold packages of loans to other financial institutions, regulators allowed them to make more loans – pumping more credit into the market. Some of these CDOs for mortgages and other types of debts (for example, credit card receivables or auto loans) were sold to hedge funds that borrowed as much as one hundred times their own capital to invest in innovative financial instruments. Some CDOs were sold to banks' own off-balance sheet entities known as conduits or strategic investment vehicles (SIVs) or simply left on the banks' books. As *Financial Times* analyst Gillian Tett has observed, "[t]hat made a mockery of the idea that innovation had helped to disperse credit risk" or that these CDOs were being sold at market prices. Banks "typically valued them by using theoretical calculations from [complex computer] models."[4]

Another innovative financial instrument, credit default swaps (CDSs), was supposed to spread the risks inherent in ownership of assets like CDOs. CDSs are akin to insurance policies. Creditors purchase them to protect themselves against the risk of default. Sellers of CDSs collect fees for taking on the risk that a loan will not be repaid. CDSs are a type of derivative, a financial contract whose value is "derived from" the value of other contracts for tradable items, in this case CDOs. There can be multiple CDS contracts issued on a single CDO. Since these CDSs can be bought and sold among parties that have no direct interest in the original loans themselves they are more like other speculative assets, such

---

[2] Paul Krugman, *The Return of Depression Economics and the Crisis of 2008,* New York and London: W.H. Norton, 2009, p. 168.
[3] Mark Pittman, "Evil Wall Street Exports Boomed With 'Fools' Born to Buy Debt", Bloomberg, October 27, 2008.
[4] Gillian Tett, "Lost through destructive creation." *Financial Times*, March 9, 2009.

as pork belly futures, than insurance policies. As long as markets remained calm and loans were mostly repaid on schedule, issuers of CDSs earned substantial fees relative to their capital investments. Since CDSs are technically not insurance policies, they do not fall under regulations requiring insurance companies to have sufficient capital on hand to cover claims.

By the end of 2007 the nominal value of CDSs had ballooned to an extraordinary 62 trillion US dollars which was more than the gross domestic product of the entire world, estimated at 54 trillion US dollars. But "the maximum amount of debt that might conceivably be insured through these derivatives was 5 trillion US dollars."[5] When the US market for sub-prime mortgages collapsed, the CDS market was thrown into turmoil. As CDS issuers had insufficient capital to cover their losses, markets seized up. For example, insurance giant American International Group (AIG) had to be rescued by the US government because it could not cover its exposure to CDSs.

When panic and fear swept through financial markets in 2008, the ensuing market crash spread to Europe and into the global South. Investors seeking to cover their suddenly vulnerable positions in financial markets started to pull capital out of developing countries, including those with small levels of perceived risk, causing their stock markets and currencies to plunge. Commodity prices and export earnings for developing countries tumbled slowing growth in some and pushing others into recession.

Falling remittances from family members who had migrated to the North were an added burden for populations who had done nothing to cause the crisis. As a result of the crisis, the number of chronically hungry people in the world would increase by 75 to 100 million in 2009 alone. Up to 51 million are expected to lose their jobs in 2009. The World Bank's chief economist for Africa predicts that 700,000 children may die over the next few years.

Regulators failed to restrain risky financial practices

The financial crisis was, in part, the consequence of the failure of regulators to rein in practices involving highly risky transactions financed by borrowed funds. As the size of the market for CDSs grew, US officials, with one notable exception, refused to consider putting regulations on credit derivatives. At an April 1998 meeting of the President's Working Group on Financial Markets, Brooksley E. Born, the head of the Commodity Futures Trading Commission, warned of the need to regulate financial derivatives. Ms Born's efforts were stubbornly resisted by Treasury Secretary Robert Rubin and his then deputy, Lawrence

---

[5] James Crotty, *Structural Causes of the Global Financial Crisis: A Critical Assessment of the 'New Financial Architecture'*. Amherst: University of Massachusetts, 2008, p 35.

Summers, who told Congress that Born's efforts to expose the risk posed by derivatives were "casting a shadow of regulatory uncertainty over an otherwise thriving market."[6]

Wall Street executives lobbied furiously against new regulations. Federal Reserve Board chairman Alan Greenspan told Congress that, "Regulation of derivatives transactions that are privately negotiated by professionals is unnecessary."[7] Then in September of 1998 a hedge fund called Long-Term Capital Management (LTCM) announced that it could not cover 4 billion US dollars in losses on its highly leveraged deals. LTCM was founded in 1994 by two mathematicians who later won a Nobel prize in economics for inventing a formula that claimed to accurately predict market behaviour. For a while it seemed to work, earning the firm returns of over 40 percent per year. LTCM invested borrowed funds that were many times larger than its own capital. At the time of its demise, "LTCM had accumulated 1.2 trillion US dollars in notional positions on equity of 5 billion US dollars."[8]

LTCM's undoing was precipitated by external events reflecting the globalization of financial markets. Their supposedly sophisticated computer models could not have predicted the fallout from the 1998 Russian default that occurred in the wake of the Asian financial crisis. At the time Federal Reserve Board chairman Alan Greenspan acknowledged that he did not fully understand the rapidly changing dynamics of global financial markets.[9]

Immediately after the fall of LTCM, Brooksley Born told a Congressional committee that its demise should serve as a wake-up call. Despite her warnings, in 1999 the US Congress repealed the Depression-era Glass-Steagall Act, which had separated commercial banks in which deposits are government-insured from more lightly regulated investment banks. Commercial banks took advantage of this opportunity by expanding their off-balance sheet operations that are not accountable to regulators. Then Congress passed the Commodity Futures Modernization Act of 2000 that exempted derivatives such as CDSs from regulation.

A 2004 decision by the US Securities and Exchange Commission (SEC) allowed investment banks to set their own net capital requirements, enabling them to incur debt-to-net-capital ratios as high as 40 to 1.[10] Moreover, rules adopted by the Basel Committee on Banking Supervision at the behest of the financial industry enabled commercial banks to set their own

---

[6] Anthony Faiola, Ellen Nakashima and Jill Drew, "What Went Wrong", *Washington Post*. October 15, 2008.
[7] Ibid.
[8] Garry J. Schinasi, *Safeguarding Financial Stabilit,* Washington: International Monetary Fund, 2006, p. 182.
[9] Ibid.
[10] Robert Weissman et al., "Sold Out: How Wall Street and Washington Betrayed America", Washington: Essential Information, 2009, p.17. http://www.wallstreetwatch.org/reports/sold_out.pdf

capital reserve requirements, "based on subjective factors of agency ratings and the banks' own internal risk assessment models."[11] US regulators not only failed to block widespread predatory lending practices, but also stopped individual states from enforcing consumer protection laws against predatory practices. The Credit Rating Agencies Reform Act of 2006 prevented the SEC from regulating credit rating agencies even when the SEC knows their standards are flawed.[12]

Krugman maintains that in addition to the financial assets held by banks, whether on their own books or in arms-length off-balance sheet entities like SIVs, there is a whole other "shadow banking system" involving what he calls "non-bank banks". This shadow system entails transactions involving lightly supervised or unregulated markets for such things as asset-backed commercial paper, auction rate preferred securities and tender option bonds.[13] The riskiest assets were often traded by highly leveraged hedge funds. The end of the housing bubble triggered a classic run within the shadow system where declining values forced asset sales in a self-reinforcing process.

Although in theory the new innovative products were supposed to make investment less risky as the risks would be spread among many investors, Gillian Tett observes that, "Many of these new products were so specialized that they were never traded in free markets at all."[14] She concludes that the "wave of innovation reshaped the way markets work.... [It was] so intense that it outran the comprehension of most ordinary bankers – not to mention regulators."[15]

Speculation overtook investment in real goods and services

Lightweight regulation of the official banking sector and the lack of regulation over the shadow system allowed highly-leveraged speculative activities to become further detached from the real economy of goods and services. But expectations of double-digit returns on financial investments could not continue while real economies were expanding at less than 5 percent per year. Marcos Arruda cites a study by François Morin concerning how "the value of speculative transactions worldwide reached a new plateau of 1,122.7 trillion US dollars" in 2002. This included 699 trillion US dollars in derivative transactions; 384.4 trillion US dollars in exchange transaction; and 39.3 trillion US dollars in financial investments. "The

---

[11] Ibid., p. 18.
[12] Ibid., p. 20.
[13] Krugman, op. cit., pp. 161, 163.
[14] Tett. op. cit.
[15] Ibid.

total is 34.76 times the 32.3 trillion US dollars in goods and services, i.e. the real economy" produced that year. "In 2002 hedge fund products accounted for 50 percent of … business in London and New York."[16]

As John Maynard Keynes famously remarked, "Speculators may do no harm as bubbles on a steady stream of enterprise. But the position is serious when enterprise becomes the bubble on a whirlpool of speculation."[17] As the 2008 market meltdown demonstrated, exotic derivatives like CDSs proved to be what Warren Buffett aptly called "weapons of mass financial destruction".[18]

Blind faith in markets

The speculative frenzy that bid up US housing prices to unrealistic levels and the wild over-investment in derivatives were justified by a fundamentalist belief in the infallibility of markets and driven by human greed. As former Federal Reserve Board chair Alan Greenspan belatedly admitted,

> Once a bubble emerges … an inbred propensity in human nature fosters speculative fever that builds on itself, seeking new unexplored leveraged areas of profit. Mortgage-backed securities were sliced into collateralized debt obligations and then into CDOs squared. Speculative fever creates new avenues of excess until the house of cards collapses.[19]

Archbishop Celestino Migliore, the Vatican's Special Representative to the United Nations observed,

> At its root, the financial crisis is not a failure of human ingenuity but rather of moral conduct. Unbridled human ingenuity crafted the systems and means for providing highly leveraged and unsustainable credit limits which allowed people and companies alike to pursue material excess at the expense of long-term sustainability.[20]

---

[16] Marcos Arruda, "Profiting Without Producing: The Financial crisis is an Opportunity to Create a World Solidarity Economy" Rio de Janeiro: PACS Instituto Politicas Alternativas para o Cone Sul, 2009.

[17] John Maynard Keynes,. *The General Theory of Employment, Interest and Money,* 1935, chapter 12. http://www.marxists.org/reference/subject/economics/keynes/general-theory/ch12.htm

[18] Sinclair Stewart and Paul Waldie, "How it All began" *The Globe and Mail.* 20 December 2008, B1-B5.

[19] Alan Greenspan, "We need a better cushion against risk", *Financial Times.* March 26, 2009.

[20] Cited in Mary Corkery. "KAIROS Calls for a Moral Response to the Economic Crisis", Toronto: KAIROS Canadian Ecumenical Justice Initiatives, January 23, 2009.

Figure 2: US and developing countries external debts and foreign exchange reserves[27]

(Billions of US dollar equivalent)

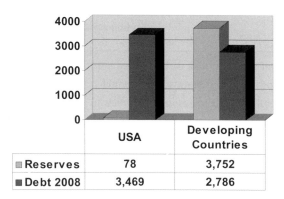

	USA	Developing Countries
Reserves	78	3,752
Debt 2008	3,469	2,786

As of September 2008, China's foreign exchange reserves were worth almost 2 trillion US dollars. India, South Korea, and Brazil each had accumulated more than 200 billion US dollars in reserves. The ten so-called "emerging countries" invited to the first G20 summit in Washington in November of 2008 held almost 3 trillion US dollars in reserves or approximately twice as much as all the G7 countries combined.

Figure 3: G20 foreign exchange reserves

(Billions of US dollar equivalent, September 2008)

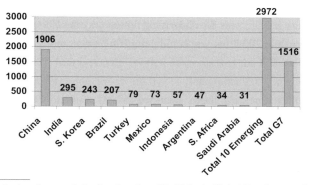

---

[27] Data for Developing Country Debts is taken from World Bank *Global Development Finance 2009*. The debt figure is for Long Term Debt for all developing countries at the end of 2008. The estimate for developing country foreign exchange reserves is for 2007 since no comparable data is yet available for 2008. The data for US debt is the net international investment position of the United States at the end of 2008 as reported by the US Department of Commerce. The data for US foreign exchange reserves is from the International Monetary Fund's Time Series Data on International Reserves and Foreign Currency Liquidity table.

Instead of using the foreign exchange built up through trade surpluses to meet urgent national needs, developing countries lend trillions of dollars to the US at very low interest rates. Thus the hard-earned savings of low-income countries are misdirected to subsidizing over-consumption in the US.

Surplus Asian savings reinvested in US assets reflect the asymmetry of the post Bretton Woods monetary system based on the US dollar as the principal reserve currency. As Jane D'Arista explains,

> ... the international reserve function of the dollar-based key currency system creates a uniquely ironic imbalance in the global economy as the current account surpluses of emerging economies are loaned to the US to finance the public and private borrowing that supports its growth.[28]

D'Arista adds,

> ... one of the more pressing issues in dealing with global imbalances is to find ways to recycle these countries' savings back into their own economies in support of development strategies that increase demand and income more equitably across their household and business sectors and reduce dependence on exports for growth.[29]

As the UNCTAD Task Force notes, the absence of a cooperative international monetary system to manage exchange rates facilitated increased global imbalances. Just as in Asia in the late 1990s, currency speculation brought a number of countries to the verge of default and dramatically fuelled the current crisis. Developing countries had to pay risk premiums to access credit from the same financial markets that spread the crisis to innocent bystanders. A new global reserve system and exchange rate regime is urgently needed to maintain global stability, to avoid the collapse of the international trading system and the imposition of pro-cyclical policies on crisis-stricken countries.

The IMF – part of the problem, not the solution

The International Monetary Fund must bear part of the responsibility for the crisis, due to the deregulation and liberalization policies it has promoted. Prior to the 1980s the IMF primarily

---

[28] Jane D'Arista, "A More Balanced International Monetary System", in Jan Joost Teunissen and Age Akkerman eds. *Global Imbalances and Developing Countries: Remedies for a Failing international Financial System,* The Hague: FONDAD, 2007, pp 133-134.

[29] Ibid. p. 134.

advocated policies of fiscal restraint and currency devaluation as the way to address balance-of-payments deficits. However, during the 1980s the IMF also began to urge countries with balance-of-payments problems to adopt measures to attract private foreign investment. Accordingly, its structural adjustment programmes removed obstacles to the entry and exit of foreign capital. Thus the IMF neglected its own articles of agreement, which authorize member countries "to exercise such controls as are necessary to regulate international capital movements."[30]

In the late 1990s the IMF's managing director, Michel Camdessus, even tried to amend the articles of agreement to allow the fund to demand the liberalization of capital account transactions, in addition to the power it already held to prevent restrictions on current account payments.[31] An analysis published by the IMF itself in 2006, *Safeguarding Financial Stability*, warned that although liberalized financial policies have tremendously benefited the private sector, their inherent market imperfections also created the potential for "fragility, instability, systemic risk and adverse economic consequences."[32]

By 2007 the IMF was undergoing a severe crisis of legitimacy. Its reputation was at an all-time low due to the failure of the structural adjustment programmes imposed on debtor countries to achieve even the fund's own stated goals. The neoliberal policies imposed between 1980 and 2005 resulted in Southern countries experiencing lower rates of economic growth and declining social development indicators relative to what was achieved between 1960 to 1980.[33] Robin Broad and John Cavanagh succinctly summarize their failure: "Structural adjustment in practice has damaged environments, worsened structural inequalities, failed even in the very narrow goal of pulling economies forward, and bypassed popular participation."[34]

Many countries repaid loans from the IMF in order to escape from its dictates. In 2006 Brazil and Argentina were the first to pay off their loans. They were soon followed by Bolivia, Serbia, Indonesia, Uruguay and the Philippines, all of whom either immediately repaid their debts or announced their intention to escape from dependence on the fund. The trend continued into 2007 when Russia, Thailand and Ecuador decided to pay off what they owed and Angola ended talks on new loans.

---

[30] See David Felix, "IMF: Case of a Dead Theory Walking", *The Progressive Response*, vol. 4, no. 15. April 11 2000.
[31] David Crane, "Plan to open capital flows suffers blow", *The Toronto Star*, October 1, 1999.
[32] Garry J. Schinasi, *Safeguarding Financial Stability*, Washington: International Monetary Fund, 2006, p. 17.
[33] Mark Weisbrot, Dean Baker and David Rosnick, *The Scorecard on Development: 25 Years of Diminished Progress*, Washington: Centre for Economic and Policy Research, 2005.
[34] Robin Broad and John Cavanagh, *Development Redefined: How the Market Met Its Match*, Boulder: Paradigm Publishers, 2009, p. 33.

As the financial crisis grew in scope and devastation during 2008, the IMF managing director Dominique Strauss-Khan recognized an opportunity to rescue the fund from its crisis of legitimacy. He prepared a "global regulation strategy" for the November G20 summit in Washington.[35] The key elements included:

- A new loan facility within the IMF to relieve the short-term liquidity problems;
- Increased resources for the Fund;
- A role for the IMF in drafting new financial regulations.

Mr Strauss-Kahn explicitly welcomed a plan proposed by UK Prime Minister Gordon Brown for persuading developing countries to lend substantial amounts of their foreign exchange reserves to the fund. Brown's initiative echoes proposals advocated by prominent private financiers who also advise the softening, but not the elimination, of IMF conditions in order to win support from developing countries.[36]

Mr Strauss-Khan once told the *Wall Street Journal*, "The legitimacy of the IMF relies upon the capacity to have everyone on board, including those countries with which there have been problems in the past."[37] The financial crisis presented an opportunity to bring back to the fold even those countries that had distanced themselves from the fund, by promising them more voting power when the next quota review is completed in 2011.

When the G20 finance ministers met in São Paulo prior to the Washington summit, they produced a communiqué referring to the need to reform the Bretton Woods institutions, "in order to increase their legitimacy and effectiveness." Hence Brazil and Argentina – that just two years earlier had been the first to pay off their loans and proclaim their wish not to have any future dealings with the fund – endorsed calls to enhance its legitimacy.

When the G20 leaders met for a second time in London in April 2009, they promised to treble the lending resources available for the IMF to 750 billion US dollars.[38] While the G20

---

[35] Dominique Strauss-Khan, "Je proposerai au G20 un plan de nouvelle gouvernance mondiale", *Le Monde,* 31octobre 2008. An English translation was subsequently posted to the IMF web site at http://www.imf.org/external/np/vc/2008/103008.htm

[36] See for example Michael Bordo and Harold James, "The Fund must be a global asset manager", *Financial Times*, 20 October 2008; William Rhodes, "The Fund must act to protect emerging markets", *Financial Times*, 23 October 2008; George Soros, "America must lead a rescue of emerging economies", *Financial Times,* 28 October 2008; Jean Eaglesham and Ben Hall, "Brown calls for worldwide bail out fund", *Financial Times,* 29 October 2008.

[37] Cited in Broad and Cavanagh, op. cit., p. 94.

[38] See John Dillon, "G20 Rehabilitates IMF, Marginalizes UN", *KAIROS Policy Briefing Paper* No. 17, Toronto: KAIROS Canadian Ecumenical Justice Initiatives, April 2009. http://www.kairoscanada.org/fileadmin/fe/files/PDF/Publications/policyBriefing17G20vsUN.pdf

Under the Keynes plan all countries in deficit within the clearings union would have access to credit in the form of bancor. As members of the union they would not have to fear running out of foreign currency.

Keynes foresaw banks in union members countries using domestic money to settle up overseas accounts with their central bank. Using bancor, central banks then settled outstanding overseas accounts within the clearings union. Instead of countries being indebted to each other, each country was a debtor or creditor with the union.

The difference was hugely important. Without access to bancor credit, indebted countries were forced to cut back spending, increase taxes, devalue their currencies and raise interest rates. With access to bancor – they could spend on domestic priorities.[43]

Despite several modifications made to accommodate domestic and international interests, Keynes' plan did not become the basis for the Bretton Woods system. Rather the proposal drafted by Harry Dexter White, the Assistant Secretary at the US Treasury, became the basis for the Bretton Woods system. Under pressure from Wall Street, the US Treasury wanted a system based on the dollar as the principal means of payment and reserve currency. As Michael Moffitt explains, "[a]t Bretton Woods the decisive factor was not the intellectual merits of the White plan versus the Keynes plan but the reality of American power."[44]

In 1944, just as today, the Wall Street bankers did not want a truly international monetary system that would cost them all the lucrative fees they earn from managing transactions. Moreover, the US Treasury was then, and still is now, unwilling to give up what Charles de Gaulle called the "exorbitant privilege" that accrues to the nation that issues the world's principal reserve currency. This privilege enables it to print money at will and pay for imports or overseas assets with dollars whose future value may well deteriorate.

A new global reserve system

Fortunately, viable alternatives to continued reliance on the US dollar as the central reserve currency exist. Starting in 1969, the IMF began to create special drawing rights (SDRs) as a type of international reserve asset that can be held by central banks. The 1984 report on

---

[43] Duncan Cameron, "*China wants G20 to create a global currency*", March 31, 2009, http://www.rabble.ca/columnists/china-wants-g20-create-global-currency

[44] Michael Moffitt, *The World's Money: International Banking from Bretton Woods to the Brink of Insolvency*, New York: Simon and Schuster, 1983, p. 20.

The International Financial System: An Ecumenical Critique drafted by the World Council of Churches Advisory Group on Economic Matters explained the advantages of a reserve system based on SDRs:

- "It can be internationally managed" (unlike the US dollar where domestic needs may lead to policy decisions detrimental to the international community);
- The "initial acquisition [of SDRs] does not entail a real cost in the way acquiring a reserve currency does" for any country or monetary union that does not issue a hard currency. (Entities that issue hard currencies can print more dollars, euros or yen etc.); and,
- "It is possible … that within globally agreed SDR issues, a bias in favour of poor and vulnerable economies can be built into SDR allocation to make a contribution to redistributing global access to liquidity in favour of poor and vulnerable economies thus linking prudent international reserve creation and economic development of poor and vulnerable economies."[45]

Whereas in the 1970s there was an active discussion of establishing a "link" between any new issue of an international currency and the needs of low-income countries, the recent decision by the G20 to approve a one-time issue of SDRs worth 250 billion US dollars has ignored this possibility. Instead the SDRs will be distributed according to each country's share of IMF voting rights, with 60 percent of this new money going directly to developed countries. If low-income countries were to receive a larger share of SDR allocations, they could exchange them for dollars, yen, euros or sterling to spend on meeting urgent needs.

Under the G20's plan, only 19 billion US dollars worth of the new allocation of SDRs would potentially go to the poorest countries because of their low quotas within the IMF. However, many low-income countries may not be able to access even a portion of this amount because they would have to pay market interest rates on any funds used and "the latest fund programmes for low-income countries … prohibit poor countries from borrowing at market interest rates."[46] According to Eurodad, low-income countries' "borrowing is limited to thresholds of what the bank and the fund consider to be sustainable debt loads" as calculated by the bank/fund debt sustainability framework.[47]

---

[45] R.H. Green ed., *The International Financial System: An Ecumenical Critique,* Report of the Meeting of the Advisory Group on Economic Matters, Geneva: World Council of Churches, 1985.

[46] Eurodad, "Finance ministers in Washington fail to deliver on G20 promises", Brussels: European Network on Debt and Development, 27 April 2009. http://www.eurodad.org/whatsnew/articles.aspx?id=3603

[47] Ibid.

While a new allocation of SDRs could serve a moderate redistributive function in the short term, a more important discussion has begun concerning the role that an SDR-like asset might play in a new global reserve system. Zhou Xiaochuan, governor of the Peoples' Bank of China, has proposed an expanded role for the SDR going beyond its role as a reserve currency held by central banks. He suggests that the SDR also be used

- as "a widely accepted means of payment in international trade and financial transactions";
- for "commodities pricing, investment and corporate book-keeping. This will ... effectively reduce the fluctuation of prices of assets denominated in national currencies and related risks"; and
- in "SDR-denominated securities".[48]

Zhou Xiaochuan further proposes that, "the basket of currencies forming the basis for SDR valuation should be expanded to include currencies of all major economies."[49] Similarly, the Commission of Experts on Reforms to the International Monetary and Financial System, appointed by Rev. Miguel d'Escoto as President of the UN General Assembly, recommends the use of an international asset like the SDR in a new global reserve system. The UN expert panel, chaired by Joseph Stiglitz, says a new reserve system is needed to overcome the imbalance created by developing countries' excessive accumulation of foreign exchange reserves and the instability of the current international reserve system, with its overdependence on the US dollar whose future value is likely to deteriorate given the USA's enormous international debt.

In Stiglitz' words,

> The existing system, with the US dollar as reserve currency, is fraying. The dollar has been volatile. There are increasing worries about future inflationary risks. At the same time, putting so much money aside every year to protect countries against the risks of global instability creates a downward bias in – aggregate demand – weakening the global economy.[50]

While the US government and Wall Street have dismissed the idea of replacing the US dollar with the SDR as unfeasible, the UN panel of experts says that a new global reserve system is "feasible, non-inflationary, and could be easily implemented." Pedro Páez Pérez, Ecuador's

---

[48] Zhou Xiaochuan, *Reform the International Monetary System,* Beijing: People's Bank of China, March 23, 2009. http://www.pbc.gov.cn/english//detail.asp?col=6500&ID=178

[49] Ibid.

[50] Joseph Stiglitz, "Reform is needed. Reform is in the air. We can't afford to fail", *The Guardian*, March 27, 2009.

former Minister of Economic Policy Coordination, told a UN hearing that such a reserve system could be implemented within six months.

On 30 October 2008, Páez Pérez presented a proposal for a crisis response agenda from the South to a UN General Assembly hearing on the crisis.[51] That agenda begins with the launch of the Bank of the South, wholly owned and controlled by Argentina, Brazil, Bolivia, Ecuador, Paraguay, Uruguay and Venezuela, with an authorized capital of 20 billion US dollars. It also envisions the establishment of stabilization funds entirely controlled by Southern countries and joint consultations on setting credible exchange rates through regional monetary agreements.

Agreements among Southern countries to use their own currencies instead of dollars or euros or yen for intra-regional trade could lead to the establishment of regional central banks and common reserves funds from which Southern countries could borrow instead of having to seek funds from the Bretton Woods institutions. South American countries are also discussing eventually creating a common currency. While this vision of South-South cooperation might be implemented first among South American countries, Páez Pérez suggests that the same kind of cooperation could occur in other regions, eventually opening the way for a new global financial architecture.

Conclusion

When economies begin to recover from the current crisis there cannot simply be a return to business as usual. Indeed, attempts to prop up the old order are not only unlikely to succeed but may also prevent the introduction of the kind of measures needed to genuinely overcome the crisis. As the *Financial Times* columnist Martin Wolf has written, "The world economy cannot go back to where it was before the crisis, because that was demonstrably unsustainable."[52]

Many civil society groups view the crisis as an historic turning point – the end to a fundamentalist belief in unfettered free markets and an opportunity for a new beginning. As the former World Council of Churches General Secretary, the Reverend Doctor Samuel K̶ ritten, "What we need are brave and new measures to correct this unjust and ur   tem in order to prevent such a crisis from occurring once agai

---

51   f "The Ecuadorian Proposal for a Crisis Response Agenda from the South"
      ral Assembly on October 30 by Minister Paéz Pérez, visit www.un.org/ga/

52   "Why the 'green shoots' of recovery could yet wither", *Financial Times*, 2
53   uel Kobia, "Letter to G20 countries on the Global Economic and Financi
      hurches, 27 March 2009.

THE CRISIS: FROM IMPACTS ON THE DEVELOPING WORLD TO A CALL FOR GLOBAL SOLUTIONS

Dr Marie-Aimée Tourres

September 2007, the crisis officially begins

This is a very brief summary of the beginning of what was later called the sub-prime crisis.[1] In September 2007, the most unexpected news hit the worldwide media. The British bank Northern Rock was declared to be in trouble and was to get an emergency loan from Britain's central bank on 13 September. Not long afterwards, the bank was nationalised. Over the next twelve months the banking and financial sector remained in the headlines and for the worst reasons. Financial giant Citigroup and US investment bank Merrill Lynch saw their shares drop, reporting increasing and worrying losses and eventually the resignation of their CEOs. In March 2008, Bear Stearns was forced to accept a buyout by US investment bank JPMorgan Chase at a fire-sale price of 2 US dollars per share to avoid bankruptcy. The deal was backed by the Federal Reserve, providing up to 30 billion US dollars to cover possible Bear Stearns losses.

After months of growing troubles and losses, the US government had to take over the two mortgage giants Fannie Mae and Freddie Mac on 7 September 2008. The US investment bank Lehman Brothers was not exempted, facing increasing financial crisis. The stock prices of other financial institutions also fell sharply, including those of Merrill Lynch, the insurance giant American International Group (AIG), and Washington Mutual, the largest US savings and loan bank.

Three major events happened in the banking industry on "Black Monday", 15 September 2008. Lehman Brothers, the fourth largest investment bank in the US filed for Chapter 11 bankruptcy protection after a huge loss in the mortgage market. On the same day, Bank of America acquired Merrill Lynch for 50 billion US dollars, while in an historic move, the US federal government bailed out AIG with an 85 billion US dollars loan, giving the government control of the firm. Once the crisis started to cross the Atlantic, financial institutions such as Swiss bank UBS and the UK's biggest bank HSBC, were not exempted from the meltdown.

---

[1] See chapter by John Dillon for more detailed background of the crisis. Also see Paul Mason, *Meltdown, the end ʰe age of greed*, Verso, 2009. Economics editor of BBC *Newsnight*, Paul Mason has covered globalization and ʳstice stories from many locations around the world. His book tells the story of the roots of the US and UK's ʰris and the financial crash which follows in a very simple and easy-to-read manner.

At that time – which was not so long ago – the newspapers headlines were "Financial panic", "Economic catastrophe", "World economy in danger" and "What next?" Over the following two years, what had started as a sub-prime crisis was followed by a cascade of further crises: financial, security, economic, environmental, food and water, energy and social. The consequences are still evident. Nonetheless, at the end of summer 2009 new headlines started to appear such as "Rays of recovery" and "Sustainable US recovery is on the way". The phrase "green shoot" has started to sprout everywhere. We may wonder if we are victims of over-optimism or if we are purposely being brainwashed by the media, which tries to keep boosting consumer confidence with made-up stories. Incidentally, we may also ask who is really concerned and who is able to feel this imminent recovery.

In June 2009, Goldman Sachs announced that its employees could expect the biggest bonus payouts in the firm's 140-year history after a spectacular first half of the year. To add to the picture, billionaire investor Warren Buffet – who invested in Goldman Sachs at the height of the financial crisis for 5 billion US-dollar share –made a 4.1 billion US dollar (2.5 billion British pounds) paper profit on the money he invested[2]. The resurrection of the guaranteed bonus and such a return on investment can be seen as shocking news. It is also worrying. Did no one learn from recent events? Are greedy bankers and investors back already?

It is hard to believe that the social, economic, ecological and political consequences can be so easily swept away. Martin Wolf in his weekly *Financial Times* column is right and can cut short concerns that the big investment banks that survived the credit crunch may derail financial regulation reforms, "Those who expect a swift return to the business as-usual of 2006 are fantasists."[3]

Even if the worst of the financial crisis is behind us, it does not mean it is over. For instance, the issue of bad assets remained unsolved in many ways. A big part of the current recovery is underpinned by massive explicit and implicit taxpayer support, as highlighted by Martin Wolf. Indeed, the ordinary person is still suffering. The green shoot is not yet at everyone's doorstep. In July 2009, the European Trade Union Confederation (ETUC) issued a report with an interesting title supporting this position, entitled "Green shoot … of casino capitalism". The report warns about the early return of a "casino capitalism" economy,

> [...] with OECD governments massively saving the banking system from its own "toxic asset" mess [...], and with high amounts of liquidity being available, financial

---

[2] *The Guardian*, "Goldman to make record bonus payout", 21 June 2009. Also *Telegraph*, "Warren Buffet makes a 4bn US dollars profit on Goldman Sachs stake", 24 July 2009.
[3] 14 July 2009.

markets have recently started to move some of the liquidity being available from "safe haven" assets (long term government bonds) into commodity markets.[4].

The report also expressed its deep concern about the deteriorating jobs situation in Europe as unemployment is rising quickly.

The contrast between what seems (already) to be a recovery at the Goldman Sachs or JP Morgan end of the banking and financial sector and the daily reality of ordinary people remains a striking truth. We have reached a stage where finance has been totally disconnected from the real economy and where an ethical access to wealth is becoming a pressing issue. In his book *Agenda For a New Economy, From Phantom Wealth to Real Wealth*, David Korten, president and founder of the People-Centred Development Forum wrote, "Wall Street's phantom-wealth machine has created prospective claims and related expectations far out of proportion to the real wealth available to satisfy them."[5]

The current crisis is the best example of where phantom wealth – money disconnected from the production or possession of anything of real value – can lead. As Korten says, the situation is "Wall Street capitalism versus Main Street markets." The latter is the world of local businesses and working people producing real goods and services to provide livelihoods for themselves and communities, people like you and me, who are paying the highest cost. We cannot allow the moral corruption of Wall Street to bring down our entire economy or our nations. This includes the developing world as a whole. The world economy is in a state of great uncertainty, and allowing us to better monitor the human impact of the crisis.

How the developing world has been hit

The world has become a complex place and it is unlikely that there is a single cause of anything we observe. Interestingly, the current crisis originated with rich-world lenders, not emerging-market or developing-world borrowers[6]. The negative impact on developing economies has been substantial although they did not cause the problem.

The global economic crisis was transmitted through multiple channels, but we can rightly say that there are three main ones. The first channel is that of banking failures and reductions in domestic

---

[4] http://www.etuc.org/a/6302

[5] 2009, page 66.

[6] This result was also highlighted earlier by Martin Wolf, from *the Financial Times*. He has consistently warned about the coming danger of the scale of the global imbalance (saving, investments, trade, and government debt). He summed up the situation in his book, *Fixing global finance,* The Johns Hopkins University Press, 2008: "Capital now flows upstream, from the world's poor to the richest country of all [the US]".

lending. Fortunately this time, the very small number of foreign-owned banks and the low level of financial integration with world markets helped to limit its direct effect on the banking sectors of most African and Latin American countries. The indirect effect was more important. The soaring prices of stock market shares and houses in the US reduced the disposable capital of the corporate and banking sector in the Western world, leading to a reduction of their will and capacity to invest in the developing world to sustain their growth. The more dramatic consequences were not long in coming: there was a rise in unemployment, leading to a fall in demand and government revenue and therefore a shortfall of money to fight poverty and hunger.

The global South has been hit by a sharp drop in export earnings. This second channel of transmission deeply affected developing countries, which experienced a reduced demand for goods (agricultural, raw materials and minerals) and services from developed countries, especially the US. Tourism has slowed sharply due to a slowdown in business travel and a fall in domestic consumption of luxury goods and hotel bookings. This has especially affected the small island states like Mauritius. Lastly, this has a substantial impact on the commodity-dependent countries since September 2008 when the oil price began a drop of 70 percent during the second half of the year.

The third main transmission channel is related to capital/financial flows. Private investment flows, trade credit and remittances, especially from migrant workers in the US and Europe, are several sources of finance dramatically hit by the current crisis. As for direct foreign investments, their levels are dwindling (with a fall of 54 percent in the first quarter of 2009 according to UNCTAD). Net private capital flows to emerging economies in 2009 will be down substantially from 2008. Net flows are now projected to be about 141 billion US dollars for the year as a whole, less than half of the 392 billion US dollars estimated for 2008, and far below the record level of 890 billion US dollars in 2007.[7]

Also, following the 2002 Monterrey Consensus on Financing for Development, the developed countries agreed to give 0.7 percent of their gross domestic income (GDI) to official development assistance (ODA). With growth slowing down, the absolute volume of ODA aid has sharply decreased. The doubling of aid from G8 donors to the developing world by 2010 is now unlikely to happen. The rise of new donors such as China and Japan are, consequently, a blessing.

The end results of the above have a direct impact on the fiscal revenues and on least developed countries (LDCs), and on government expenditure capacity in developed economies. From

---

[7] The Institute of International Finance, June 2009

an economic crisis, we have moved to a pending social and human crisis with potentially severe political consequences in some parts of the world.

Imbalanced growth coupled with a phantom economy

The irony of the history is sad to observe. The developing world, including the emerging economies or the South, are the ones which have in their own way sustained and/or contributed to world economic growth and, more specifically, growth in the Northern Hemisphere. They have historically been the growth engine, as the table below shows.

Table: Contributions to global demand, consumption and investment in percent and percentage points[8]

	1995	2000	2005	2006	2007
Real GDP					
Global (1)	3.8	4.8	4.2	4.7	4.5
US	0.6	0.9	0.8	0.7	0.5
Euro area	0.6	0.8	0.3	0.5	0.5
Other advanced industrial (2)	0.4	0.6	0.4	0.5	0.5
Emerging economies (3)	2.2	2.5	2.7	3.0	3.0
Real consumption (4)					
Global	3.5	4.7	4.3	4.5	4.7
US	0.7	1.2	0.8	0.8	0.7
Euro area	0.5	0.6	0.3	0.4	0.3
Other advanced industrial	0.4	0.4	0.4	0.4	0.5
Emerging economies	1.9	2.5	2.8	2.9	3.2
Real investment (5)					
Global	4.6	6.4	7.7	7.1	5.7
US	1.4	1.5	1.5	0.6	-0.5
Euro area	0.5	1.0	0.6	1.0	0.8
Other advanced industrial	0.3	0.4	0.8	0.8	0.5
Emerging economies	2.4	3.5	4.8	4.7	4.9

(1) growth in the economies listed, in %, weighted by 2005 GDP and PPP exchange rates.

(2) Australia, Canada, Denmark, Japan, New Zealand, Norway, Sweden, Switzerland and the UK.

(3) Argentina, Brazil, Chile, China, Colombia, the Czech Republic, Hong Kong SAR, Hungary, India, Indonesia, Korea, Malaysia, Mexico, the Philippines, Poland, Russia, Saudi Arabia, Singapore, South Africa, Taiwan, Thailand, Turkey and Venezuela.

(4) Private final consumption expenditure.

(5) Gross fixed capital formation.

---

[8] Data sources: IMF, Datastream national data; in BIS 78th annual report, June 2008.

Also, in some cases, the growing national consumption from emerging economies helped US exports, while in other cases, developing countries were lending their foreign reserves to developed countries at a very low interest rates and borrowing back at higher rates. Under the neoliberal framework, there is a tendency for capital to flow frantically into one asset bubble after another, with the financial system as the channel. The capital flows towards the Western countries – and especially the US – were mediated by Wall Street.

Since the 1997 Asian crisis especially, the central banks of emerging markets such as China have been building up a substantial amount of foreign reserves. This is a liquidity creation scheme that relies on the dollar's favoured position in international trade and as a reserve currency. The combination of these factors resulted in a global macroeconomic imbalance which, slowly but surely, put the world as a whole in an unsustainable situation.

Since the 1990s, the global financial system has created gross instability in the world economy. We can also correctly say that the imbalanced global situation has been in part increasingly characterised by the nature of its global liquidity. The dominance of a new financial system, derivatives and a debt-fuelled growth model is in reality only a little over ten years old. The derivatives, such as futures, options and other similar financial instruments – which were originally made to manage risk - quickly appealed to smart investors, who found loopholes in the system, deregulation and new technology allowing the emergence of the wider global derivative market use in making profit instead. The speed and the way in which this new finance system grew and began to disconnect from the real economy were exponential and crazy.

However, not everyone saw what was happening as a problem. For Alan Greenspan, then Federal Reserve chairman, derivatives were contributing to a safer financial system with reduced systemic problems. Opposed to this view was the world-renowned investor Warren Buffet, for whom derivatives were a "financial weapons of mass destruction."[9] History shows us who was right.

In fact, the words "irrational exuberance" seem best to describe what the economist Robert Shiller, a professor at Yale University, observed in 2000.[10] Shiller's observation prompted

---

[9] "We try to be alert to any sort of mega catastrophe risk, and that posture may make us unduly apprehensive about the burgeoning quantities of long-term derivatives contracts and the massive amount of uncollateralized receivables that are growing alongside. In our view, however, derivatives are financial weapons of mass destruction, carrying dangers that, while now latent, are potentially lethal," excerpt from Warren Buffett's speech to the Shareholders of Berkshire Hathaway Inc., p. 14. http://www.berkshirehathaway.com/letters/2002pdf.pdf

[10] The definition of the term irrational exuberance has its origin in a speech given by Alan Greenspan on 5 December 1996. It became his most famous quote.

him to warn that the stock market has become a bubble as early as March of that year. This phenomenon worried him to the extent that he decided to entitle his book, which became a New York Times best-seller, *Irrational Exuberance*.[11]

Nouriel Roubini, professor of economics at the NYU Stern School of Business, was another person pointing out the risk of expanding bubbles within such an imbalanced environment.

> The crisis was caused by the largest leveraged asset bubble and credit bubble in the history of humanity, where excessive leveraging and bubbles were not limited to housing in the US but also to housing in many other countries and excessive borrowing by financial institutions and some segments of the corporate sector and of the public sector in many and different economies: a housing bubble, a mortgage bubble, an equity bubble, a bond bubble, a credit bubble, a commodity bubble, a private equity bubble, a hedge funds bubble are all now bursting at once in the biggest real sector and financial sector deleveraging since the Great Depression.[12]

The inverted pyramid in the figure below demonstrates how disconnected real and virtual money has become. Updated at the beginning of 2010, the global liquidity pyramid describes the elusive nature of the shadow financial system. It is easy to see that the value of the financial economy is much bigger than that of the real world on which is it based. The bottom part, reflecting the power money of reserve cash, accounts for a mere 1 percent of global liquidity and is opposed to the top part, which represents interest rate and credit derivatives. This top part, added to securitized debt, represents a spectacular amount of virtual money. This is no less than the equivalent of 1058 percent of the world GDP.

Although it is difficult to evaluate the real state of the liquidity pyramid, the trend is worrisome. Despite the 2007 financial turmoil and its domino-effect consequences, the share of derivatives and its equivalent in terms of world GDP has increased. It was respectively 75 percent and 802 percent in 2007.[13] This is an indication that the virtual financial system is still rolling. Wall Street continues to run the government somehow, rather than the reverse.

---

[11] 2000.

[12] 9 October 2008, RGE Monitor website http://www.rgemonitor.com/roubini-monitor/253973 or Contreinfo website : http://contreinfo.info/article.php3?id_article=2237

[13] See chapter by Roel Aalbersberg for more comments on this pyramid.

Figure : Liquidity Pyramid[14]

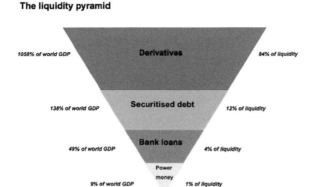

The liquidity pyramid

Crisis rescue: from what has been claimed and agreed...

Despite a general tendency to compare the current crisis to the Great Depression of 1929, actions taken by the G8 governments have helped to avoid a similarly disastrous episode. The US government opted for a round of various plans including the bailing out and recapitalization of banks and insurance companies, starting with the Paulson plan in September 2008. This three-page plan put in place in panic by the then-Treasury Secretary Henry Paulson, came to an amount no less than 700 billion US dollars.

At the international level, the G20 met for its Summit on Financial Markets and World Economy on 14–15 November 2008, where G20 leaders announced unprecedented stimulus packages and policy responses to offset the effect of the financial collapse. The summit acknowledged the severity of the economic situation and came out with a few key objectives, ranging from bank supervision, transparency on accounting standards to less protectionism, just to name a few. All members actively supported a policy of lowering interest rates as part of the solution to the problem.

A second G20 summit followed in London in April 2009. Tax haven and hedge fund issues were part of the agenda, while the rejection of any sort of protectionism was re-iterated. The group also re-affirmed its commitment to the millennium development goals (MDGs) and their pledge to increase ODA. The IMF, its actions and administration,especially towards

---

[14] Independent Strategy Ltd. Used with permission.

the poorest and hardest-hit countries, was also up for discussion. It was then announced that a total of 1.1 trillion US dollars – a tripling of finance – would be made available via the institution to boost the world economy. Timothy Geithner, the 75th and current US Secretary of the Treasury, said that a new realignment of power at the fund would be given to new members in a way beneficial to emerging markets. The IMF quota review has been brought forward from 2013 to 2011. He also proposed a reduction in the size of the IMF's executive board from 24 to 22 by 2010, and to 20 by 2012, paralleling the end of the EU and US headships at the IMF and the World Bank respectively.

However, the good news from the G20 must be taken cautiously. The G20 is not the 192 UN member countries and therefore the outcomes of the summit cannot be the same as if they resulted from a UN summit. We must monitor what comes next and what has actually been done so far and compare it to the big. International finance and sustainable economic development for all must not exclusively belong to those who participated in the London summit.

Many of these and other policies are merely short-term or temporary fixes, like sticking plasters. The long term effects on the *real* economy of the stimulus packages, lower interest rates and other monetary policies implemented by various governments have not really been examined as they should have been. The real impact of the indirect and possible dire consequences remains to be seen when the time comes to pay back the national budget deficits incurred during the crisis.

... To what has really been done

At the time of the AGEM09, many issues remained unaddressed. Data estimations indicating the total extent of the crisis and subsequent recovery were still being either discussed or faced a lack of consensus. The are several key issues. One glaring example is the agreement to avoid any sort of protectionism until 2010. This did not have many echoes in reality. Despite a pledge by the G20 leaders in November last year to avoid protectionist measures, 17 of the countries have since put in place 47 new measures that restrict trade at the expense of other countries' new trade restrictions, according to a World Bank report.[15]

The reform of international financial institutions has not made much progress. The increased resources of the IMF have surely contributed to the rehabilitation of the institution in its duty toward the developing world. As John Dillon pointed out in his chapter, the IMF was

---

[15] Elisa Gamberoi and Robert Newfarmer, "Trade protection: Incipient but worrisome trends", World Bank, *Trade notes,* number 37, 2 March, 2009. http://siteresources.worldbank.org/NEWS/Resources/Trade_Note_37.pdf

undergoing a severe crisis of legitimacy by 2007. The current crisis is giving the institution a new role to play.[16] Although the IMF will work hand in hand with the United Nations and its agencies, the latter has been marginalized in the process. The quota-share revision, agreed upon in April 2008, was still under discussion in summer 2009, because the G20 could not reach a new allocation to satisfy them all.

The IMF and the G20, which control about 85 percent of the world economy, agreed to help the developing world by using additional resources from the IMF. In April 2009, the leaders committed 1.1 trillion US dollars to combat the financial crisis, mainly channelled through the IMF. Seven hundred and fifty billion US dollars is to be given via the IMF and split as follows: 500 billion US dollars consists of new resources which, if realised, would be in addition to the 225 billion US dollars that the IMF had available from existing quota-based resources. (Incidentally, by July 2009 only the 100 billion US dollars committed by Japan in February had actually been formally signed off, the rest being only intentions or commitments. The tracking is not easy to do because the communiqué available at the time did not provide a real breakdown of the sum.) The balance of 250 billion US dollars were issued via the IMF's reserve asset, the special drawing rights (SDR),[17] and injected into member nations' treasuries (186 countries) on 28 August 2009. This disbursement is by far the largest general SDR allocation in the IMF's six-decade history.

Although, the IMF stressed that, "nearly 100 billion dollars of the general allocation [would] go to emerging markets and developing countries, of which low-income countries [would] receive over 18 billion dollars,"[18] the largest of the new SDR allocations [would] go to the most advanced economies because of their relatively heavier quotas. The United States, the biggest stakeholder, [would] get a combined SDR allocation of 30.4 million SDR, or roughly 47.3 billion dollars.

Separately, the total created under the special allocation would amount to SDR 21.5 billion (about 33 billion US dollars) and made available on 9 September 2009. According to the IMF, "the special allocation will make the allocation of SDRs more equitable and correct for the fact that countries that joined the fund after 1981 – more than one fifth of the current IMF membership – had never received an SDR allocation."

---

[16] Also see John Dillon, "G20 rehabilitates IMF, marginalizes UN", *Policy briefing paper*, Kairos, no. 17, April 2009.

[17] The SDR is an international reserve asset, created by the IMF in 1969 to supplement its member countries' official reserves. Its value is based on a basket of four key international currencies, and SDRs can be exchanged for freely usable currencies.

[18] IMF, "IMF Governors Formally Approve 250 Billion US dollars General SDR Allocation", Press Release No. 09/283, 13 August 2009. http://www.imf.org/external/np/sec/pr/2009/pr09283.htm

mean that everyone must have the same income. It means giving a high priority to assuring everyone an adequate livelihood supporting human dignity and avoiding extremes of wealth and poverty.

We must revisit the focus on GDP figures as the only measurement of how a country, a region or the world is doing. It is amazing how often the IMF revises its forecast upward or downward, based on just the previous quarter digit. Growth is not the problem *per se*; it is the direction of growth that causes concern.

The role of the state and government has also to be revised with respect to social collectives. It is the right and responsibility of the population of every country to control their own economy and social priorities according to their needs and values, and to keep its national sovereignty as long as the cost of their decisions does not fall onto others. After all, Asia achieved its impressive growth by doing the opposite of the Anglo-Saxon model. The government used state intervention, trade protectionism and exchange rate manipulation to develop their economies, reduce poverty and educate their populations.

A call for global solutions

Solutions have been offered by the G20 and the IMF but some have not yet been effectively implemented. We have also seen their limits and their agenda and how it is still too often servicing their own interests. Many proposals are more cosmetic than the real, radical reforms we need. Yet we shall acknowledge some of the G20 commitments such as the extra fund of one trillion US dollars made available to speed recovery or their strong stance against corruption. But again, this is more a bandage, a temporary fix, than a real reform. In fact, reading the G20 London Summit statement,[21] the words "agreement" or "proposal" are king. How much real action will follow if they do not directly involve G20 interests or face pressure from lobby groups? The low carbon tax proposition is a good example.

The United Nations Conference on the World Financial and Economic Crisis and its Impact on Development, which concluded on 26 June 2009, was the first opportunity for all countries of the world to discuss the crisis on an equal footing. We must recognize that the G20 took prompt and unprecedented action. However, what they called for – and their use of G20 money – was at first more panic action to save themselves than it was inclusive of the poor countries indirectly hit. If we are not inclined to dismiss the prompt and unprecedented

---

[21] http://www.londonsummit.gov.edu.uk/en

actions taken by the G20, Dr Rogate Mshana, in a lecture given during the 33rd Assembly of the United Congregational Church of Southern Africa in August 2009, highlighted some disturbing points of the reality.

> Close observation reveals that the G20 have put themselves as drivers fighting against global recession despite the fact that they are part of the problem. Their stimulus package is more than 40 times the amount needed to eradicate poverty and address climate change but most of this money went to save institutions which were responsible for the crisis in the first place. The lack of mentioning the role of the UN G192 is alarming. The proposals they made are to repair the current destructive system instead of transforming it democratically.[22]

The recommendations and follow-up processes we would like to offer must be comprehensive. There are alternative proposals reflecting and addressing the root causes of the economic crisis more thoroughly. Indeed, we believe that the United Nations, which maintains an image of fairness, is among the only institutions capable of pushing through these necessary measures, involving all 192 member countries.

First of all, to correct the global current imbalance, we must have real and active counter-cyclical policies for all, not a double standard with one set of solutions for the G20 and the rest of the world at its mercy. Developing countries are seldom in a position to afford a rescue and stimulus package. Our policies must support domestic banks in the developing world, especially those which can play an active role in helping develop the agriculture sector and the small and medium enterprises[23]. The process of long-term lending to the poorest has to be revised and real interest rates kept low. Macroeconomic policies like public investment and innovative public-private partnerships to boost economic demand and help vulnerable countries are an essential requirement. The microfinance system, which appears to be more resilient during times of crisis than any other system, has to be strengthened.

Regional arrangements should be allowed to support and/or complement G20 summit initiatives. As much as the respect of the sovereign state is essential, the recognition of

---

[22] Lecture in honour of the Late Rev. Joseph Wing given during the 33rd Assembly of the United Congregational Church of Southern Africa -UCCSA, 24th August 2009, Molepolole, Botswana.

[23] On a broader scale, Paul Mason, op.cit., sees Minsky-style solution applicable to the current banking situation as an alternative: "a socialized banking system plus redistribution is, I believe, the ground on which the most radical of the capitalist re-regulators will coalesce with social justice activist. [...] It is also possible that a socialized banking system, by allowing the central allocation of financial resources, could be harnessed to the rapid development and large-scale production of post-carbon technologies," p. 163.

regions and communities to empower themselves is equally important. Initiatives such as the Asian Monetary Fund, ALBA, or the Bank of the South should be encouraged to handle regional matters and to empower people in the global South. It is also vital to reconcile trade regimes with the new realities.

We need to reconsider the idea of a truly global reserve currency and create new regulation for these global foreign reserves. The use of an international asset like the SDR in a new global reserve system has been recommended by the Commission of Experts on Reforms to the International Monetary and Financial System, appointed by Rev. Miguel d'Escoto. In fact, China and Russia also made a proposal in March 2009, but in vain. They faced the unsurprising resistance of the US and the EU regarding the creation of an extra SDR or suchlike. New regulation of global foreign reserves is part of the international financial architecture we call for. We cannot go on with the current imbalance or international reserves management. Its excess is mainly a reaction by Asian countries to the way the Asian crisis was handled by the IMF in 1997–98.[24] The instability of the US dollar has been proven many times and consequently an alternative, both international and regional, to this declared "planetary currency" is the way to avoid future crises linked to currency and exchange rate issues.

Although the task is not an easy one, a global tax system needs to be developed. Put into a framework of economic theory, the current global situation does not follow the Pareto optimum – "when someone is better off, no one is becoming worse off" – at the international level. Unfortunately, the reality is very much otherwise and a more adequate solution would embrace the economic theory of the Kaldor-Hicks efficiency. According to that premise, when a change leaves some people better off, those better off compensate the losers and still remain better off themselves. This can be done though the collection of global taxes. Ultimately, tax revenues are indeed the only sustainable source of development finances.

The use of tax revenues could take many possible forms, from the elaboration of common standards to minimize tax avoidance opportunities, to multinational agreement to allow states to tax transnational corporations on global unitary basis, with an appropriate mechanism to allocate tax revenues to a developing world fund or the IMF. This redistribution could

---

[24] Malaysia was the only hit-country which refused to go under IMF during the Asian crisis. Its crisis management and especially the imposition of capital controls in September 2008, remains a sensitive issue. See Marie-Aimée Tourres, *The tragedy that did not happen, Malaysia's crisis management and capital controls*, ISIS Malaysia, 2003. Also the article by Robert Wade on the revision of the original World Development Report 2000 on poverty, "Showdown at the World Bank", *New Left Review*, issue 7, Jan-Feb. 2001: "the long section on the need for capital controls was cut to a fraction of the earlier draft's and mention to Malaysia's experience was dropped altogether. [...] Capital control appears only as transitional measures en route to free-market."

also refer to taxes on polluting activities such as carbon tax, or to taxes on international financial transactions, especially if related to portfolio investments or speculative currency transactions. In parallel, as suggested by Ocampo, former UN secretary general, an international debt court should be created.

The question of speculation on commodities, especially food and energy, needs to be eradicated through the creation of public mechanisms to monitor speculative behaviour. Indeed, the word "regulation" is always emphasized when related to financial markets, but we also need other types of regulation on things such as the commodity market, especially for Africa.

Between August 2007 and September 2008, the price of every tradable commodity on earth went crazy; not only oil but also gold, aluminium and sugar. Rice had doubled in price in the year to March 2008. All this affected the developing world. This issue has to be handled soonest. Following the surge in raw material prices and the current meltdown of the financial market as something from which to make money, those who can move their money out of structured finance are doing it. Wall Street firms are expanding their commodity desks. Hedge funds investing in commodities are growing, with new funds being set up in 2009. In 2002, there were only 53 hedge funds making money on commodities. This number grew to 310 in 2007 and 450 in 2008.[25] This is a very worrying trend due to the destabilising impact this can have on many developing countries. Hedge funds speculate on commodities including crude oil, natural gas, biofuels, raw materials such as nickel and aluminium, and also corn and soybean crops.

Another set of necessary actions relates to the Bretton Woods group and other international bodies. Part of the solution to our current problems is a complete radical revision of the IMF and other Bretton Woods institutions. As Joseph Stiglitz rightly highlighted, "today's institutions are not adapted to today's issues."[26] This means a few things. The age of globalization calls for a better global governance; indeed, basic democratic governance, more legitimate and adapted to today's issues, should be the guideline. This includes a revision of the quota system and of memberships. The IMF has mentioned some revisions but the deadlines, when given, are too far away.

Complementary to the above, other new institutions need to be established. As David Korten advocates in his book,[27] "we must now come together to create the institutions of a new

---

[25] http://seekingalpha.com/article/77282-a-commodity-hedge-fund-in-every-pot

[26] Joseph Stiglitz is the Chairman of the Commission of Experts on reforms of the international monetary and finance system set up by the UN. This commission is called, as a short form, the "Stiglitz commission".

[27] *Agenda for a new economy, from phantom wealth to real wealth*, Berret-Koehler publication, 2009, p. 161

economy based on a values-based pragmatism that recognizes a simple truth: If the world is to work for any of us, it must work for all of us." If everything is going global, especially finance as it is today, this requires minimum supervision at a global level. We cannot act globally and restrict our monitoring to the local level. A comprehensive global regulatory regime has become a necessity.

A supervisory body such as an international credit agency is one possibility. This would help to regulate and reform the credit agency industry into proper independent supervision institution(s), based on more transparency regarding credit ratings and strict regulation of the management of conflicts of interest. The establishment of an international bankruptcy court with the authority to cancel illegitimate debt and arbitrate debt issues is another one.

Additionally, no single government can solve the economic problems we are all facing now at the global level. Yet with a communitarian action, a truly and genuinely concerted action, this can be done. A global economic council could be created under the auspices of the United Nations, whose power would be strengthened. This institution would be given the same status as the UN Security Council.[28]

The measure of our wealth – which has traditionally been calculated against GDP – needs to be revised. GDP is the economic indicator used in the press and in any communiqués from the G20, THE IMF or similar institutions. The limit of this economic performance indicator is that it focuses on financial values before life values. The GDP measure as it is now tends to encourage policies that promote the growth of phantom wealth at the expense of real social and environment wealth. Physical and mental health, wellbeing, equity, natural environment and ecological footprint are not part of the current calculation. If GDP alone was all right up to now, an aging society, increasingly severe health problems in part due for example to rising obesity, climate change and its consequences, environmental degradation due to unsustainable development management by some emerging economies and/or thirst for natural resources and energy by countries like China and Russia, have all to be captured in the calculation of national wealth.

Lastly, the acute economic slowdown has several implications in terms of the provision of social services and protection programmes. It is important to ensure that the most vulnerable, such as women and children, have access to and can still meet their needs for food, energy, shelter, education and healthcare. There is a real risk that governments will sacrifice their

---

[28] This idea was echoed by German Chancellor Angela Merkel early February 2009 with her suggestion about a UN/World Economic Council.

commitment to fight climate change and environmental degradation in favour of economic survival and funding more immediate priorities. It is a duty of the G20 and all of us to help to ensure that the preservation of the environment is not a secondary priority but a parallel action.

This is just the first step

Without a doubt it is going to be a slow process, but we need to find a new paradigm of economic development. It will take a comprehensive and integrated approach, with a clear understanding that to ignore any issue is to jeopardize the prospects of addressing other issues successfully.

Regardless of how long it will take, the first step is to get started when we are still in chaos and disarray. This has to be done with a real reformation, not just piecemeal measures rolled out temporarily, only to revert back to "business as usual" as soon as possible. AGEM09, along with a few United Nations bodies' work, could be the genesis of a follow-up process to expand the UN's role. We need to work together with civil society in support of the UN's efforts to engage a process of fundamental reordering of our priorities for humankind. It is hoped that our call to strengthen the role of the United Nations development system in response to the economic crisis and its impact will be heard. The participation of people and civil society organizations in the thinking and policy-making processes around a clearly defined navigational chart is essential, including the promotion of decentralized governance structures and participatory democracy.

The dynamic of the next growth will be shaped by the willingness of ordinary people to impose limits, values and sustainability on the new economic development paradigm. Every new era in capitalism poses new questions of social justice. In this process of pragmatic, critical thinking, people from all walks of life including sociologists, ecologists, philosophers and theologians should be included, alongside economists.

it was weaknesses in the economy and in its corporate structure and dynamics that gave rise to the crisis – the collapse in stock and share values was just one manifestation. He points out that the collapse of the investment trusts and the systems led by holdings, moved by an insatiable appetite for easy profit, "effectively destroyed both the ability to borrow and the willingness to lend for investment."[7] All this took place without any of the necessary regulations by the authorities and the private sponsors of the speculative merry-go-round showed absolutely no sense of responsibility. And the same thing happened again 80 years later! At the end of his study, Galbraith writes that in 1929 the economy was fundamentally insecure. He points to five weaknesses that, leading always to greater indebtedness, signalled disaster. They can be held up for comparison with the weaknesses running through the world's financial architecture today, further aggravated by the tendency for globalization to transmit the magnitude of any economic or financial crisis at the centre to the systemic and planetary levels.

Poor distribution of income

In 1929, 5 percent of the population controlled nearly one third of all personal income. Income concentration is even higher today in the USA, where the wealthiest 1 percent controls 20 percent of the country's revenues, and the mean wage rose a meagre 0.1 percent from 2000 to 2007. It was low pay that led families to take out loans to pay school, housing and health costs (private health insurance rates rose 68 percent in the same period). Meanwhile, money that could be expanding supply of goods and service migrated to financial speculation, increasing imports and causing deficits.

Poor corporate structure

The United States enterprise in the '20s, says Galbraith, "had opened its hospitable arms to an exceptional number of promoters, grafters, swindlers, impostors, and frauds. […] a kind of flood tide of corporate larceny." He points to the vast new structure of investment trusts and holdings as the main corporate weakness, because dividends from companies operating in the real economy (infrastructure, transport and recreation) went to pay off interest on the bonds of upstream holding companies. In econo-speak, this meant a major risk of devastation by reverse leverage: any interruption in dividends left the bonds insolvent, bankrupting and bringing down the whole structure; the temptation to speculate more and more – instead of producing – was joined by deflationary pressures that limited earnings and brought corporate pyramids tumbling down! Income was earmarked to pay debts, it was impossible to borrow to refinance debts or make new investments... It is "hard to imagine a corporate system

---

[7] J.K. Galbraith, *The Great Crash of 1929*, Time Inc., New York, 1962, p. 188.

better designed to continue and accentuate a deflationary spiral."[8] Today's global financial system is suffering the same illness, with its mammoth bank structures and globalized financial firms issuing massive types of bonuses, titles and derivatives, making it possible to maximize profits with sheer speculation and to divert private tax money to tax havens and secret jurisdictions. The behaviour of today's globalized corporations is just as badly distorted – or worse. Proof of this are the financially and ethically scandalous bankruptcies of mega-corporations like Enron, Worldcom/MCI and other Tyrannosauruses; not to mention the corporate fiascos of LTCM, Bear Stearns Bank, finance giants Lehman Brothers and Merrill Lynch, and the bail outs with public money of mega-corporations like Fannie Mae, Freddie Mac, AIG, GM, and on and on.

Poor bank structure

The failings here were laid bare by domino-effect bankruptcies brought on by fear and lack of confidence. In the first half of 1929 alone, 346 banks failed. In a context of depression, "as income, employment and values fell, bank failures could quickly become epidemic," and the damping effect on spending and investment reinforced the depression still further. Today, the lack of rigorous regulation and the excessive freedom afforded to investment banks, a range of financial institutions and stock markets themselves to issue various types of money and to speculate, added to the financial channels and destinations that facilitate capital flight, tax evasion and money laundering, combines high financial yields with very high risks for the banking system as a whole.[9] Laws are not strictly enforced, while the means to dodge them proliferate.

Poor state of external accounts

For over a decade following World War I the USA enjoyed a trade surplus, to the point of using that favourable balance to pay off its debts to Europe. In turn, countries with trade deficits with the United States paid the US in gold and borrowed from United States private banks to bridge the gap. Loans to politically and economically unstable countries, President Hoover's high protectionist tariffs, debtor countries' payment difficulties, a number of insolvent loans and declining US exports all contributed to widespread vulnerability, especially among farmers. In the present day, the United States corrected trade deficit was around 800 billion US dollars in 2007. With China alone, the USA has liabilities of over 1 trillion US dollars in National Treasury bonds. Its total external debt leaped from less than

---

[8] Ibid., pp. 180-181.

[9] Bruno Gurtner and John Christensen, "The Race to the Bottom: incentives for new Investments?" Tax Justice Network, Bern, Switzerland. Paper presented at the Seminar "Beyond Bretton Woods: the Transnational Economy in search for New Institutions", Mexico City, October 15-17, 2008.

2 trillion US dollars in 1980 to more than 5 trillion US dollars in 2007, half of it held by the strongest Asian economies.[10] Were it not the owner of the international exchange currency, the USA would be even more vulnerable than it already is.

Poor economic intelligence

After the crash of September–October 1929, most advice from economists "was almost unanimously perverse." Attempts to expand income available for consumption and to maintain capital investment by tax reductions had practically no effect whatever, except to favour the highest-income groups: investment, wages and employment were maintained only as long as that meant no financial disadvantage to companies; from that point on, policies almost entirely pushed the economy towards the brink. Balanced-budget fundamentalism reigned: public spending could not be increased to boost purchasing power and alleviate impoverishment; nor could taxes be cut further. After 1930, this rule or formula had to yield to pressure from mass unemployment. In addition, United States gold stocks grew enormously up to 1932. Two risks haunted the economy: abandoning the gold standard and feeding inflation. Instead, however, the country entered the most violent deflation of its history. Advisors saw an embedded risk of uncontrolled price increases. That fear reinforced calls for a balanced budget. It limited interest rate cuts, and the abundant credit and easy borrowing conditions. The refusal to use fiscal and monetary policies in those circumstances meant refusing all affirmative government economic policy. Economic advisors were unanimous in decrying all available measures for controlling deflation and the depression: "a triumph of dogma over thought," concludes Galbraith shrewdly. Today, influential advisors are fixated on reviving the economy by any means. They are, at least temporarily, abandoning neoliberal dogma and injecting massive amounts of public money into banks, companies and foundations. As a sop to taxpayers, they are taking considerable portions of these economic agents' equity into state control. On 15 November 2008, at the Washington D.C. meeting of the G20, the presidents of the wealthiest and "emerging" countries decided to adopt a common plan of action designed just to alleviate the impacts of the current financial crisis.[11] The USA and Britain refused to back the creation of standardized global regulations and an international agency with the power to monitor the activities of the international financial system in order to make compliance with the rules compulsory. No one talked about attacking the contributing factors of the crisis, nor about redefining the model of development that the financial system is there to serve, and which is also coming to the end of its life. The heads of state and their advisors seem blind to the main issue, which is to get to the root of the problem.

---

[10] Martine Bulard, "Uma Nova Geopolítica dos Capitais", in *Le Monde Diplomatique Brasil*, November, 2008, p. 12.
[11] *O Globo*, 16 November 2008, p. 28.

All in all, any similarity between the crash of 1929 and the crash of 2007–2008 is no mere coincidence! Other signals of a death foretold come from a number of political and economic articles, among them an essay published in Brazil and Switzerland at the start of the Brazilian crisis of 1999, which reads:

> The unlimited right of governments and companies to issue these papers has led to the world's markets being inundated with virtual money, because a large part of the papers are launched on the supposition that, sooner or later, the government or company will be able to turn them into real wealth and so redeem them for the value that they are supposed to represent. This supposition belongs to the subjective sphere of the economy, that which operates on the basis of non-material values like confidence, foresight, hope and so on. Now, when the government or company does not manage to repay the bearer of their moneys, it becomes insolvent, thus proving that the supposition was false and that the confidence and hopes deposited in them were mistaken, for lack of proper planning, rules and supervision to ensure that the game was played correctly and cleanly – and because their monies were only virtual […] Today we are witnessing a casino economy at the world level and, with it, an almost unavoidable risk of worldwide financial, social and economic crisis […] In practice, neoliberal capitalism is responsible for the casino-economy that has globalized in the world today.
>
> The disease manifest in the hypertrophy of money and over-indebtedness can only be surmounted by a national and planetary system of planning and regulation, capable of liquidating these ailments at their root. Capitalism itself is unlikely to set up such a system, since the capitalists do not want to see that this is a disease – and one that could be fatal to the system itself. When they do realize, they are unwilling to take radical curative measures, because these measures too could be fatal to the system! In fact, capitalism is increasingly squeezed between these two pressures: on the one hand, pressure for the various forms of money issues and indebtedness to be planned and for capital flows to be regulated; and, on the other, the risk of bankruptcy throughout the capitalist system if it fails to adopt these measures.[12]

This curious paradox compounds the lack of any long-term pragmatic vision on the part of the "pragmatic" governments and businessmen who worship the market and money as gods.

---

[12] Marcos Arruda, "Globalização Financeira Neoliberal: Grave Enfermidade do Capitalismo", 1999.
  http://www.jubileubrasil.org.br/somos-credores/globalizacao-financeira-neoliberal-grave-enfermidade-do-capitalismo/?searchterm=Marcos percent20Arruda

The roots of the financial crisis

The world has been flooded with virtual money, paper wealth that does not correspond to any material goods, speculative money, convertible into material fortunes while trust prevailed. If the real connection of that money were to fail – in the case that millions of debtors in the real estate sector failed to pay their mortgages as the interest rates went up steadily in the US – the whole chain of virtual money would collapse. And it did.

What explains such irrational behaviour from economic agents? Firstly, an objective factor: the divorce between real and virtual money and the increasing prevalence of virtual money; the commoditization of money and currencies, houses, land, food, natural resources and everything that can become the object of speculation; in one word, the massive creation of fictional wealth. Secondly, a subjective factor: greed, the voracity to accumulate material wealth beyond its use value, the ego of accumulation. The outcome has been overindebtedness of individuals, families, enterprises and states, the over-concentration of financial gains and the stagnation of purchasing power (real money) in relatively too few hands.

Financial institutions serve a certain mode of development. The existing ones have served the ideology of neoliberal capitalism that reduces development to endless growth and the unlimited search for profits and capital accumulation by private actors, regardless of the costs for society and for the natural environment. An international financial architecture will be new if it is aimed at strengthening their members' *capacity to plan and manage sustainably their own endogenous, democratic and sustainable socioeconomic and human development.*

Corporations repeat and repeat this motto, "We are too complex to be regulated. Give us the freedom to regulate ourselves." Scandals like Enron and WorldCom, the recurrent financial crises, the collapse of the real estate sectors in the US, UK, Spain, etc., and the profound socioeconomic crisis of 2008 onwards prove that corporations know only deregulation! And by promoting the logic of deregulation, multilateral financial institutions, namely the IMF, the World Bank and the regional banks have constantly violated their statutes and frustrated their mandates. One example: the island of Jersey, one the current European fiscal havens, has a law of reverse taxation: the wealthier you are, the less you are taxed. Fiscal havens provide legal tools that facilitate fiscal evasion and capital flight. Derivatives and complex financial products are "weapons of self-destruction"[13] and express the endless thirst for the highest profits at whatever cost. Neoliberal capitalism has promoted a recent systemic shift from entrepreneurial

---

[13] Warren Buffett, speech to the Shareholders of Berkshire Hathaway Inc., p. 14.

investment risk to risk taken by parasites who speculate in order to achieve immediate gains at any cost. Transnational corporations (TNCs) not only prevail over the economies of nations and the world, but also influence government policy using legal and illegal means. They are key actors in the perverse transfer of capital and natural resources from the South to the North. Extreme inequalities of income and wealth are the result.

Profiting without producing

This, in a word, is the corporate governance keynote of the advanced stage of world capitalism: profiting without producing. While 1.2 billion men, women and children suffer and die of hunger in the world, others make fortunes without producing, just by speculating. From the standpoint of the majority of the earth's inhabitants and ecosystems, such an economic system is irrational, inefficient and immoral. Added to which, it continuously reproduces a profound division of societies and our species into social classes that transcend national territories and are globalizing. The nomenclature "Global North" and "Global South" thus appropriately and accurately identifies how humankind is divided into social classes by the system of capital – and even more cruelly now that financialization has brought all its deficiencies, inequalities, violence and insecurity to the point of paroxysm. So what does that financialization look like in figures?

In 2002, writes François Morin,[14] the value of speculative transactions worldwide reached a new plateau of 1,122.7 trillion US dollars. That's right: one quadrillion, one hundred and twenty-two trillion and 700 million dollars, including 699 trillion in transactions with derivatives, 384.4 trillion exchange transactions and 39.3 trillion in financial investments. That total is 34.76 times the 32.3 trillion US dollars of transactions in goods and service, i.e., the real economy.

Nonetheless, in the years that followed, the situation got even worse. Between 1993 and 2002 transactions in products guaranteeing derivatives rose from 200 trillion US dollars to 300 trillion US dollars. From 2003 to 2004 that went from 300 trillion US dollars to 874 trillion US dollars! Note that, in 2002, hedge fund products accounted for 50 percent of the day's business in London and New York. These funds' activities are opaque and speculative: instead of applying with a view to reducing risks, they have come to seek futures applications, which are riskier but more profitable if they secure a lower buyback price. Hedge fund products include organized, standardized and easily tradable market products; and swap contracts. The former represent

---

[14] F. Morin, *Le Mur de l'Argent*, Seuil, Paris. http://www.moulinier.info/article-23674632.htm, 2006.

23.8 trillion US dollars, their turnover rate is high and they are purely speculative transactions. Swap contracts totalled 122.5 trillion US dollars and turnover is low.

World stocks of financial products stood at 186.3 trillion US dollars in 2002, that is 4.62 times larger than that year's world GDP, plus goods and service imports, all of which came to 40.3 trillion US dollars. Thus, it is clear that financial transactions have nothing to do with economic activity – but the financial bubble is both real and menacing.

Figure 1: Speculation versus real economy (in trillions of US dollars)

2002

	Financial Speculation	**Real Economy Goods and Services**
Transactions	1,122.7	32.5
Stock of products	186.3	40.3

Source: François Morin, 2006.

Let us focus on the outcome of the crisis for the different actors of the global casino[15]:

- Global GDP lost 3.7 trillion US dollars in 2009, as compared to 2008.[16] Global trade volume of goods and services fell 11.9 percent. The world lost 4.5 trillion US dollars in exports. Global sales in 2009 were the lowest since 1937. Global industrial production retreated 15 percent. Global trade volume of goods and services fell 9.5 percent.
- Unemployment in major advanced economies jumped from 5.45 percent in 2007 to 5.89 in 2008 to 8.24 in 2009. Unemployment in China reached 20 million in 2009. Japan exports fell 46 percent in 2009 and imports fell 32 percent.
- Emerging countries' GDP fell 1.1 trillion US dollars in 2009 vis-à-vis 2008.[17] Latin American exports fell 24 percent.
- Even more relevant, private financial flows to emerging countries and other developing countries fell from 664.48 billion US dollars in 2007 to 129.52 billion US dollars in 2008, to 52.49 billion US dollars. The total value of this capital flight in three years was 749.02 billion US dollars! This shows how uncommitted financial capital is with respect to anything other than its own interest and greed.

---

[15] Data to be found in the IMF website: http://www.imf.org/external/pubs/ft/weo/2009/02/weodata/weoselagr.aspx
[16] From 60,917.48 billion US dollars in 2008 to 57,228.37 billion US dollars in 2009.
[17] From 18,686.01 billion US dollars in 2008 to 17,594.49 billion US dollars in 2009.

- Net foreign direct investment in emerging and developing countries fell nearly 48 percent between 2008 and 2009. Add an increasing trade deficit due to the collapse of global demand and, from the viewpoint of the establishment, the situation became dramatic and demanded seeking new foreign loans to balance the current accounts and to serve the existing foreign debt.

- The external debt of those countries jumped from 4,306.8 billion US dollars in 2007 to 4,575 billion in 2009. The added total debt service for these three years was 3,688.26 billion, confirming that, "the more they pay, the more they owe" – the dreadful vicious circle of endless indebtedness.

- In 15 months up to January 2009 the US became 16.5 trillion US dollars poorer. This amount is worth more than one US GDP, and more than 12 Brazilian GDPs. Most families in the US invest mainly in real estate and in capital markets, and these were the two areas that fell most steeply.

All in all, the global economy being highly dependent on the US currency, there was no means to avoid financial turmoil when the US economy was hit by the 2007–2008 speculation earthquake. And the worst casualties were, once more, the poorer social classes and the poorest countries.

Speculation

If you stand between two mirrors and look into one of them, what do you see? An endless succession of images of yourself. In the other mirror, another endless stream of images of yourself. But only one you is real! "Speculate" comes from the Latin *speculum*, a mirror. It produces money from money and not by producing any real wealth. But why do that? It is a consequence of the fetishization of money, of greed, a thirst for gain, for accumulating money without limit.

On that point, economist Muhammad Yunus is quite right in his interview in *O Globo* newspaper.[18] He is mistaken, however, when he says that the capitalist system is not responsible. There certainly is a culture of maximising profits, but there is also a system of institutions and social relations that embodies that culture. The core and ethic of capitalism is to accumulate profit, money, capital, material wealth – and the only people who matter are those who have capital. That capital is created by human work, but to capital, working men and women are merely "factors of production", along with capital-money, raw materials,

---

[18] 12 October 2008.

machinery, land, energy and so on. Therefore, it is the system of globalized capital that is responsible, in the first and last place, for the financial crisis that is shaking the world: its compulsion to grow indefinitely, its mode of "development" and "progress" (which comes down to a pattern of compulsive production, consumption and predatory exploitation of ecosystems), its universe of values (greed, selfishness and competition)[19], and its institutions of global governance, particularly the IMF, the World Bank and the WTO.

What did the financial crisis do to the world's billionaires?

The number of billionaires fell from 1,125 to 793. Their fortunes retreated from 4.4 trillion US dollars to 2.4 trillion US dollars from 2008 to 2009. The three richest – Bill Gates, William Buffett and Carlos Slim – had an aggregate loss of 68 billion US dollars up to 23 February 2009. Their fortunes shrank from 180 billion US dollars to 112 billion US dollars. Yet, out of the 50 African countries only three (Algeria, Nigeria and South Africa, mainly exporters of oil and minerals) had higher GDPs (current US dollar prices) than the added fortunes of these three individuals in 2009!

Crisis of insolvency and corporatocracy

When the US Federal Reserve Bank raised the prime rate nearly 5 percentage points, massive numbers of real estate owners could no longer pay their debts: confidence in the whole financial system began to collapse. A large number of debtors failed to pay, as had already happened in the early 1980s with the external debts of countries of the South.[20] The investment banks, insurance companies and other finance companies that had acted as croupiers in the global casino and went bankrupt were salvaged with public funds! But there was no compassion for the over-indebted countries of the Southern hemisphere when they suffered the effects of the United States' unilateral interest rate hikes in the late 1970s. Most of those debts were in dollars, under flexible interest rate provisions.

The Citizens Audit of the debt, part of Jubilee Network Brazil, calculated that if the interest rate on dollar loans had remained at its historical mean level (of around 6 percent), Brazil would have paid off its external debt by 1989 and would even be entitled to 161 billion US

---

[19] I am not stressing here the moral dimension of these values, but the fact that they are a source of imbalance and unhappiness, 'naturally' inherent in the structure of the market-profit-consumerism system. The change has to be structural and systemic, if we want to overcome these values and replace them with a culture of sharing, altruism and cooperation – the only path to social harmony, happiness and fulfillment.

[20] Marcos Arruda, *Prometeu Acorrentado – Os Grandes Grupos Econômicos, O Endividamento Externo e o Empobrecimento do Brasil*, Documento de Trabalho, PACS/PRIES-CS, 69pp, Rio de Janeiro/RJ, 1988.

dollars from its foreign creditors in interest overpaid between 1973 and 2006.[21] Remember that nearly half of Brazil's external debt was brought into being by illegitimate governments under the military dictatorship. While Ecuador set an example for the continent by conducting a thorough audit of its external debt, thus laying the technical and legal foundations for sovereign renegotiation with its creditors, the Lula government turns a deaf ear to civil society organized in the Jubilee Network Brazil (which is pressing for a thorough audit of Brazil's public debt), meanwhile insisting on maintaining the masochistic cycle of increasing public debt, high interest rates and unmanaged exchange.

The embarrassing question to be asked in the current crisis is: who is insolvent? Apparently, the poorer families who grasped the opportunity of low mortgages rates and irresponsible loans; private financial and banking firms in the US; then, all those who bought junk bonds from them seeking easy and quick gains. In reality, the US government is the largest debtor. Chossudovsky shows that, as it transfers public funds to private hands, arguing that they are alleviating the banks' burden of bad debts and non-performing loans, in fact these massive amounts are being used by a few mammoth corporations to consolidate their position in the global financial system.[22] This is a clear indication that the crisis is intensifying the trend towards global monopoly, as we shall see below.

In early 2010 the US economy shows unequivocal signs of bankruptcy.[23] In a recent article, Porter Stansberry recalls the Greenspan-Guidotti rule[24] to show that the US total reserves – adding 300 billion US dollars in gold, 58 billion US dollars in oil, and 136 billion US dollars in foreign currencies – is about 500 billion US dollars, or one quarter of the nation's short-term debt. The only way for the US to avoid bankruptcy and/or default will be, once more, to use its power as the printer of global currency, but this will raise the risk of a global crisis of hyperinflation and the final collapse of the US dollar.

Chossudovsky goes further, unveiling the real power of corporatocracy over the US state.

> The mainstream media suggests that the banks are being nationalized as a result of TARP, In fact, it is exactly the opposite: the state is being taken over by the banks, the state is being privatized. The establishment of a worldwide unipolar financial system

---

[21] Auditoria Cidadã da Dívida, Boletim No. 12, 31 May 2005, Brasília, DF. http://www.divida-auditoriacidada.org.br/

[22] See Michael Chossudovsky in http://www.globalresearch.ca/index.php?context=va&aid=15254

[23] http://www.silverbearcafe.com/private/02.10/bankrupt.html

[24] "to avoid a default, countries should maintain hard currency reserves to at least 100% of their short term foreign debt maturities."

is part of the broader project of the Wall Street financial elites to establish the contours of a world government. In a bitter irony, the recipients of the bail out under TARP and Obama's proposed 750 billion US dollars aid to financial institutions are the creditors of the federal government. The Wall Street banks are the brokers and underwriters of the US public debt, although they hold only a portion of the debt, they transact and trade in US dollar-denominated public debt instruments worldwide. They act as creditors of the US state. They evaluate the creditworthiness of the US government, they rank the public debt through Moody's and Standard and Poor. They control the US Treasury, the Federal Reserve Board and the US Congress. They oversee and dictate fiscal and monetary policy, ensuring that the state acts in their interest. Since the Reagan era, Wall Street dominates most areas of economic and social policy. It sets the budgetary agenda, ensuring the curtailment of social expenditures. Wall Street preaches balanced budgets but the practice has been lobbying for the elimination of corporate taxes, the granting of handouts to corporations, tax write-offs in mergers and acquisitions etc, all of which lead to a spiraling public debt …

Public opinion has been misled. The US government is in a sense financing its own indebtedness: the money granted to the banks is in part financed by borrowing from the banks. The banks lend money to the government and with the money they lend to the government, the Treasury finances the bail out. In turn, the banks impose conditionalities on the management of the US public debt. They dictate how the money should be spent. They impose "fiscal responsibility"; they dictate massive cuts in social expenditures, which result in the collapse and/or privatization of public services. They impose the privatization of urban infrastructure, roads, sewer and water systems, public recreational areas; everything is up for privatization.

Crisis of confidence

At the peak of the crisis, even banks have stopped lending to one another. Mistrust started to reign supreme and the state was required to channel funds into cleaning up the accounts of speculative agents and boosting consumer credit. In psychological terms, the aim was to defuse the crisis of confidence that tends to make people and companies prefer not to spend and not to lend. With no credit and no demand, industrial companies' stocks are building up, while they cut back on production and payrolls, and the whole system starts to fall apart. In Brazil, it was discovered that private banks and large industrial corporations had been speculating with derivatives and exchange – without their shareholders or investors suspecting the risks involved![25] Now they are suffering significant losses. By 18 November 2008, the government announced "anti-crisis package" measures worth 373.5 billion Brazilian reais, including massive input from the national economic and social development bank, BNDES, to facilitate lines of credit for large and medium-sized firms, tax breaks, and lines of financing for foreign automobile assembly plants. Quicker and more effective would be to apply reforms to redistribute income and wealth in Brazil, which has long been promised, but never done.

Intensifying trend towards monopoly

The news of Brazilian Itaú's buyout of Unibanco – to form the largest banking conglomerate in the Southern hemisphere, with assets valued at 575 billion Brazilian reais – comes as no surprise. This is the natural movement of capitalism towards increasingly oligopolistic markets. It generally intensifies during cyclic crises of over-production or over-speculation, like the one facing the world at present.

This movement is suicidal, because the scope of what can be termed "market" is narrowing. Where there is no free interaction between supply and demand – runs the capitalist doctrine – there is no genuine market, but rather a kind of monopolistic dictatorship. The monopoly's power to manipulate prices, needs and desires to satisfy its own insatiable thirst for profits prevails over all other criteria or ethics.

In the context of the world financial crisis which began to release toxic gases in 2007 and erupted for the first time in September 2008, this movement forms part of the intensifying trend towards monopoly capitalism, as amply examined by writers ranging from Marx to Paul Sweezy, Paul Baran and Harry Magdoff. Monopoly,[26] oligopoly or cartel are a compound problem: they confine the activities of less-wealthy or less-powerful actors; they manipulate prices at their whim, seeking maximum profit and imposing a levy of exploitation on buyers and consumers; they externalize costs at will, burdening consumers, taxpayers and the environment; they gain ever greater power to influence centres of power, funding electoral

---

[25] See cases of lies or uninformed advice from bank and financial institution staffs to their clients in Izique, Claudia, *Horas Diabólicas*, in the magazine EU&, Valor Econômico, 17-19 October 2008, pp. 4-7.

[26] *Monopoly* is exclusive control of a market by one single seller. At the other extreme is *monopsony*, which is exclusive control of a market by a single buyer. Every person, community or enterprise is a human quantum within the natural-social system (noosphere-biosphere) it belongs to, just as every cell in the body is a vital quantum inseparable from the organism it forms part of. What happens when one cell decides to grow without limit, to feed off the others until it is finally the only cell in the organ or even in the organism, is fractally proportional to what happens when one person, enterprise or country takes a similar decision!

campaigns and sowing corruption among public servants and government authorities in order to obtain ever greater benefits and enjoy virtually absolute impunity; and so on. More serious still, however, is that the bigger the corporation, the smaller its ability to adapt to changing social and environmental conditions. That is why I do not hesitate to use the Tyrannosaurus allegory to describe them, comparing them with the giant dinosaurs that vanished in the Late Cretaceous period, when there was rapid, planet-wide climate change. Nor do I hesitate to call the political system that prevails today in capitalist countries, including Brazil, a "corporatocracy" – a term used by John Perkins in his striking book on the strategies of the United States empire.[27]

Those who praise the Itaú buyout of Unibanco and all the other mergers and buyouts that are taking place around the world[28] seem to ignore some important facts. The first is that this new conglomerate holds assets equal to about 25 percent of Brazil's 2007 GDP. Even though the total worth of these assets is small compared with major banks in the North, it is highly significant in relation to Brazil's national income. Note that, in the years preceding the crisis, these two banks enjoyed extraordinary profit margins, a significant portion of them from their speculative activities and by virtue of their holding internal public debt bonds, which yield the highest rates of interest anywhere in the world.[29] Note also that Itaú and Unibanco together surpass Bradesco (assets of 422.7 billion Brazilian reais) and Santander-ABN Amro (328.1 billion Brazilian reais). On 21 November 2008, Banco do Brasil announced it was purchasing a 71.25 percent stake in *Nossa Caixa*, raising it to second place in the saurian stakes, with assets of 512.4 billion Brazilian reais. This trend towards concentration is also advancing in the USA, supported by the US government. Here are two examples:

- The three largest banks – Bank of America Corp., J. P. Morgan Chase & Co. and Citigroup Inc. – held 21.4 percent of all deposits in the United States at the end of 2007; with the government-backed sales of bank assets – of Washington Mutual Inc.

---

[27] John Perkins, *Confissões de um Assassino Econômico*, Cultrix, São Paulo, 2004.

[28] In Brazil, 2009, mergers and acquisitions mobilized nearly US dollars 90 billion, or 32% less than in 2008. There is a clear trend towards market concentration and capital centralization, strongly backed by the Lula government with funds from the National Bank for Economic and Social Development and the Bank of Brazil. President Lula's strategy is to support the creation of competitive Brazil-based mega conglomerates with potent global reach. Precisely the opposite of what the Workers' Party was elected for, i.e., to reshape the economy towards an endogenous, sovereign, democratic and sustainable mode of socioeconomic and human development.

[29] According to economist Adriano Benayon, "in 2007, the profits of 31 banks operating in Brazil increased to 34.4 billion Brazilian reais, that is 43.3% real growth over 2006, when profits reached 25.05 billion Brazilian reais. Return on assets grew from 21.2% to 24.3%. That real growth of 43.3% by those 31 banks – which include the group of five with the largest profits – exceeds the latter's percentage growth of 30.6% or 27.89 billion Brazilian reais in 2007. From 2005 to 2006, the real increase was 19.73%" (*Brasil de Fato,* 12 March 2008).

to J.P.Morgan and of Wachovia Corp. to Citigroup – the big three came instantly to hold 31.3 percent of all deposits.[30] Other, smaller banks are being snapped up by the bigger banks, aggravating bank concentration in the USA.

• Freddie Mac and Fannie Mae – the two government-sponsored insurance companies that were thrown an 85 billion US dollar lifeline by the US Treasury – held 740 billion US dollars in credit between them in 1990; 1.25 trillion US dollars in 1995; 2 trillion US dollars in 1999; 4 trillion US dollars in 2005. In September 2007, just before they were bailed out, their assets totalled 5.4 trillion US dollars, 45 percent of all mortgage finance in the USA or roughly half the United States GDP! The guarantees of these two colossal financial dinosaurs underwrote 97 percent of all mortgage lending. They were the end of the real estate chain, they were those who sold insurance on debt papers, which had multiplied unchecked in a greedy irresponsible spiral. This acceleration in the value of their assets resulted from the real estate bubble of 2001–2006 and the speculative tidal surge brought on by flourishing financial engineering.[31]

The second fact is that the new oligopolistic tyrannosaurs are emerging precisely as the moment of their extinction approaches, certainly because the financial crisis is surely going to worsen over the next two or three years. And that is not hard to foresee, given that world economic policy authorities are unwilling to examine the deep-seated causes of the crisis:

• a Himalayas of speculative money, with no basis in the real economy, and for that very reason no chance of being salvaged out of public funds;
• the free hand given to central banks and financial agents to manipulate the usury rate at will; the lack of regulations to ensure that finance serve as a tool for investment in production;
• the tax havens, the secret jurisdictions and the thousand-and-one channels for tax and exchange evasion offering refuge all over the world;
• the irresponsibility of the major banks and industrial corporations seeing abundant, easy profits in financial speculation;
• and, permeating all this, the compulsion to grow, to consume, to grow more, to consume more, and to inundate the earth with garbage and refuse of all kinds.

---

[30] The Wall Street Journal, 2 October 2008, in *Valor Econômico*, p. C5.
[31] Ibrahim Warde, "Fannie Mae e Freddie Mac vão para o brejo", in *Le Monde Diplomatique Brasil*, October, São Paulo, 2008, p. 15.

II - Trends

> This is the limit for capital: the limits of the earth.
> Leonardo Boff

The system centred on capital, profit, the ideology of scarcity and unlimited economic growth for companies and the material economy has no intrinsic ability to generate anything beyond itself. As long as the geographical area of the planet has permitted it to expand, it has advanced, multiplying and globalising goods, services, markets and the appetite for consumption. This system that promotes greed, voracity, the scarcity fix and permanent competition among people, companies and nations has come to the beginning of the end – without managing to accomplish what it calls "development" and "progress" for all peoples and citizens, but in fact depredating or lethally jeopardising the best part of the earth's natural resources and ecosystems. We live at a point in human history when a civilization, its cultural ideas and its mode of social, economic and political organization, is heading for extinction. Meanwhile, budding and meshing within it are factors that herald a new civilization and a new paradigm for being human and living on earth.

The risks of systemic global crisis stemming from the way the economy is currently organized and operated are compound. Elsewhere I have gone into them in some detail:

- the risk of collapse in the global financial system;
- the risk of social upheaval on a continental or even planetary scale;
- the risk of major armed conflicts with strong potential for nuclear escalation and for proliferating worldwide at some unpredictable point;
- the risk of large-scale ecological crisis, particularly under the effects of global warming, given the lack of will among the powerful to take radical measures in time to reduce and mitigate the various consequences (greenhouse gas emissions, tropical forest fires, rising atmospheric and oceanic temperatures, melting of the icecaps, rising sea levels, altered sea currents, and scarcity of fresh water), which in turn become the causes of still more warming;
- the risk of an energy crisis related to the quick decline of fossil fuel reserves in face of increasing global demand for oil; and
- the risk of a food crisis due to the massive conversion of productive land from food production to the production of agro fuels.

Any one of these risks could, on its own, bring on planet-wide disaster and, if they were to happen together, it could be catastrophic to human life on earth.

Another financial crisis has happened, more virulent than the former ones. As pointed out above, it is essentially global and systemic. The financial crisis threatens the real economy with the risks of *stagflation* (industrial stagnation combined with mass layoffs and high prices resulting from financial costs), *deflation* (continuously falling prices, caused by overproduction and surplus stocks immobilized by the market collapse brought on by an abrupt loss of purchasing power among consumers and national currencies), and even *depression*. That is when the financial crisis becomes a dramatic economic and social crisis – there is no investment, demand collapses, production grinds to a halt, employment and purchasing power evaporate and staples become scarce and expensive. Impoverishment becomes endemic and the risk of social chaos is imminent. To these must be added the risks resulting from the tendency for global warming to intensify exponentially.

At this point the king has no clothes: capitalism bares its chaotic true nature and there is imminent risk of elites resorting to war. Now war has two lightning effects: it reactivates the economy through weapons production and trade, which involves complex production chains in manufacturing death; and it distracts people from the systemic crisis and from pressing for radical, far-reaching social and economic change. Capitalism is an entropic system, which tends to reduce everything and everyone to merchandise and to make more and more extravagant use of energy with no concern for replacing it or for the resilience of the systems it commands (from economic and financial systems to ecological systems). All agents, in their historical time and place, are forced to take part in a breakneck race against all comers to grab the carrot of happiness for themselves to the exclusion of all others. The carrot, however, dangles from the tip of the stick of material wealth, which in turn is tied to each competitor's back. The result is the inevitable tendency of the world capital system to dissipate energy and to chaos.

However, our complex matrix of likelihoods comprises yet another scenario. It falls to those who perceive these trends and who wish to prevent civilization as a whole from crumbling into a shambles, to link up their awareness and will in webs of non-hierarchical relations connected by the synapses of mutual help, affection and an openness to others as diverse and complementary beings. The end of this stage of history can be the dawn of a new age, a time when the noosphere transcends this money-grubbing era that has shackled it to material treasures. Such a time will harbour respect for life, for its diversity and its incessant upward movement towards greater complexity and spirituality. In such a time humankind will be attuned to the cycles of nature and the mysterious rhythms of the universe.

III - Alternatives

The tsunami of unreal wealth that has inundated the planet is destined, for better or for worse, to ebb. All the public monies in the world put together cannot save it or cover the speculators' losses. If the authorities should try to do so, they would flood the world with another tsunami of unreal wealth, closing a catastrophic and irrational vicious circle. If they fail to change the rules of the financial game, hyperinflation or stagflation, more wealth concentration and deeper trenches between social classes will be unavoidable. The decision taken by those who met at the G20 in São Paulo, and then in Washington D.C., in November 2008, and the measures taken by national and global authorities ever since, barely scratched the surface of the problem. An accommodation was reached between the neoliberals and the advocates of a "new capitalism" with a greater state presence. The former can countenance a state presence only for as long as it takes to set national and global finances to rights, after which it should withdraw so that the gains can be privatized. Meanwhile, the costs are to be socialized. After that, it will be business as usual … until the next crash. The latter feel the state should remain, regulating, overseeing and redistributing the surplus produced by society. But each state should act on its own initiative, with no organic arrangements among states and only discretionary compliance with whatever rules are enacted to discipline financial flows.[32]

Their promise to detail these corrective measures within the six months since that meeting was no consolation: the crisis continues corroding the structures, and we all know that unless the measures are radical and urgent, the world financial system will tend to spontaneous combustion in a matter of months or very few years, with terrible consequences for the real economy and particularly the working classes and the excluded.

The measures to be adopted are short-, medium- and long-term. They depend on their authors' strategic goals. So the sponsors of solutions to the crisis fall into three types. Firstly, those who restrict themselves to the surface symptoms and propose *ad hoc* reforms "so that things return to normal as soon as possible." Their assumption is that "normal" is good for everyone. They would be satisfied with temporary state interventions to transfer public money to banks and corporations at risk of failure, thus salvaging their capacity to offer credit and boost GDP in the short term. Their horizon seems limited to cushioning the impacts of the financial crisis and stimulating countries' domestic demand by fiscal measures.

---

[32] Declaration published following the G20 meeting on 15 November 2008 in Washington D.C. (www.oglobo.com.br/economia)

The social democrats of various persuasions, echoing Keynes, advocate a state-controlled economy, at least as long as the crisis lasts. They talk about placing finance at the service of business and the citizenry. And they plan to "refound global capitalism" by completely reforming the financial system.[33]

Lastly, there are those who envisage a conceptual movement towards comprehensive development for humankind – person and society – that should be endogenous, sustainable and based on solidarity. That, in turn, entails global economic planning, starting from the community and returning to it with complementary resources and investments at the national and regional level to support and leverage local development that is plural, concerted and harmonious. For such development to occur there is an urgent need for a new financial architecture that integrates the local level with national, continental and global levels and, in that context, resignifies the role of the United Nations as a potentially effective institution of global governance. It is on that perspective that I offer the following proposals. They imply strategies and work to change the power correlation, which are the responsibility of social movements.

At the national level:[34]

(1) Restore people's power to plan and to pursue their own development, individually and collectively, from the local and community level up to the national and global level, combining social management with state management. Capital is apparently allergic to planning. In fact it is not, but it only accepts that private firms should have the right to plan. The central planning paradigm has proved a failure, because it imposed targets and processes on people from above. In the view of an ethical economy, social planning and self-management are combined with state planning and macro management in order to design the best and most efficient development plans! Finance should be seen as just one means, because the end should always be to develop the material and immaterial potentials of the human person and collectives, and to achieve comprehensive wellbeing and happiness. Endogenous, democratic, sustainable, solidarity-based development is essentially bound up with meeting human needs and fully achieving rights, particularly the rights to a decent life, to democratic sharing of productive goods and resources, to wellbeing and happiness. Such development cannot be evaluated and measured by present indicators of wealth. The whole

[33] Nicolas Sarkozy, in *O Globo* newspaper, 16 October 2008, Rio de Janeiro.

[34] To those wanting more detail of the proposals submitted to the Brazilian authorities, I would recommend reading Reinaldo Gonçalves, *Crise Econômica: Radiografia e Soluções para o Brasil,* monograph, 24 October, UFRJ, Rio de Janeiro, 2008; and Ivo Lesbaupin, *Lições a tirar da Crise Econômica Internacional,* monograph, Iser Assessoria, Rio de Janeiro, October, 2008.

(5) Declaring that finances and money are, in their essence, a public service. Therefore, their priority should be to serve to generate purchasing power, equity and wellbeing for all. Keynes' advice should not be forgotten: the country that wishes to have control over its own development must have control over its own finances. Financial activity should not be an end in itself, and its prime motivation should not be profit, but rather to serve to create wealth to meet human and social needs and to support the integration and sovereign, democratic, solidarity-based development of the peoples of Latin America and the Caribbean. That should be the purpose of public banks such as Bank of the South, BNDES, Banco do Brasil, Caixa Econômica Federal and the state banks.

On the international level:

(1) Creating internationally orchestrated, compulsory regulations and levies on financial stocks and flows; and bringing financial institutions partly under government and inter-government control.

(2) Creating institutions at the national, continental and global levels with the power to enforce such rules and impose sanctions on agents who breach them.

(3) Dismantling tax havens and secret jurisdictions, which, through undemocratic secrecy, permit laundering of illegal money and capital and exchange evasion.

(4) Radically reforming multilateral financial institutions, their principles, functions and modes of operation, so that they fulfil their respective roles as orchestrators of the equitable, sustainable development of peoples, and regulators of world financial equilibrium at the service of such development.

(5) Recognizing that this is not just a finance crisis. It is yet another crisis in the capitalist mode of production, in the system of power centred on capital and on the mega-corporations that hold it. It is a crisis in the neoliberal economy that has dominated the planet for the last three decades. And it signals another, more deep-seated crisis: it is a multidimensional, systemic crisis, a crisis of our civilization, which affects the objective and subject dimensions of human and social existence on the planet and calls the system of globalized capital into question. The working classes submission to the capital class worsened and expanded when, in present times, the already retrograde "producing by exploiting the work of others" began to regress into the now prevailing "profiting without producing". The labour surplus from all society has becomes fodder for speculative parasites. They fatten without limit, to bursting point, which the globalized capitalist world is approaching perilously and unhesitatingly.

(6) Promoting sustainable globalization in solidarity. Thoroughly solving the crisis entails recognising the need for a new model of global development that does not rest on selfish, materialist greed, nor the uniformity of one-track thinking, but rather on responsibility, plurality and solidarity among societies and cultures, with enough material abundance, with unlimited production and exchange of non-material goods, and with new indicators in place to measure human wellbeing and happiness. It should rest on a pattern of conscious consumption directed to sustainable economic degrowth for the elites and planned growth within the limits of natural and intergenerational sustainability for the oppressed or excluded majorities; while avoiding waste and applying to our relations with nature the principle of the four Rs: reduce, reuse, recycle, respect.

The world financial system will collapse in ruins, certainly and with disastrous consequences for the socio-economy and the environment planet-wide, unless those who wield institutional power decide to change radically the role of money and indebtedness, and the underlying meaning of development.

IV - Gross national happiness (GNH): towards another development

"Always more" fills the heart with cholesterol plaques instead of happiness!
Jean-Luc Gérard [37]

Not all the news is bad though. A new indicator of wealth is coming into use and it has the power to realign the whole axis of economic activity and development policy. It obliges governments (planning goals, public budget, public policies), banks, corporations and value-added chains to redefine their operating goals in terms of a new index embodying a comprehensive, multidimensional concept of wealth.

In October and November 2008, events on the gross national happiness (GNH) index took place in Campinas and Porangaba in Brazil, with participants meeting for a weekend at a time, over 1000 at Sesc (São Paulo), 250 at Unicamp (Campinas) and some 150 at Parque Ecológico Ecovillage (Porangaba). Impeccably organized by the monk Susan Andrews, and her extremely efficient team, these three events – plus numerous interviews with the spoken and print media – were attended by three members of the government of Bhutan, a tiny country in the Himalayan foothills between India and China, where the GNH has been applied for the past 12 years with outstanding success; and Michael Pennock and his wife Martha, from Canada. Michael, a health specialist, spoke on the subject of gross national

---

[37] Gérard, Jean-Luc, 2008, "Manifeste à l'usage des jeunes générations. Penser autrement au sein de la nouvelle civilisation numérique, : marier le cœur et la raison", dossier Pangea 2008, Lucerne.

In Brazil, as in other countries, a movement is taking shape to popularize an index of human and social wellbeing and happiness the purpose of which is to influence the way people, institutions and governments measure wealth, and how they behave. The GNH index is a very powerful tool for encouraging aware consumption, for supplanting the logic of profit by the logic of integral development of persons and communities, and fostering the adoption of public policies directed to increased satisfaction, wellbeing and happiness of the entire populations of their respective territories.

Given the threat of global crisis, the GNH movement offers a practical vision of another possible economy. It is conducive to convergence among movements such as the Solidarity Economy networks[40] that seek to reconceptualize the economy, taking as their central value the human person as a relational being, that is, as a multidimensional being, at the same time individual and social;[41] and the movement for integral, self-managed human development,[42] as a process directed to realising the potentials, qualities and attributes of the human person that can generate individual and social life of quality and increasing happiness.

Additional References

Alan Greenspan, Chairman, Board of Governors of the Federal Reserve System, Statement before the Committee on Banking, Housing, and Urban Affairs, United States Senate, February 24, 2004.

Alan Greenspan, "Repel the calls to contain competitive markets", in *Financial Times*, August 4, London, 2008.

Frédéric London, "O dia em que o Fed se tornou socialista", in *Le Monde Diplomatique Brasil*, October, São Paulo, 2008.

Joan Martínez Alier, *Languages of Valuation*, paper presented at the Seminar "Beyond Bretton Woods: the Transnational Economy in search for New Institutions", Mexico City, October 15-17, 2008.

---

[40] Euclides Mance, *Redes de Colaboração Solidária: Aspectos econômicos-filosóficos, complexidade e libertação*, Editora Vozes, Petrópolis, 2002, pp. 42-52 and Luis Francisco Verano Paez & Alejandro Escobar Bernal, "Elementos ideológicos y politicos del modelo de Economía Solidaria", in *El Modelo de Economía Solidária: una alternativa frente al neoliberalismo*, Colacot, Bogota, Colombia, 1998.

[41] Marcos Arruda, *Humanizar o Infra-Humano: A formação do Ser Humano Integral – Homo evolutivo, práxis e economia solidária*, Editora Vozes, Petrópolis, pp. 171-222.

[42] Marcos Arruda, *Tornar Real o Possível: A formação do Ser Humano Integral – Economia solidária, desenvolvimento e o futuro do trabalho*, Editora Vozes, Petrópolis, 2006, pp. 151-218.

WORLD FINANCIAL CRISIS: CHALLENGES AND OPPORTUNITIES FOR CHINA
WHAT IS AT STAKE IN THE CURRENT FINANCIAL ARCHITECTURE

Xiao Lian

The US sub-prime mortgage crisis led to world financial crisis

The proportion of US sub-prime mortgages was less than 14 percent of total US mortgages (less than 1.5 trillion US dollars), yet it has led to an ongoing international financial crisis that has landed the world economy in the most difficult situation since the 20th century's Great Depression.[1] US financial and economic problems, triggered by the mortgage crisis, are not only an adjustment in its economic cycle but also an outbreak rooted in the intrinsic contradictions of capitalism. The international financial system we have today is one that is based on injustice: it is a system wherein the global poor are essentially subsidizing the rich.

Unless we deal with the internal contradictions of capitalism and with deregulated financial markets, unless we establish a new financial architecture in the world, not only will we fail to handle the current world financial crisis, but we will be unable to avoid the recurrence of a world financial crisis. Under the current capitalist system, the so-called free market, developed countries manipulate the entire international system. There are about 5,000 financial specialists who control the world's financial markets. Other countries, especially developing countries, do not understand how these specialists package different portfolios that combine toxic sub-prime mortgages with bonds and other financial instruments to sell to buyers worldwide. A lack of transparency in the international market system led to the crisis that is now spreading rapidly throughout the world.

The crisis has been characterized by a financial chain reaction in six stages:

1) Hedge fund companies met with market failures due to speculation in sub-prime mortgages (the case of AIG is one example).
2) Insurance companies were overextended because they could not compensate for losses incurred by their largest customers.
3) Investment banks declared bankruptcy (for instance, Lehman Brothers; Bear Stearns).

---

[1] WCC AGEM2009, Geneva.

economy would contract by 1.7 percent this year compared to growth of 1.9 percent in 2008, the first global decline since the Second World War. Growth would actually decline in Central and Eastern Europe, Central Asia, and Latin America and the Caribbean. About 53 million more people would be trapped in poverty this year, subsisting on less than 1.25 US dollars a day, because of the crisis. In parts of Africa, South Asia and Latin America, the struggle is for food or no food.[3] This crisis is threatening the achievement of the millennium development goals.

It is too expensive for the US to overcome its own financial crisis led by sub-prime mortgages, so the US would like to push the G7 and G20 together to address the current crisis, which will require great changes to international architecture. Here are some of the reforms that are highly recommended: adjustments in rates of interest among the G7, especially between the US and the other members of the G7; interest adjustments among G7 and G13; interest adjustments among the G13; and interest adjustments among G20 and non-G20 countries in the rest of the world. Given this overview, I agree with the point made by the World Council of Churches in its call for a new international financial architecture under the auspices of the UN, a decision-making body which would include many more voices.

The reasons behind the current world financial crisis

This crisis is attributable to a variety of factors. In an address at Davos, Switzerland in January 2009, Chinese premier Wen Jiabao identified these major reasons for the crisis:

- inappropriate macroeconomic policies of some economies and their unsustainable model of development characterized by prolonged low savings and high consumption;
- excessive expansion of financial institutions in a blind pursuit of profit;
- lack of self-discipline among financial institutions and rating agencies and the ensuing distortion of risk information and asset pricing;
- failure of financial supervision and regulation to keep up with financial innovations, which allowed the risks of financial derivatives to build and spread.[4]

Beyond the reasons described above, I believe that the unreasonable international financi currency system is also one of the main reasons for the crisis. The US dollar is being us as a international super currency with special power to determine prices for internatio

---

[3] Zoellick urges G20 leaders not to forget poor, Agencies, 1 April 2009.
[4] Wen Jiabao, Premier of the PRC, at the World Economic Forum Annual Meeting, 28 January 2009, Davos.

trade (over 80 percent of trade is determined by the US dollar) and define foreign reserves (64 percent of total world reserves). It would be far too easy for the US to transition from its own crisis and burden the whole of the world by devaluing the US dollar, especially when a financial crisis has taken place in the US.

Challenges in China

1. Challenges in macro-economic phenomena

In 2008 the growth of gross domestic product in China declined to 9.0 percent, compared with two-digit growth in each year of the past two decades. It is estimated by international institutions that China's GDP growth rate will continue to decline by 5.6–7.5 percent, although the Chinese government promises to keep up its economic growth by 8.0 percent. The fiscal deficit will reach 950 billion RMB (139 billion US dollars), with a 3.0 percent of GDP deficit. The real estate market has dropped 30 percent, which will lead to more than 60 industries shrinking. Adjustments in the real estate market will continue for 2–3 years, at least.

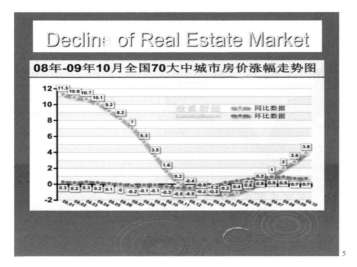

2. Challenge in Chinese economic growth model

China has achieved 30 years of continued fast economic growth in the world, under the model that materials and markets are located outside China but manufacturing takes place in China. China keeps its economic growth rate high through this combination of inexpensive natural resources and cheap Chinese labour, and has accumulated over 2 trillion US dollars in foreign reserves, 70 percent used to buy US treasury bonds and other government bonds

---

[5] Chart used with permission from the Chinese National Statistic Bureau, 2009.

economic growth involving firstly a substantial increase in government spending and the implementation of a structural tax cut. It has rolled out a two-year programme involving a total investment of RMB 4 trillion, equivalent to 16 percent of China's GDP in 2007.

Secondly, interest rates will be frequently cut and liquidity increased in the banking system. The central bank has cut deposit and lending rates of financial institutions five times in a row, with the one-year benchmark deposit and lending rates down by 1.89 percentage points and 2.16 percentage points respectively. Thirdly, large-scale industrial restructuring and rejuvenation program will be implemented, alongside active encouragement of innovation and upgrading in science and technology. Fifthly and finally, the level of social security will be substantially raised to accelerate the improvement of social safety.[9]

China's role in the current world financial crisis

China has become the largest contributor to the IMF after the United States and Japan. Following the G20 Summit in London, China has contributed 50 billion US dollars to the IMF, the largest contribution by a developing nation during an economic crisis. China's contribution indicates it is committed to fulfilling its responsibility as an economic power and wants to push for the implementation of the IMF's plan to boost global credit recovery, economic growth and employment.

China has become a member of the newly established Financial Stability Board (FSB). But even before that it had been willing to undertake more international responsibility with other FSB members, and its contribution proves it is ready to do everything possible to support the IMF's and the World Bank's financing programmes. The country's 40 billion dollar contribution should boost global fluidity and greatly increase the IMF's capacity to help its member economies tackle the global financial crisis.

Though China is the world's third largest economy, it is still a developing nation. Its contribution to the IMF does not have much to do with its burgeoning foreign reserves because its per capita GDP stills rank below 100 in the world despite having about 2 trillion US dollars in foreign reserves. It is unfair and unrealistic to judge a member economy's proportion of increased contribution to the IMF only according to its foreign reserves. A wide range of factors, such as an IMF member economy's stage of development, its per capita GDP and the structure and composition of its foreign reserves should be taken into

---

[9] Wen Jiabao, Premier of PRC, at the World Economic Forum Annual Meeting, 28 January 2009.

account when deciding how much it should contribute. The degree of a donor country's dependence on foreign reserves to ensure its economic security should also be an important factor in gauging its contribution to world financial bodies.

The existing IMF contribution structure and the way member economies share the votes do not reflect the changing pattern of the world economy. For instance, China, Brazil, India and other developing countries have achieved rapid economic development in recent years and their economic influence has been on the rise on the world stage. But the IMF's contribution quota and voting share have not undergone any major change. That is why it is necessary to reform the IMF and make it adapt to the fast-changing world economy. Member economies' proportion of contributions to the IMF and their voting rights should be decided by their economic aggregate and per capita GDP. Hence, China's 50 billion dollar contribution is far more than its voting share in the international financial body. China's contribution to the IMF and its voting share should be commensurate with its rising economic status in the world.

The IMF's existing 85-vote mechanism has to be changed to make it more representative and to ensure that the voices of emerging economies and developing countries, including poor African nations, carry more weight. The US is said to hold 17 percent of the IMF vote share, and the European Union holds 32 percent. Such a voting arrangement is tantamount to extending the US and EU the privilege to veto any major resolution, which is unfair to the huge number of developing countries.

For more effective international economic cooperation, China should urge the World Bank and the IMF to carry out some necessary reforms and listen more carefully to the voices of developing countries. Developing nations' presence in the World Bank should be increased to 50 percent, not the 44 percent proposed by World Bank president Robert Zoellick. The established IMF provisions should be revised to reduce Washington's unreasonable privilege. The reform of the IMF and the World Bank should also ensure that emerging economies have a greater say in electing the heads of international financial institutions, and that the elections are more transparent. Besides, candidates should be chosen on the basis of their overall merits, the most important being their ability to provide developing countries' representatives with access to the high-level decision-making organs.[10]

China's drastically increased contribution to the IMF should increase member economies' recognition of China as a market economy. China should make this recognition a precondition

---

[10] Xiao Lian, "A financial body in need of urgent reform", China Daily, 9 April 2009.

for the help it is extending to the IMF to increase its liquidity. It is not fair for some IMF member economies to enjoy the benefits that China's contribution will bring even as they refuse to recognize the country's economic status. Such a system is also detrimental to the establishment of a new international financial system.

How to avoid excessive, destabilizing currency speculation

The range of the IMF's special drawing right (SDR), long dominated by the US dollar, Japanese yen, euro and pound sterling, should be widened. China, for its part, should accelerate the development of the yuan and other currency into an international currency and try to include it in the SDR. Simultaneously, measures should be taken to push for the development of the SDR as a super-sovereign international reserve currency.

It is suggested that SDRs be considered as a new global currency. A proposal was made by China's central bank governor, Zhou Xiaochuan, on 23 March 2009, to establish a super-sovereign reserve currency after reviewing the inherent vulnerabilities and systemic risks in the existing international monetary system.[11] It remains very risky to rely entirely on a single currency for international payments. Therefore, we hear the call for the world to consider an alternate currency controlled by the IMF as the world's standard currency. As a result of the current worldwide financial crisis, China is urgently promoting the RMB as the regional currency of choice instead of the US dollar. China is in effect praising its own currency and asking the world to use the RMB more often.

Since the current currency exchange rate is extremely volatile, China's first priority is to stabilize its own currency exchange for across-the-border exchange with neighbouring nations. It foresees a three-step approach in internationalizing the RMB, initially limiting the use of RMB to China's trading partners who belong to the ASEAN; next, extending this use to neighbouring nations such as Russia, Japan, India and Korea;and finally, using the RMB globally for trade. The hope is for the RMB to replace the US dollar and become the standard currency of the world.[12]

---

[11] "China's proposal on int'l monetary system constructive", Xinhua, 2 April 2009.
[12] Jordan_c_fan, "Hot talks on the 'Super Currency'", bbs.chinadaily.com.cn 27 March 2009.

THE BLOOD-STAINED SILVER LINING

Alexander Cobham

Can there be a silver lining to a crisis which is expected to increase the number of people living in severe income poverty by more than 200 million in two years, leaving more than one billion people in chronic hunger, potentially adding nearly three million extra infant deaths by 2015, while governments face even greater struggles to provide the most basic services as revenues fall and private capital flows plummet?[1]

Yes. It's a blood-stained silver lining, touched by the unnecessary deaths and undermined lives of so many women, men and children. But it is there, if the will exists among policymakers to grab it, and if the momentum can be built among faith communities and civil society organizations, in countries of the global South and the North, to leave politicians with no choice.

The crisis should not cloud judgements, or memories. It is not the case that before the first bank fell in 2007, all was well. The world was not on the road to poverty eradication, even if the unsustainable economic growth rates had continued for fifty years. The benefits of that growth were not evenly shared, and the underlying economic, social and political structures and systems were directly responsible. In addition, the failure to effectively manage human exploitation of the planet means that massive political commitment is now needed to reverse course and ensure environmental sustainability. The crisis is causing great hardship – but it cannot be forgotten that this is only a worsening of a situation that has long existed, characterised by massive hardship throughout the "good times".

As Christian Aid sets out in its call to action, *Poverty Over*,[2] the crisis can be a moment of opportunity. It is a time for new thinking and for new models, for new objectives and new efforts. But only a global social movement can build the pressure for change that can ultimately deliver the eradication of poverty – not only poverty of low incomes, but poverty of life more completely, putting an end to illiteracy and untreated illness, to political oppression, social exclusion and economic marginalization. The World Council of Churches can play an important role in building and supporting that movement.

---

[1] All statistics taken from World Bank, *Financial Crisis: What the World Bank is Doing* (updated 1 July 2009). http://www.worldbank.org/financialcrisis/bankinitiatives.htm

[2] Christian Aid, *Poverty Over*, 2009. http://www.christianaid.org.uk/Images/poverty-over-report.pdf.

This chapter does not seek to cover the vast waterfront of change that is needed to end poverty. Instead, it focusses on a more specific analysis of the financial crisis, its causes and the solutions. Here too there is a silver lining. The same liberalization and lack of transparency in financial markets that were the fundamental causes of the crisis also contributed to a much longer-term process that creates and exacerbates poverty: the failure of effective taxation in many countries. Measures to make future crises less likely can therefore do much to address the longer-term obstacles to poverty eradication. While the human costs of the crisis cannot be undone, this would be a true silver lining – striking a great blow for poverty eradication efforts.

Information and the financial crisis

The roots of the grave problems now facing developing countries lie thousands of miles away from most of their borders, in the fever that surrounded the United States' sub-prime mortgage market and in the boardrooms of what were, until recently, the most powerful financial institutions in the world.

Information and the customer

It has long been recognized that financial markets are different from others, in that they are more highly dependent on information. If you sell me a banana, you care only that I have the money to pay for it immediately. If you make me a loan, however, you will usually want to know whether I have the means to pay you back. That will require information about how solvent I am, as well as my probity. If you know that I have assets (a house), a steady income (a sound job) and a reputation for repaying my debts (good credit history), you will probably make the loan. If you cannot find out any of these things, you probably won't.

If, however, you have an incentive for making the loan, regardless of whether or not I can keep up the repayments, you may well decide to lend to me anyway. This is the story of the US sub-prime mortgage crisis that triggered the present financial maelstrom.

In recent years, mortgage brokers in the US were systematically engaged in obtaining customers by whatever means they could, knowing that they would be paid on the basis of every loan made, regardless of the customer's subsequent ability to repay the borrowed money. This behaviour, which in retrospect appears almost criminally negligent, was encouraged by banks keen to extend credit in the full confidence that the loans made could then be shifted along the chain and sold en bloc on the international market for collateralized debt.

Those who ultimately owned the mortgages were in no position to judge their true value, for they knew nothing of the mortgagees' ability to pay. As customer after customer defaulted, mortgage after mortgage turned out to be worthless, leaving serious question marks over the value of the mortgage "bundles" that had been sold on. The credit-rating agencies, which should have been assessing the risk factor, merely exacerbated matters. They helped design, often for large consultancy fees, the financial instruments through which the mortgages were passed down the chain and sold on.

Arthur Levitt, former chairman of the Securities and Exchange Commission, which protects investors in the US, has argued that "the credit-rating agencies suffer from a conflict of interest – perceived and apparent – that may have distorted their judgement."[3] Whether faced with a conflict of interest or not, the agencies seem to have fundamentally failed in their role of ensuring efficient risk evaluation across the market.

Information and the banks: the role of trust

Just as a financial market needs information to function efficiently, so banks also require information about other banks if they are to do business with them. It's a world in which reputation is all. The nature of standard banking is to accept savings deposits (to borrow from customers) and use that money to make loans to other customers, either individuals or businesses, loans which are then repaid by the customer, with interest. The interest rate paid by borrowers is higher than that given by the bank to depositors. This is the bank's margin. The difficulty is the "maturity mismatch": customers may wish to access their savings quickly, while banks cannot retrieve the loans they have made at the same speed because invariably the money will have been invested, in housing in the case of many individual borrowers, or in business enterprises.

Any bank in the world would face closure if enough customers demanded their money back at once, as no bank holds all the customers' savings in cash. It is critical then that withdrawals remain within normal parameters. A panic-stricken run on a bank will take down even the soundest institution. For this reason, banking regulations demand that there are strict limits on the amount of loans a bank can make (or other financial assets it can create or acquire) in proportion to its equity.

As the current financial crisis unfolded, while depositors largely kept faith, the banks (and other financial institutions) effectively did not; they stopped lending to each other. Even the

---

[3] Quoted in R. Lowenstein, "Triple-A failure", *New York Times* magazine, 27 April 2008. http://www.nytimes. com/2008/04/27/magazine/27Credit-t.html

shortest-term markets (such as overnight loans) seized up, and the lending that did take place incurred interest rates far higher than the central banks' policy rates. Put simply, the banks had stopped trusting each other. As mortgage bundles turned out to be potentially worthless, the banks became aware they did not know the value of each others' assets or likely future income streams, and nobody wanted to be left holding loans that could not be repaid. Part of this uncertainty stemmed from factors outside the banks' control, such as the likely future performance of the housing market and the economy, which determine, respectively, the value of mortgage and business-loan books.

A far greater part of the problem, however, was a direct result of the way in which banks and other financial institutions has been operating in recent years, in particular the lack of transparency surrounding their assets and liabilities. This lack of transparency is partly the result of the complex way in which banks exploit the difference in banking regulations between countries where they do business in a process known as "regulatory arbitrage". In effect, without wanting to draw attention to their activities, they seek out the legal jurisdictions that will put the least restriction on their activities and charge the least tax on their profits.

Opacity is also the result of the sheer complexity of the new derivatives – for instance, collateralized debt obligations (CDOs) and credit default swaps (CDSs) – that were created to "slice and dice" the sub-prime debt, and the dangerously small number of people within financial institutions or regulatory agencies who fully understood how these new financial instruments worked. As long as the markets were going up, few people questioned the true value of such derivatives, but plummeting prices and rocketing defaults in the US housing market eventually forced a reassessment as investors tried to work out who was really hurting.

As bank share prices fell, reassessment also took place in the money markets. Banks started to question the wisdom of lending to each other, knowing what their own assets and liabilities looked like and so naturally questioning the positions of others. The problem was often one of perception. Bank A may have considered Bank B a sound institution. However, if no one else in the market was prepared to lend to Bank B, then Bank A wouldn't either, to minimize the risk of default.

Once the crisis broke, the banks compounded the lack of trust by refusing to come clean about what they were really worth. This refusal may have arisen in part from a genuine inability to value their assets, but it had every appearance of being a pretence that there was no real problem. This perceived bluff served only to unnerve investors further, delaying the resumption of normal business and prolonging the crisis.

In short, the massive bail out operations that have been necessary are the result of the disappearance of trust between banks and other financial institutions. Only the power of state support has proved able to restore that trust; hence part-nationalization as a solution in many cases.

Information and regulation

There is a further reason for lack of transparency in the banking sector: banking secrecy. Previous large-scale corporate bankruptcies – such as those of Enron and WorldCom – exposed nests of hidden transactions and liabilities, primarily located in tax havens. These structures misled investors about the true value of the companies' assets and liabilities, whether intentionally or not. The current wave of bankruptcies is no different. The UK parliament saw a session on the nationalization of Northern Rock bank descend into farce, as it became clear that the government – the new owner – did not know either who owned the Rock's Jersey-based offshore vehicle, Granite, or what, if anything, it was worth.[4] The run on the bank may have been more about panic than fully informed judgement by customers, but that run seems quite reasonable in the light of the subsequent balance-sheet revelations.

In fact, this was part of a wider process – the development of what the Basel-based Bank for International Settlements (the "bank for central banks") has referred to as the "shadow banking system". In fact, they asked, "[h]ow could a huge shadow banking system emerge without provoking clear statements of official concern?"[5] This is the setting-up of banks, bank-like institutions and funds, including hedge funds, private equity operations and structured investment vehicles – conduits used by mainstream investment banks and others – in jurisdictions (tax havens) outside the main financial centres and outside their regulatory reach.

The growth of opacity

The aims are to escape the type of regulation that banking activities usually face and to reduce the tax bill – even if most actual activity remains in the financial centres and not in the havens. One result is greater opacity, keeping the detail of arrangements largely out of sight (and out of mind) of more stringent regulators.

The regulations these institutions are trying to avoid are those that aim to ensure the solvency of banks and similar institutions by requiring that they maintain some minimum level of

---

[4] This issue – like many involving opacity in the crisis – was first raised and investigated by the campaigning accountant Richard Murphy: see http://www.taxresearch.org.uk/Blog/. See also *Hansard* Column 281, 19 Feb 2008. http://www.publications.parliament.uk/pa/cm200708/cmhansrd/cm080219/debtext/80219 0023.htm

[5] BIS, *78th Annual Report*, Bank for International Settlements, Basel, 2008, p. 138. http://www.bis.org/publ/arpdf/ar2008e.pdf?noframes=1

capital to guard against adverse scenarios. In recent years institutions have made increasing efforts to avoid this fundamental check on systemic solvency. One well-developed example of the key part that regulation (or lack of it) played in this crisis relates to Ireland, although over time many more examples will emerge in many different jurisdictions. Jim Stewart, senior lecturer in finance at Trinity College, Dublin, has highlighted the role of that city's International Financial Services centre (IFSC) in the crisis.

As he notes,[6] Ireland "streamlined" its regulation on setting up funds so that "if the relevant documents are provided to the regulator by 3 p.m., the fund will be authorized the next day." This is in spite of the fact that "a prospectus for a quoted instrument is a complex legal and financial document (a debt instrument issued by Sachsen Bank ran to 245 pages) so it is unlikely it could be adequately assessed between 3 p.m. and the normal close of business (5 p.m.)." Ireland was by no means alone in this – there has been a "race to the bottom" in the regulation of such activity. In Luxembourg, for example, it is possible to set up a hedge fund with "pre-authorization approval" as long as the regulator is informed within a month. Moreover, the regulator will not make any checks on elements such as the capitalization of the fund promoter, unlike in Ireland.

The Financial Times noted in April 2008,

> Historically, European asset managers' default option was to look to the Cayman Islands, Bermuda or the British Virgin Islands. But more recently European jurisdictions (chiefly the Channel Islands, Ireland and Luxembourg) have been streamlining regulation and beefing up services to get a piece of the ever-growing hedge-fund action. On the margins, the Isle of Man offers a cost-effective solution and Malta is seen as a domicile for the future.[7]

By 19 July 2008, funds facing problems had been identified as located at the IFSC, according to Stewart. In addition to four German banks with problems at IFSC-located funds, which required almost 17 billion euros of German state aid, Stewart notes that Bear Stearns, one of the largest banking collapses earlier in the crisis, had "two investment funds and six debt securities listed on the Irish Stock Exchange, and it also operates three subsidiaries in the Dublin IFSC through a holding company" – a holding company which managed to finance 11,900 US dollars of assets for every 100 dollars of equity.

---

[6] J. Stewart, "Shadow regulation and the shadow banking system", *Tax Justice Focus:* The Research Edition, July 2008, pp 1-3. http://www.taxjustice.net/cms/upload/pdf/TJF_4-2_AABA_-_Research.pdf

[7] Financial Times, "Europe stocks shoppers' must-haves", *Special report: Fund markets*, 7 April 2008. http://www.ft.com/cms/s/0/2ff2e92c-043a-11ddb28b-000077b07658.html

Compared to the international consensus (the Basle II capital accord) that banks should not exceed 1,250 US dollars of risk-weighted assets for each 100 dollars of shareholder capital (that is, they should have shareholder capital equal to at least eight per cent of their risk-weighted assets, as a cushion to absorb losses without hurting depositors), that ratio is a striking indication of the extent to which the shadow banking system is responsible for the enormous growth of credit in recent years. The type of assets that such a bank would finance would include loans, and the purchase of shares, bonds, related options and derivatives. In this way, regulatory arbitrage led directly to greater credit creation and higher asset prices – and so was at the very heart of the long boom that is ending so badly.

Stewart goes on to note that the Irish regulator, the Financial Services Regulatory Authority, appears to consider itself responsible only for "Irish banks" – those with headquarters in Ireland – and hence to question whether anyone had ultimate regulatory responsibility for oversight of investment structures of banks headquartered elsewhere. The German regulator appears to have had at best minimal oversight of the Irish operations of German banks. This is one example of a potential loophole in global regulations covering holding companies located outside the jurisdiction in which their headquarters are registered. Far from being a problem only for Ireland, it is a common theme in analyses of the shadow banking sector. The *Financial Times* argued in an October 2007 editorial that "the supervision of so-called 'conduits', off-balance sheet vehicles which borrow money, finance loans and generally behave just like banks," was of great concern. "Most of this activity is regulatory arbitrage – it exists to avoid the restrictions placed on banks – and supervisors appear to have ignored it." Indeed, the paper continued, "[i]f there is to be reform then this is the place to start."

Who pays?

In the present crisis, when banks have got into trouble the costs have been borne by national governments (that is, the taxpayers) and the bank shareholders – neither of which groups appears to have had sufficient information to discipline company behaviour effectively. There can surely be no better argument for stronger regulation and greater transparency. Shareholders require information so they can value businesses accurately. National governments require information to ensure that they can regulate business, in order to protect themselves – or rather, to protect taxpayers – from bearing the costs of activities in which they do not share the returns.

Needless to say, the banks do not appear to have repatriated the profits from their shadow activities in order to contribute to the societies that have ended up covering their risk, through paying taxes. In the financial sector, more or less the full risk remains in the with growing loan defaults and tighter borrowing conditions. Businesses that could borrow faced higher costs when they could least afford it and bankruptcies soared. Unemployment followed, slashing consumption further and undermining the prospects of those businesses with relatively strong financial positions.

Countries with substantial sovereign wealth funds can be split into two groups: those with natural-resource wealth and those who had close experience of the East Asian crisis. The latter group does not exist by coincidence – a clear decision was taken to build up vast reserves of foreign exchange so that, no matter what came to pass, they would not suffer such dictated terms again. Once meltdown was reached in that crisis, it became clear that protecting economies required careful, extended support for their financial sectors. Countries able to follow that course – that is, those that did not have to rely on the IMF to bail them out in return for policy control – did so as far as they could.

Wall Street or Main Street?

It is therefore foolish to suggest, as strands of political discourse have done during the current crisis, that there exists a stark choice between helping Wall Street or helping Main Street – the financial markets or the real economy. The reality is that abandoning the former at the very moment of their greatest weakness would have devastating effects for the latter. However, it does not necessarily follow that support is warranted for the specific multi-billion-dollar bail outs across Europe and the US. But there is no doubt serious action was needed, as banks had become almost completely unwilling to lend to each other, and then only at interest rates much higher than the policy rate – in effect, creating the conditions of the IMF bail out during the East Asian crisis.

Part-nationalization may have offered the best chance of restoring trust among banks and ensuring that some lending continued. What is critical is that these steps are followed up with others to ensure that business lending (to small and medium-sized enterprises in particular) is sufficiently protected, so that balance-sheet consolidation in the banking sector does not provoke more of a spike in unemployment than is absolutely necessary. The other lesson from the East Asian crisis is that policymakers should be particularly focused on the longer-term path of inequality, which is likely to have been increased by both the boom and the bust – with implications for poverty, especially now. Greater costs of social welfare systems are guaranteed, but in addition greater redistribution during the downturn would reduce the long-term costs for social stability and the damage to the lives of the least well off.

It is a sad fact that such crises, even if rapidly reversed, cause long-term damage through, for example, periods of malnutrition during infancy and childhood. Higher inequality is also often identified as a barrier to future economic growth.[20]

For both instrumental and direct reasons, then, policymakers should take care to control the extent of both poverty and inequality. The inevitable constraints on fiscal policy (given levels of public debt) should not mean that the poorest in societies pick up the tab for financial-market excesses. The presumption in favour of international financial liberalization, regardless of the lack of evidence of any benefits and with clear evidence of grave costs, must surely end. But the role of trade regulation is also relevant, as the Director-General of the WTO, Pascal Lamy, has pointed out.

> Trade in goods and services represents only about two per cent of international transactions but it takes place in one of the most internationally regulated environments ever created. No such regulations exist for international finance …

Yet current trade negotiations include a powerful process aimed at liberalising services. In this context, the new obligations on the movement of European Union capital and entry of EU service-providers – including, most obviously, financial services – being demanded by the European Commission in negotiations over economic partnership agreements with African, Caribbean and Pacific nations, might weaken and destabilize the financial sector in developing countries. Just as rich countries are currently doing, developing countries need to review their financial regulation and conduct impact assessments to determine the type of regulation and liberalization that will benefit development – and not allow themselves to be forced into liberalization through trade deals.

Finally, it must be absolutely certain that where support is given to countries facing problematic capital reversals, the IMF in particular must not hypocritically return to its policy stance of the late 1990s, which it has already acknowledged was flawed. Sadly, the early evidence is not promising – for example Iceland, a relatively wealthy country but dramatically weakened by the crisis, in accepting IMF support, was required to raise its interest rate to 18 per cent "in order to attract foreign capital."[21]

---

[20] See e.g. World Bank, *World Development Report: Equity and Development*, Oxford: Oxford University Press/World Bank, 2006.

[21] Financial Times, "Iceland lifts rates to 18 percent from 12 percent", 28 October 2008, http://www.ft.com/cms/s/0/5465d1ac-a4d5-11ddb4f5-000077b07658,dwp_uuid=a36d4c40-fb42-11dc-8c3e-000077b07658.html

secrecy jurisdictions (tax havens) into line. An initial success for development was the G20's decision to stress the importance of ensuring the wider group of developing countries also benefited from the greater transparency being demanded.

Nonetheless, the approach thus far has hinged on requiring secrecy jurisdictions to sign a number of bilateral tax information exchange agreements (TIEAs). Sadly, TIEAs have demonstrably failed to deliver effective information exchange even for the most powerful tax authorities – because the burden of proof on the requesting jurisdiction is so high, and the restrictions on the requested jurisdiction so limited. This limitation would be even more powerful for developing countries with much more limited capacity in their tax authorities to pursue the necessary investigations for a successful request. In addition, developing countries face the added obstacle that their political power is much more limited and hence the key secrecy jurisdictions are not willing to negotiate, far less to sign, TIEAs with them.

The solution, advocated by Christian Aid and a range of engaged NGOs and others including the Tax Justice Network, is a multilateral agreement requiring *automatic* exchange of tax information between jurisdictions. This would ensure that developing countries truly benefited from the greater transparency, and could take measures to stem the corrupt and tax-dodging illicit financial flows out of their own jurisdictions. Failure to act in this arena would reflect a decision by the international community to leave untouched the infrastructure that facilitates and supports all manner of illicit outflows, undermining developing countries' finances and promoting corruption.

Financial regulation

Finally, the analysis set out in this paper makes absolutely clear that there can be no continuation of the ideologically-motivated demands for greater financial liberalization and deregulation that developing countries have faced from donors and the international financial institutions for more than two decades. As noted above, even key economists at the IMF have now found and accepted evidence that greater reliance on foreign finance undermines growth. The additional concerns that liberalization may promote inequality and poverty-inducing instability should make the default policy position one of great caution. Instead, it appears that further liberalization remains the kneejerk response.

Also noted above is the tendency for policy thinking at the IMF (not to mention among academic economists and leading NGOs) to be well ahead of the actual recommendations being made by IMF country teams. In this case, the historic ideological strength of views on financial liberalization means that the weight of evidence alone may not be enough to drive change. Policy space must be opened up for developing countries to choose their own levels of, and approaches to regulation, according to independent evidence and advice, and without facing misplaced ideological disapproval for doing so. This does not mean that economies should be closed to foreign finance, nor that there is any obvious uniformly appropriate combination of state and private banking, nor that the case for specific capital controls is unassailable. A full debate is needed, drawing on the lessons of the good times as well as the bad, and leading to a more well-founded analysis of suitable country-specific priorities.

Conclusions

Business as usual in world financial markets would mean continuing and powerful obstacles to development. Above all, the crisis has created a window of opportunity for a global social movement to demand greater transparency, appropriate regulation and space for countries to pursue truly evidence-based rather than ideologically driven policy. NGOs, including the important faith-based communities such as that represented by the World Council of Churches, have a responsibility to exploit this window of opportunity to push for real change – change that can eliminate some major structural and systemic obstacles to hopes of global poverty eradication.

The crisis has had, and will continue to have, devastating human consequences in the poorest countries. Any silver lining will be stained in that blood – but that makes it all the more pressing that the possible benefits are indeed obtained.

Additional References

The Distressed Debt Report, 27 November 2007. http://distresseddebt.dealflowmedia.com/reports/112707.cfm

Financial Times, "The right response to Northern Rock", Leader, 1 October 2007. http://www.ft.com/cms/s/0/3771a632-6fd1-11dc-b66c-0000779fd2ac.html

LIFT YOUR LAMP ABOVE THE BUSHEL: THE ROLE OF THE ECUMENICAL MOVEMENT IN FACING THE GLOBAL FINANCIAL CRISIS

Roel Aalbersberg

Credit crunch

At the heart of the present global financial crisis is the sudden "credit crunch"[1] that has already dealt its lethal blows to a good number of formerly large and influential institutions, and that is still threatening to eat away at the very foundations of the global financial and economic household. A credit crunch, in the definition given by Investopedia, is "an economic condition in which investment capital is difficult to obtain."[2] If that is a definition to go by, it means for many millions of entrepreneurs, especially in the Global South, that they have been living with a credit crunch for ages – in a permanent credit crisis, really. For whatever private capital is available in the South has always had a tendency to flow into directions that avoid the "poorer quarters": it flows to the cities and avoids the countryside, it flows to industry and avoids the more volatile agricultural sectors, it flows into the hands of men rather than those of women.

Credit seems to have its particular likes and dislikes. It is not impartial. On the contrary, it is choosy, and the central value on which its choices are made is obvious: profit – as much, as soon, as easy and as risk-free as possible. It was therefore a particular privilege for me, a few years ago, to meet with a group of 150 women in a South India rural area who had managed to create their own inroad into the world of credit. I was there as a member of a group attending a regional conference of ECLOF, the Ecumenical Church Loan Fund.

The women are all members of the Ponni Self Help Groups Federation in Manikandam Block, a province of the state of Tamil Nadu. The Ponni Federation is just one of the clients of the ECLOF India micro credit programme. The self help groups (SHGs) are groups of five people (often women) that operate as one economic unit. Every group starts as a saving group, with each of the members setting aside a small but fixed amount of rupees a month. From the combined savings, the individual members can take out a loan in situations of acute need – often for so-called unproductive purposes such as a funeral or treatment of a family member at a hospital. Once well established, four SHGs may join to form a self management

---

[1] Speaking of credit: I owe a debt of gratitude to Karin Koolmees for critically reviewing earlier drafts of this paper.
[2] See: www.investopedia.com/terms/c/creditcrunch.asp

group (SMG) with access to outside credit. The Ponni Federation is composed of 20 such self management groups and counts 400 members – in this case, all women.

The programme of the visit contains some festive music and dances, but mainly speeches: by the Chair, the Vice-Chair, the Honorary Chair, followed by presentations of various length by representatives of all 20 self management groups in the federation. Nevertheless, we do not get bored of seeing and hearing the pride and joy of the women as they report on their challenges and successes, and we share in the excitement and applause of the entire assembly. The stories we hear are not just about savings, credits and book-keeping ledgers – certainly, that too – but also about going together as a group to meet with the local government official and making him see to it that the muddy path to the school is upgraded, so that the children do not get their clothes dirtied every day on the way home. Or about the new identity cards for all group members, provided by ECLOF and carrying their photographs: "Now we really are somebody. Now our voice is heard!"

Credit is extended here on the basis of a different set of values. ECLOF's policies and priorities are directly opposed to those of "normal" credit: prioritizing rural credit and for-agricultural loans, and a strong preference for female clientele. In doing so, ECLOF, born of the ecumenical movement even before the World Council of Churches saw the light, shows its ecumenical family traits: a hunger for justice and a commitment to the cause of the poor and the marginalized.[3] It is a sign of hope. Yet it represents little more than a drop in the ocean of money that makes the world go round and that has now shown its frightening capacity to bring it all to a grinding halt.

All the money in the world

In her presentation at the AGEM09[4] on the causes of the current financial crisis, Dr Marie-Aimée Tourres shared a picture showing the nature of the global liquidity.[5] It is a strong image that has stayed on my mind since. It depicts all the world's money[6] as an upside-down pyramid.

---

[3] For more information on ECLOF and its work: see www.eclof.org
[4] AGEM: Advisory Group on Economic Matters, created by the WCC to help churches respond to the global financial crisis. Earlier AGEMs had been formed to respond to crises in 1979 and 1984.
[5] Independent Strategy Ltd, 2010. Used with permission. The original picture was taken from a memorandum of Independent Strategy Ltd on "New Monetarism", 26 April 2006, http://www.instrategy.com/docs/products/New_ Monetarism260406.pdf.
[6] For the sake of readability, I use the word "money" here for liquidity. I realize that it is a wider term than liquidity, which refers to "money readily available for use".

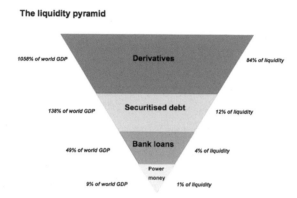

The liquidity pyramid

1058% of world GDP — Derivatives — 84% of liquidity

138% of world GDP — Securitised debt — 12% of liquidity

49% of world GDP — Bank loans — 4% of liquidity

9% of world GDP — Power money — 1% of liquidity

The bottom segment, the "real money" (coins, bank notes), forms the tiny tip of the pyramid. This tiny tip represents only 1 percent of total liquidity in the world and about 9 percent of the world's gross domestic product (GDP). This is basically the money people have in their pockets and their current accounts and which they use for their daily needs, shopping and paying their bills. On top of this is a segment that could be called "broad money" and which consists of bank loans, which we use to run our businesses and to buy our homes and whatever else we would like to have but cannot (yet) afford. This covers 4 percent of total liquidity and 49 percent of the world GDP. These two segments together are what, some 40 years ago, we used to know as the sum total of liquidity.

On top of that "money as we knew it" has come a much bigger segment of securitized debts (basically, long-term loans converted into marketable securities), covering 12 percent of total liquidity (or 138 percent of world GDP). On top of that again, another enormous segment has grown of derivative financial markets, representing no less than 84 percent of global liquidity and a breath-taking 1058 percent of the world GDP.

What this picture points out is that most of the money that goes around in the world today is virtual, unreal, imaginary, fake, wind. But on this "wind", big and influential financial institutions have been built, including many banks. Entire economies rest on it and the lives and livelihoods of millions are entangled with it. The picture could also be seen as a huge balloon, filled with hot air, and carrying a tiny basket full of passengers high above the solid ground.

Now that we witness the "wind" escaping from the balloon, and its ability to keep us all afloat drastically diminishing, we wonder how on earth we are going to amend this situation – or even where to start. Indeed, the immediate reaction of many governments in the wealthy North has been to pump in massive amounts of more hot air into the leaking balloon.

Where are we heading?

One may wonder whether what we are witnessing today – the bankruptcy of financial institutions formerly deemed invulnerable, the dramatic increase of unemployment, the sudden lack of funds for investment, the mortgage crisis in the US and elsewhere – is really the full crisis, or whether these are just the first signals of worse to come. What if, indeed, all these events are just the warning signs of a tsunami that is still miles away from us? What if it is just the receding sea water we see, revealing all kinds of muddy and ugly things on the sea bottom, formerly hidden from our eyes, with all kinds of fish, big and small, struggling and dying in it? What if the real tsunami is yet to come and hit our shores with a giant wave that will destroy all that we hold dear? What else could we do than grab our children and run for the hills!

What is clear is that this crisis will affect both the Global North and the Global South. Since this is primarily a financial crisis, it is likely that the immediate effect will be on those with the largest stakes in the world of finance. It will turn out to be less easy to shift the burden of this crisis entirely to the South, as has been the case in other world crises. This time, the North will not be spared – the North where generations have lived with little or no experience of shortage, poverty or hunger, and where the skills to make ends meet, the skills to cope, are under-developed, to put it mildly.

What if poverty is coming (back) to these regions – not in a limited number of geographical and social pockets in the North, but as an endemic phenomenon, with thousands and millions of jobless, homeless, income-less, *poor* people? What would be the effect, for instance, of rampant poverty on the world's major superpower, the USA? What if the Obama administration, in which so many have invested such high expectations, is seen as "failing to deliver"? Would the race card be played again? Would the unity, the Union, hold? Thirty years ago, the falling apart of the USSR was utterly unthinkable. Yet it happened. Could it happen to the USA this time?

Some experts maintain that indeed the worst is still to come.[7] Others suggest that we have seen the worst now and that there are signs of a new equilibrium.[8] All have to admit, however,

---

[7] E.g. Alar Tamming & Krassimer Petrov, "Credit Crisis – The Worst Is Yet To Come", 8 December 2008, www.financialsense.com/editorials/petrov/2008/1208.html or the International Monetary Fund, "Worst days of US crisis may lie ahead", in The Guardian, 15 June 15 2009, www.guardian.co.uk/world/2009/jun/15/imf-us-recovery

[8] E.g. Warren Buffett, the world's richest man according to Forbes magazine, was reported to say on May 3rd 2009: 'The worst of the crisis in Wall Street is over' (www.bloomberg.com/apps/news?pid=20670001&sid=aMWbId0 HNwOk) or Martin Fridson (Fridson Investment Advisors, New York) as quoted by Reuters on July 17th 2009: 'We are well past the worst of the credit crisis' (www.reuters.com/articlePrint?articleId=USTRE56G46E20090717).

that they did not see this crisis coming. Many are observing the unfolding drama like the proverbial chicken observing a thunderstorm – they take note of what they see, but cannot make any sense of it. Indeed, economics as a science is living some of its darker moments. Jean-Philippe Bouchaud said lately,

> Compared to physics, it seems fair to say that the quantitative success of the economic sciences is disappointing. Rockets fly to the moon, energy is extracted from minute changes of atomic mass without major havoc, global positioning satellites help millions of people to find their way home. What is the flagship achievement of economics, apart from its recurrent inability to predict and avert crises, including the current worldwide credit crunch? Why is this so?[9]

In an effort to answer his own question, Bouchaud points out that in economics, unlike other sciences, assumptions play a more important role than facts.

> Classical economics is built on very strong assumptions that quickly become axioms: the rationality of economic agents, the invisible hand and market efficiency, etc. An economist once told me, to my bewilderment, "These concepts are so strong that they supersede any empirical observation." As Robert Nelson argued in his book, *Economics as Religion*, the marketplace has been deified.[10]

What are we to do?

What is to be the role and agenda of the ecumenical movement in all this? It would be presumptuous to suggest that we as Christians hold the answer to the crisis. We are involved – both as instigators and as victims of the crisis – just like anyone else. We are as flabbergasted and dumbfounded as any other commentator or analyst. We have no blueprints to bring to the table.

However, the observations of people like Bouchaud and Nelson who speak of the underlying assumptions or even religious beliefs on which the economic thinking of our days is based, can be taken as evidence of the value of the one thing we as Christians, as churches or as the ecumenical movement may have to offer to the world: a different and more solid set of values on which to build a new international financial and economic architecture.

---

[9] J.P. Bouchaud, "Economics needs a scientific revolution", Nature, vol.455, 2008, p.1181.
[10] Ibid. Italics by Bouchaud.

It is not for the first time (and it will not be for the last time either) that the ecumenical movement is called to face a deep crisis in the world and to ask itself the question: What should we do? It is also not for the first time that the Movement seeks the answer at a deeper level than the political and economic.

The root of the matter

What can the churches do about this? They can adopt resolutions and reports. But will that make much difference? The crisis is a crisis of motivation, of fundamental attitudes. The deep trouble lies underneath the political and economic level. The root of the matter is that at a time where history requires that humanity should live as a coherent responsible society, men still refuse to accept responsibility for their fellow-beings.[11]

Now we can of course seek to awaken a sense of solidarity with and sympathy for the needy. We do so with some success. And we must go on doing this. But that is not the radical operation which is needed. That does not lead to a changing of the structures of world-economy… No, what is needed is nothing less than a conception of humanity … It is in our Holy Scriptures that the unity of humanity is proclaimed in the most definite manner …

When it is said that God makes all things new this means above all that through Christ God re-creates humanity united under his reign. Mankind is one, not in itself, not because of its own merits or qualities. Mankind is one as the object of God's love and saving action. Mankind is one because of its common calling.[12]

The above statement, that seems to speak so eloquently to the crisis the world faces today, was actually written more than forty years ago. It is taken from a speech by Dr Willem Visser't Hooft, addressing the 1968 Assembly in Uppsala of the World Council of Churches. The crisis he speaks of is different from that of our days, and yet we sense the truth and lasting relevance of his analysis for today: the root of the problem is the refusal of mankind to accept responsibility for one another – and its solution should be sought in a unity that can only be achieved by submitting to the rules of the kingdom of God.

---

[11] The concept of a responsible humanity was advocated strongly already in the theology of John Calvin, as Rev. Dr Park Seongwon pointed out in his article: "Finding an Answer to the Economic Crisis from Calvin", in: Kukmin Daily Newspaper, 3 March 2009, where he states: "According to Calvin, economy is an act of solidarity in which human beings help each other (…) The rich are the servants of the poor and the poor are the representatives of God."

[12] W.A. Visser't Hooft, "The Mandate of the Ecumenical Movement", The Uppsala Report, World Council of Churches, 1968, pp. 318-319.

The longing for a world that is one and responsible is a dream we share with many, within the churches and the ecumenical movement and within the human family at large. We share it with many generations that went before us. So far, humanity has not succeeded in establishing something like a "world government" – and perhaps it is a good thing that it hasn't.

As Christians, we believe and proclaim, "The earth is the Lord's and all that is in it" (Ps. 24:1). And in the footsteps of Jesus we proclaim the kingdom of God – that it is near, that it is coming, that it is here. What is the relevance of this old message to the situation we face today? How is it to be "good news" to people who have just received the news that their money has vanished, their houses are forfeited, their jobs lost, their dignity gone?

To help and equip

Therefore, one of the first tasks the churches and the ecumenical movement should prepare themselves for is that of extending a helping hand to the victims of the crisis, both in terms of pastoral care and of material support. At the same time their own membership should be equipped to deal with the crisis. They should be made aware of what is happening and be encouraged to engage with it and to lift up the light given to us: the light of the values of the kingdom of God.

Speaking of this kingdom and its values, Jesus told us, "Is a lamp brought in to be put under the bushel basket, or under the bed, and not on the lamp stand?" (Mark 4:21). Now, a bushel is a basket used to scoop up grain for sale. It is a measuring-instrument, an economic tool. Evidently, Jesus does not discard economics as something evil. But he does drive home the point that economics and its tools may only work or be used properly in the light of the lamp – the light of the kingdom of God. Instead of deifying the bushel, we should apply it according to the divine guidelines given to us – the laws of the kingdom: those of love and justice, of mercy and stewardship.

If there is one thing that stands out in the charter of the kingdom it is the concern for the poor, the widow and the stranger. Whatever international rules for finance, economy or trade we try to create, one guiding principle must be, how does it affect, or better, how does it do justice to the poor, the widow and the stranger? This is the lamp we are called to lift above the bushel. Therefore, materials, tools and instruments should be devised, developed and distributed among the churches and the ecumenical movement at large, making it possible for their constituencies to engage with the issue at every level in this light.[13] Statements

---

[13] The educative material of Christian Aid (UK) for its "Poverty Over" campaign provides an inspiring example of such tools. See: http://www.christianaid.org.uk/images/poverty-over-report.pdf

and reports will not by themselves bring the solutions. We are up against powerful forces, even though we see their foundations tremble. 'In life there is no such thing as a solution. Powers are on their way. You must create them, and the solutions will follow'[14].

If we are to make a meaningful difference, a movement will have to be built that stands for the principle of justice to the poor, the widow and the stranger. This will require investments in the basis of our movement as well as the forging of alliances with other, like-minded movements and actors in the world.

To prophesy and repent

In its prophetic role, the ecumenical movement is called to cast this same light on the unjust foundations on which the present international financial and economic order was built. It should speak to nations and global institutions and their leadership, and hold them accountable for their role in the unfolding drama, as well as point out ways in which the kingdom values may be translated into a more just and sustainable architecture of international relations.

However, in order to raise a credible prophetic voice to the world, the church must take a close look at its own role in the crisis and its causes, both as a collective and individually. It has been an old but often neglected wisdom of the church that "its first act must … be, not condemnation of the world, but confession and contrition."[15] As churches and Christian institutions, as well as the individual members thereof, we are part and parcel of the financial and economic build-up that is now under the threat of tumbling down. Especially in the North – but certainly not only there – we have, knowingly or unknowingly, taken part in and benefited from the same irresponsible credit schemes and derivatives markets as so many others.

Acknowledging, naming and owning these facts are a condition for any further action to claim credibility. Repentance must come hand in hand with conversion. Nothing less will do to lend credibility to our call to others to join us on new and just roads. Such a conversion implies changes in both institutional investment policies and individual life styles. What do churches do with their money? Do they put it where their mouths are?[16] Are they transparent and accountable? How do they and their members go about paying taxes? What about

---

[14] A. de Saint-Exupéry, *Vol de nuit*, 1931, p. 151. Translation by the author.

[15] Henry van Dusen, "General Introduction", *The Church and the International Disorder*, London, 1948.

[16] An example of the contrary is given in a news item by Ekklesia (3 July 2009), connecting investments by the Church of England to exploitation of garment workers in Bangladesh, lobby groups questioning the reality of global warming and human rights violations: www.ekklesia.co.uk/node/9793. To be sure, examples on other churches and Christian institutions are not hard to come by.

consumption patterns, energy use? Can they meet the standards of justice and sustainability? What about Christian charities; do they provide the kind of detailed financial information they require from their clients? What about ecumenical donor agencies; do they make their annual reports and accounts accessible to their partners for scrutiny? Before we start preaching to others what they should do, let us try and do what we preach.

Another aspect we need to revise is our way of life as churches and as ecumenical institutions, especially so in the Global North. The church itself has been in a stage of nearly constant crisis here, with more and more people turning their backs on the church in which they grew up. Apparently, the church has no "good news" to bring to the new generations, or it has failed to find the proper wording or acts to validate its words.

When we look at the institutional life and indeed the architecture of churches and ecumenical institutions, is it not true that here, too, we can notice impressive build-ups of paid staff, synods, boards and committees, never short of reports, statements and other hot air, and sustained by a membership that decreases by the day? In our churches as well as in the ecumenical movement at large, we urgently need to reconnect with reality. We are as badly in need of a new architecture based on solid stones and masonry, as is the global finance world.

To lift our lamp above the bushel

In raising a prophetic voice to the world, the ecumenical movement faces the challenge of translating the kingdom values into a language that speaks to the world and the crisis it finds itself in. To lift our lamp above the bushel would mean above all that that economy and finance become the servants and instruments of humanity rather than the deities they have become. In more worldly terms, this implies that we are to call for a restoration of the link between the real world and finance, for the introduction of safeguards for transparency and accountability, as well as for sustainability in the arenas of finance and trade. At the same time, it implies that we are called to address greed as a major driving force behind the crisis and as a force of evil.

In order to deal with such an elusive force, new instruments may have to be invented to hold economic and financial actors accountable, at every level, including and especially at the global level. In contrast with the existing international measuring instrument of the "poverty line", an international "greed line" could be developed to expose unacceptable concentrations of power and wealth. Along with the existing World Poverty Report, a World Finance Report might be in place. Efforts to restrain the many instruments of greed might as well include the bridling of the powerful influence of greed enhancers such as advertising, commercials and gambling.From their side, the churches and the ecumenical movement should consider their own calling in holding the actors – including themselves – accountable to the standards of the kingdom of God and create the instruments to do so effectively and credibly. The time to act is now.

We see big powers shaking on their foundations. We gasp as we witness giant institutions tumble down overnight. We hear wise men stammer and become speechless. The images remind us of the downfall of Pharaoh and all his might in the sea of reeds. They remind us of the walls of Jericho tumbling down.

Now is the time, as this global crisis unfolds and deepens, to seize the opportunities[17] and to lift our lamp wherever we can, pointing the world to the kingdom values that the gospel has imprinted on us as a better and more solid base on which to build our common future.

The sea of reeds is opening up. Now, let's start walking.

---

[17] See also: The ICCO Alliance, "Manifesto for seizing opportunities. International cooperation in transition from working 'for others' to working 'with others'", Utrecht, April 2009.

THE NEED FOR MORAL VALUES: ADDRESSING YOUTH'S MORAL DILEMMA

Mariana Issa Zureikat

Introduction

The world is experiencing a series of crises: financial, environmental, food and energy, to name but a few. The causes of these crises are many, of which the simplest could be negligence; risk neglect, environmental neglect, destitution neglect and energy consumption neglect respectively. The word "negligence" is defined as conduct that falls short of what a reasonable person would do to protect another entity from foreseeable risks of harm. It is a product of human behavior that is driven by the moral values of knowing what's right and what's wrong. Thus, what is more dangerous than a financial or environmental crisis is the underlying moral and cultural crisis our world is facing.

In light of recent crises, it is evident that there is a moral dilemma in a society that treasures financial gain and considers it the main criterion for determining a person's worth. If material things are the most important in life, then is life just about materialism? Why should one even try to lead a moral life? What does it matter how we treat each other, so long as we are getting what we want? Why, then, would it be wrong to embark on any finance-generating jobs like drug dealing, which is a very lucrative business indeed? With the line dividing right and wrong slowly disappearing, we find ourselves living in societies that are devoid of moral values.

Are youth facing a moral crisis?

Graduating from university and joining the workforce is not an easy transition. In fact, since the outcome defines what kind of person one will become, it is considered one of the most crucial and difficult decisions one makes. It marks a person's coming of age; an age of accountability and responsibility. Challenged by the question of what it takes to succeed in today's life, graduates find themselves confronted with three possible destinations: money, money and money.

As graduates face a world empty of moral values and live in societies that commoditize everything, the increased crime, drug and alcohol abuse, stress-induced disease and suicide rates are consequently all indicators of the existence of a moral dilemma. Young people now find themselves questioning the way they lead their lives, the way their parents led their lives and the way society as a whole functions. If material things are the most important in life, what does the loss of material things mean?

The world now is more unequal than ever, with the gradual disappearance of the middle class and the uneven distribution of wealth. We find the majority of the world being controlled by a small number of people and corporations. Such a system raises notions about conspiracies, with a small number of people putting their own personal interests above the interests and well being of others. Subsequently, young people find themselves playing on an uneven field, where excelling in life must come at the expense of others.

Whether or not the conspiracies exist is immaterial; so long as the youth believes that the world is an unjust place comprised of corporate conspiracies, it is a trend that one can't afford to ignore. Most of the problems facing today's youth are not restricted to any particular ethnic group but affect the young people worldwide. So, how did we get here?

The evolution of the world's economic system

> Capitalism is the astounding belief that the most wickedest of men will do the most wickedest of things for the greatest good of everyone.
> John Maynard Keynes

Changes in economic thought have always accompanied changes in the economy. Economic thought evolved from feudalism in the Middle Ages to mercantilism in the Renaissance, when it was evident that trade policy must be structured in order to further the national interest. During the industrial revolution, the modern economy of Adam Smith appeared. Technological advancement, mobility between countries and previously inconceivable material luxury was becoming a reality.

Following Adam Smith's magnum opus, *Wealth of Nations*, classical economists such as David Ricardo and John Stuart Mill examined the ways the landed, capitalist and laboring classes produced and distributed national riches. Karl Marx criticized the capitalist system he saw around him. To Marx, capitalism was an exploitative, isolating and unjust system. However, most political systems based on the alternative that Marx advocated have failed to provide a functional and sustainable economic alternative, let alone to alleviate the exploitation of man.

After the wars of the early twentieth century, John Maynard Keynes led a reaction against governments' abstention from economic affairs. He was a strong advocate of interventionist fiscal policy to stimulate economic growth and prosperity. As Keynesian policies seemed to falter in the 1970s, neo-classical economics emerged with its most prominent theorist, Robert Lucas. Neo-classical ideas captured the interest of some Western countries but were not fully implemented. Critics of neo-classical economics emerged in the 1980s, the most famous being Amartya Sen, Paul Krugman and Joseph Stiglitz, who promoted free trade and globalization by introducing the theory of comparative advantage.

Our world has been driven by capitalism and the idea of free markets operating and sustaining themselves by allowing the invisible hand to work on its own. However, for demand and supply to operate, there are certain conditions that need to be observed, such as free entry and exit, a number of products and services supplied and a number of consumers. Unfortunately, this is not always the case. An example would be the fluctuating oil prices in 2008, when oil prices experienced a sudden decline. Oil prices went down from 135 US dollars per barrel in June 2008 to 36 US dollars at year-end.[1] Going back to the simple Smithian demand and supply model, oil prices are supposed to be determined by demand and supply equilibrium. Therefore, for the oil prices to drop, there should be a change in either supply or demand. A change in the quantity demanded should reflect a proportional change in price:

Price change: 135 US dollars - 36 US dollars = 99 US dollars

Percentage change: 99 US dollars/135 US dollars x 100 = 73 percent drop in price

According to the IEA Oil Market Report,[2] as shown in the graph below, oil product demand dropped from 87 mb/d in the second quarter to 85 mb/d in the fourth quarter, which corresponds to a percentage change of 2.35 percent:

Percentage change in oil demand = $\underline{87 \text{ mb/d} - 85 \text{ mb/d}}$ x 100

85 mb/d

= 2.35 percent drop in demand

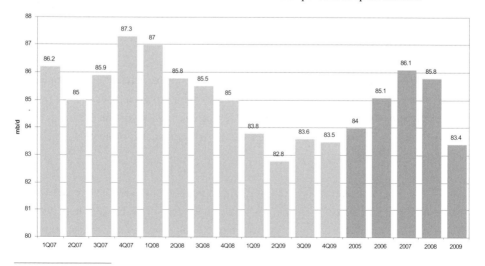

[1] John Lipsky, "Economic Shifts and Price Volatility", At the 4th OPEC International Seminar, Vienna, 18 March 2009. http://www.imf.org/external/np/speeches/2009/031809.htm

[2] "Quarterly Oil Product Demand - World", © OECD/IEA, Oil Market Report, 10 April 2009.

How could a 73 percent change in oil price result from a 2.35 percent drop in demand? Even by looking at the graph above, despite the financial crisis, demand for oil has not changed drastically. Moreover, the supply of oil also did not change drastically during that period of time; it actually increased from 1,332 billion barrels to 1,342 BB.[3] So, if neither demand nor supply account for the change in oil prices, what does?

The shift from industrial capitalism to financial capitalism

In the past, capitalism indeed increased the productivity of countries, since countries were then producing tangible goods. However, in the past two decades the world has been experiencing a shift from industrial capitalism to financial capitalism. Financial capitalism could be described as the pursuit of profit from purchasing and selling financial products such as currencies, bonds, stocks, futures, options and other derivatives. It also includes credit, the lending of capital at interest.

Financial capitalism was a result of the massive amount of corporate finance needed to expand businesses during the industrial revolution. It promoted more banks to unite specifically to create financial instruments that were ultimately targeted at the growing middle class of citizens, encouraging them to obtain more finance. Since the financial market was easily accessible, people started to buy financial instruments to earn a living instead of providing labour. People could now make more money by engaging in financial market activity rather than having a second job or working for longer hours. It enabled them to obtain wealth that would secure a comfortable retirement, thus becoming independent from government pension plans, which proved to be tentative at best.

The global financial crisis: How did we get here?

The role of financial markets is to make capital available to investors to enhance the economy's performance. Financial institutions take the savings of businesses and households and use them to make loans and investments. The financial system is supposed to allocate funds efficiently and prudently by giving special regard to risk. Unfortunately, that is not always the case.

With globalization increasing, international financial markets started to intertwine. People suddenly had unlimited investment options and started investing abroad where rates of return were more lucrative. For countries receiving capital inflows from savings, this could be highly beneficial *if* the resources were allocated efficiently. Sadly, this was not so.

---

[3] "Crude Oil Proved Reserves", EIA Official Statistics from the U.S Government. http://tonto.eia.doe.gov/cfapps/ipdbproject/IEDIndex3.cfm?tid=5&pid=57&aid=6

Financial institutions reacted to this surplus by competing for borrowers, by making credit cheap and easy to obtain for both households and businesses. Loans were poorly managed, with managers authorizing loans with no regard for creditworthiness or the client's ability to repay the loan.

As the situation escalated, financial institutions started to create new securities that included many individual loans. These securities were sold to investors and included high risk paper that neither the buyers nor sellers fully understood. With time, debtors started defaulting, sending a ripple effect throughout the financial and credit market not only in the US, but internationally.

The flaws of capitalism

There are three major flaws in capitalism. Firstly, capitalism is an amoral system. It encourages infinite competition between people, dividing them and leading to individualistic societies. Having a society where every man is for himself cannot be sustained and is most likely doomed to failure. In order to have a healthy economy in which people are dependent on one another, there is a need for a moral system to guide people's behavior; where the success of one is dependent on the other rather than opposed to it.

Secondly, industrial capitalism requires continuous growth, and since the fact that the earth's resources are finite is rather obvious, it is almost impossible to have unlimited growth in the world economy as a whole. So, with the system promoting wealth and emphasizing the importance of capital, people start abusing the earth's resources in order to increase their wealth, as population growth exceeds the expansion of available resources.

Thirdly, the system relies on people trading in financial tools rather than producing to earn an income. Eventually, this leads to people generating money from money. As the use of these financial tools expands globally the market becomes harder to control and as wealth starts to be created from such transactions, people overcome with greed start to seek more wealth and begin investing in risky assets. This leads to the volume of loans exceeding the value of collateral against those loans and then becoming greater than the amount of money available in the market. The creation of this "fictitious" wealth could ultimately be detrimental to an economy.

Capitalism and society

Capitalism is an amoral system, neither promoting nor opposing the implementation of ethics. Capitalism is much more than just an economic system; it is a philosophy, an ideology and social order where profit regulates the social structure. The interference of capitalism in politics, religion and our moral psychology is inevitable.

When living in a society that promotes competition and promises infinite wealth, people become controlled by greed. The free social mobility also poses a problem, given that classes are defined by capital. As Benjamin Franklin once said, "He that is of the opinion that money will do everything may be suspected of doing everything for money." Financial capitalism created a new type of elitism based purely on earning power and manifested in conspicuous consumption. This creates certain tensions in a society in which people aim to climb up the social ladder to enjoy its privileges. Eventually, this leads to egoism; being selfish at the expense of others. Capitalism means free markets and this freedom means the survival of the fittest. It has reduced society to individuals, who act independently with disregard to the consequences of their actions on other people and the environment. As long a person reaches his/her goal, nothing else matters. Under capitalism, taking time to be considerate is a considered a cost; a cost that no one is willing to pay.

When competition becomes a form of life, it unleashes the wolves in the sheep pen. With a system so reliant on capital, competition becomes brutal, disregarding friendship, cooperation and mutual respect between people. Eventually, the line dividing moral and immoral becomes vague and people are left with confusion, not knowing what's what.

The global casino

Gambling has been frowned upon since its inception; the majority of arguments, especially religious, consider it immoral. Gambling is the wagering of money or something else of material value on an event with an uncertain outcome, with the primary intent of winning money or material goods. Although the act of gambling or playing games of chance does not oppose justice, it becomes morally unacceptable when it deprives someone of what is necessary to provide for their needs. Also, the risk of addiction is a major concern since the passion for gambling becomes part of the fabric of our society. This ultimately leads to greed, and eventually the entertainment part of gambling is replaced by a thirst for winning. That is precisely why the gambling industry is a heavily regulated one.

Today's financial markets allow people to trade easily in financial securities with low transaction costs by allowing them to place "orders" on not only immediate, but also future transactions. Hence, engaging in financial market transactions involves speculation. By speculating, investors try to predict future market movements and, in attempts to beat the market, end up creating money from money. This has evolved into a culture of quick profit maximization.

How different is gambling from speculating? Not very. So, when the speculative transactions worldwide reach a frightening 1,122.7 trillion US dollars[4] something is definitely going

---

[4] Marcos Arruda, "Profiting Without Producing: The Financial Crisis As An Opportunity To Create A World Solidarity Economy."

wrong. Speculative actions helped nurture people's desire to quickly increase wealth, thus reinforcing a culture of materialism in which people are reduced to commodities and divided into classes based on their "market value". Money ceased to be the fruit of labour, a medium of exchange and became a measure of success.

Furthermore, speculation has added a new class of "super rich" people who own an astronomical amount of money. Current billionaires include Bill Gates, who is worth 40 billion US dollars, more than twice the amount of the Hashemite Kingdom of Jordan's GDP which was 19.12 billion US dollars in 2008.[5] This demonstrates the unequal distribution of income in the world. The creation of super wealth in which people own vast amounts of money and are ranked in magazines such as Forbes encourages people's profit maximization attitude, leading to competition over titles and labels and eventually a loss of the sense of individuality.

It's all about the money

Materialism is the simple preoccupation with the material world as opposed to intellectual or spiritual concepts. In today's world, material success and progress are the highest values in life. As societies get swept away by materialism, people become obsessed by the desire to obtain material wealth and are frustrated by the burden of maintaining that wealth and status.

As awful as the global financial crisis may seem, it might be the key to the world's salvation. The worldwide collapse of financial markets shocked the world into a rude awakening. People have now started questioning not only the system but also society and life itself. This awakening causes us to ask what is life all about. Are material things really the most important? And is material success our major priority in life?

International reactions to the financial crisis further demonstrates our preoccupation with materialism and the importance of finance in our lives. Despite facing several other serious crises, humanity chose to devote the most attention and resources to the one that involves money. The world has spent an exorbitant amount of money in an attempt to combat the crisis and mitigate its effects. What makes the financial crisis more worthy of trillions of dollars than other crises?

Conspiracies

Belief is a strong driver of human behaviour. Accompanying the financial crisis was the confidence crisis, during which people no longer had faith in financial institutions. In fact,

---

[5] CIA – The World Factbook, "Field Listing – GDP (Official Exchange Rate)" https://www.cia.gov/library/publications/the-world-factbook/fields/2195.html (Accessed April 21, 2009).

it would be safe to say that the financial crisis was triggered by people's lack of confidence. So, if the loss of faith in financial institutions shocked the globe, what would be the outcome of man losing faith in systems, nations, leaders, societies and mankind?

Recently, the media have focused on conspiracies. Videos on websites such as YouTube, showing alleged proof of the existence of conspiracies, have had an immense affect on the youth worldwide. One such example is the movie *Zeitgeist*, directed by Peter Joseph who in 2008 received an award in the annual Artivist Film Festival in Los Angeles. The word *Zeitgeist* is of German origin, meaning "the spirit of the age and its society." It describes the intellectual, cultural, ethical and political climate and morals of the era we are living in. It also talks about alleged social myths including religion, politics and banking system.

For a while, the movie reached the most viewed charts and was even translated into various languages. It claims that Christianity and all other theistic belief systems empower those who know the truth, but use the myth to manipulate and control societies. The belief that such conspiracies exist led to the youth's refusal to being associated with any institution and their failure to seek guidance from religion, the ultimate representative of morality.

Moral capitalism

Financial capitalism led to significant cultural and social changes. The moral vacuum of materialism is detrimental to economies and proves that a system that relies solely on competition and wealth maximization is unsustainable. The actual problem may not be in the reliance on competition but in the supremacy of materialism as the sole criterion for self-evaluation. However, despite the world's preoccupancy with material things we find certain exceptional people deviating from materialism and going against the system, acting in a very (God forbid!) un-capitalistic manner. What makes people who violate laws and go against the world system folk heroes?

It takes great courage to stand up to a system that governs the world, to challenge superior powers and accept the fact that ultimately you will face punishment. A recent illustration of such behavior is the Pirate Bay verdict. Pirate Bay is the world's largest torrent tracker, allowing people to find and download TV shows, movies and music for free. The establishment of this website presents very un-capitalistic behavior. So, what makes people do it?

The inherent outlook of capitalism is, "if you can't afford it, you don't get it, period." So, the people running things like the aforementioned Pirate Bay are living proof of the existence of morality and consciousness in human nature. These people realized the unfair system they live in and chose to act upon it. Therefore, it would be safe to infer that the main driver of the creation of Pirate Bay was morality, and a sense of responsibility. Those people chose to use their skills in providing something that many were deprived of.

But what will happen if everyone in society starts to disregard laws that they regard unjust? Is there not a responsibility towards society to respect the law? This brings us to the concept of responsibility and raises the question, are we all carrying out our responsibilities towards the world? This particular sense of responsibility proves to be crucial in sustaining societies and maintaining the earth's well being.

Taking responsibility: an alternative to materialism

> The willingness to accept responsibility for one's own life is the source from which self respect springs.
> *Slouching Towards Bethlehem*, Joan Didion

To be morally responsible, one must be worthy of a particular reaction such as praise or blame for having performed a particular act. Taking responsibility is, in my opinion, the first step towards the solution. With capitalism erasing the notion of moral responsibility, we are left with societies composed of individuals, acting individually, thinking individually and benefiting individually. This individuality is extremely costly. Instead, societies could start to recognize the power of collectivity; how a simple action done by millions could have a tangible outcome.

It is essential that people understand their connection to one another, and that how every action one takes, regardless how small, has an effect on at least one other human being. The financial crisis has demonstrated how people suffer from unjust actions; however, it is also important to notice the opportunity this crisis has given us. The Chinese word "crisis" is a combination of two words: danger and opportunity. And this is exactly what the crisis is, an opportunity for mankind to sort out their priorities in a responsible way, bearing in mind that the following generations will ultimately inherit the consequences of the decisions made today.

Introducing a theme of responsibility in societies might take a considerable amount of time and effort, but is most certainly achievable. At this point in our technological advancement, a vast number of people can now be reached. Advanced mediums can be exploited to send messages of responsibility throughout the world, targeting everyone, especially children and the youth. A worldwide "responsibility" campaign could be aimed at developing a culture that cherishes responsibility and considers it as an important part of the social framework. The means by which responsibility could be emphasized on a worldwide scale are available; it all boils down to a matter of willingness to execute.

The ecumenical role

The responsibility campaign could be used as a means of raising awareness about moral values and their importance as part of our social fabric. Since religious institutions are representatives of all that is moral, just and ethical, their contribution to spreading the message is fundamental. Christianity is a religion of compassion and love. It promotes equality between people and discards social barriers. It is a religion that discourages preoccupation with material things and encourages spirituality and intellectuality. In the gospel of St. Mark, Jesus points out man's tendency to become preoccupied with social laws, and states that what matters the most in life is how we treat one another.

> Again Jesus called the crowd to him and said, "Listen to me, everyone, and understand this. Nothing outside a man can make him 'unclean' by going into him. Rather, it is what comes out of a man that makes him 'unclean'." After he had left the crowd and entered the house, his disciples asked him about this parable. "Are you so dull?" he asked. "Don't you see that nothing that enters a man from the outside can make him 'unclean'? For it doesn't go into his heart but into his stomach, and then out of his body" (Mark 7: 14-19, New International Version)

The World Council of Churches is the broadest and most inclusive among the many organized ecumenical movements. The WCC has devoted itself to attaining Christian unity and has implemented programmes that call for justice, ethics and consideration for the world's unfortunate and deprived people. The WCC has set itself as an outstanding example of Christianity; it has devoted efforts to addressing various issues throughout the world, targeting everyone. Therefore, in light of the youth's moral crisis, there is no better-suited organization than the WCC to address the problem.

One possible starting point is the youth's disinterest in religion. The reason for this deviation is primarily due to the intricacy in modern-day Christianity. Interdenominational dialogues focus on intricate issues of doctrine that only those very skilled theologians can understand, let alone partake in. So, with the increasingly complex Christian denominations, young people find themselves lost whilst attempting to understand the Christian message. Consequently, the issue of belonging to a Christian denomination becomes complicated, discouraging the youth from attempting to practice or even understand religion. Instead of concentrating on what separates a Catholic from an Orthodox or a Protestant Christian, the church could simplify its teachings and aim to deliver the Christian message rather than Christian diversity. Since the World Council of Churches includes denominations collectively representing Christians throughout the world, it is the perfect representative of the simplicity and accessibility of the Christian religion.

The general perception of religious institutions is one of traditional, black-and-white institutions that dictate rather than deduce.Since today's youth values logic and reason, the incorporation of logic into religious teaching is essential. Religious institutions could attempt to contemporize by shifting from doctrinarian dictums in which people are asked to tailor their problems to fit the solution, to being more patient in understanding problems and applying the logic behind morality. This could be a much more effective way of portraying religion as a source of guidance. The WCC has already devoted considerable effort in targeting and connecting with the world's younger citizens through youth programmess. It embodies the perfect combination of factors to attract the youth's attention and interest in seeking guidance from religious institutions.

Moreover, the fact that the WCC extends a helping hand to whoever is needy, regardless of ethnic background or religion, succeeds in promoting the true image of Christianity; a religion that discards social barriers between people and promotes equality. People never touch each other so lightly that they don't leave a mark behind. Therefore, I can't help but reiterate the importance of man understanding that life is shared between human beings, and there is no better preacher of this message than the WCC. By engaging in activities that support unity and break down barriers between people, it could initiate a significant ecumenical movement promoting equality and codependence.

The WCC could further expand its educational programmes to encompass social issues and address the moral crisis. Education is a powerful tool and could impact the lives of many. By sending a message to the youth and increasing awareness about the WCC and its actions, the organization could help restore young people's faith in humanity. It could promote research that helps in the better development of nations, and be an exclusive supporter of human advancement.

Economorals

What is the outcome of studying economorals, the attempt to understand, develop and apply moral values to the study and elucidation of economic principles? The purpose of economorals would be to give moral content to economic theories. Economoralists could be the very people who specialize in incorporating moral values into economic systems in a way that renders economies efficient. The study of economorals could be extended to educational institutions, becoming an important element of social, political and economic studies. The teaching and preaching of moral values could be extended to the world's governments. Economoralists could help governments regulate and monitor the extent to which members of their societies fulfill their duties to the public more meticulously.

Time has proven that with the absence of moral values, an economy cannot be sustained. The introduction of economorals could be a way of setting moral standards as a necessity for the success of economies. As people are educated about the importance of morality – not only from a religious point of view, but also from a logical and economical point of view – the incorporation of morals into our daily lives becomes instinctive.

What shall we choose?

We live in a world that is able to find the money to develop and maintain jet fighters that cost billions of dollars[6] but is unable to find the resources to stop treatable diseases such as diarrhoea and pneumonia in developing countries. It is statistics such as these that indicate the dire need to rearrange our priorities and work hand in hand to prevent the alienation of the poor, deprived and needy.

The shift of moral and cultural behaviour poses significant concerns in our ability to sustain the world and the human race. Living in a society that is devoid of moral standards is unsustainable; it is apparent that there is a need for moral standards to guide human behaviour and ensure social welfare.

It is our responsibility to ensure that everyone is born with an equal right to the necessities of life, food, water, clothing, shelter and security. The famous Franco-Czech novelist Milan Kundera once said that the existence of such burdens is what pins us to the ground, and the heavier the burden, the closer our lives come to the earth, thus the more real and fulfilling they become. Without such burdens, we are light, flying far above the ground, far from reality, our actions becoming less and less significant. What, then, shall we choose? To live a fulfilling life with burdens and responsibilities towards one another, or continue to exist individually, having no significant impact on the world?

References

Marcos Arruda, *Profiting Without Producing: The Financial Crisis As An Opportunity To Create A World Solidarity Economy,* Instituto Politicas Alternativas Para O Cone Sul, 21 April 2009, http://www.pacs.org.br/ (see also earlier chapter).

Andrew Beattie, "Financial Capitalism Opens Doors To Personal Fortune", Investopedia, 1 May 2009, http://www.investopedia.com/articles/07/financial-capitalism.asp.

---

[6] Richard Lardner, "Jet Fighter Costs to Hit US$1 Trillion", the San Francisco Chronicle. http://www.sfgate.com/cgi-bin/article.cgi?f=/n/a/2008/03/11/national/w154215D32.DTL

British Council press releases. "British Council Youth call for 'Moral Capitalism' ahead of London Summit", British Council, Home. 1 April 2009,, http://www.britishcouncil.org/new/press-office/press-releases/British-Council-Youth-call-for-Moral-Capitalism-ahead-of-London-Summit/.

Central Intelligence Agency "CIA - The World Factbook – Field Listing - GDP (official exchange rate)",. 29 April 2009, https://www.cia.gov/library/publications/the-world-factbook/fields/2195.html.

"Cultural Materialism", Philosophy - AllAboutPhilosophy.org, 21 April 2009 http://www.AllAboutPhilosophy.org/cultural-materialism.htm.

Justin Fox, "The Comeback Keynes", *Time* magazine 23 October 2008.

John Lipsky, "Economic Shifts and Oil Price Volatility", International Monetary Fund, 18 March 2009. 11 April 2009, http://www.imf.org/external/np/speeches/2009/031809.htm.

Louis Proyect, "Finance Capitalism", Columbia University, 29 April 2009, http://www.columbia.edu/~lnp3/mydocs/economics/finance_capital.htm.

Sasika Sassen, "The End of Financial Capitalism?" The *Morung Express,* 1 May 2009 http://www.morungexpress.com/columnists/19093.html.

Andreas Saugstad, "The Moral Psychology of Capitalism", Go Inside, 14 April 2001, http://goinside.com/01/4/capital.html.

"We are all Keynesians now", The *Boston Globe,* 25 November 2008, http://www.boston.com/bostonglobe/editorial_opinion/editorials/articles/2008/11/25/we_are_all_keynesians_now/

A THEOLOGICAL REFLECTION ON THE ECONOMIC CRISIS

Kim Yong-Bock

The current financial crisis has raised not only economic policy questions, but ethical and theological questions as well, which point to the crisis of the existing capitalist market system, and to social and ecological crisis. Analysts and policy makers are still seeking economic solutions, both theoretical and practical. The US and other major economic powers are bailing out the big financial institutions with astronomical amounts of funds from their tax revenues. The economic recovery expected from this bail out will not, however, alleviate the suffering of the poor and neglected, whose already bad situation will be worsened by the "recovery" process. This is also true for the ecological crisis: attention is drawn away from it by the financial crisis, and the integral relationship of the current economy with the ecological crisis is mostly ignored.

Why ethical and theological questions?

In the first place, the financial crisis is deepening and accelerating the suffering of people throughout the world, and is aggravating ecological destruction. Radical questioning is needed, beyond the issue of policy adjustment, because the suffering and destruction have reached the stage of ultimate crisis. Remembering the arrogant claims of the economic regime and its advocates – and their promises to eradicate hunger and poverty – we recognize them as hypocritical, and realize the need to deal with the deeper ethical and theological problems posed by the myopic, destructive policies and systems that dominate life today.

Some regard the current situation as a temporary crisis that can be overcome through policy measures and "economic recovery packages". Such thinking is a denial of the reality of suffering and destruction that have been produced by the uncontrolled greed of the current economic regime.

While the beneficiaries of the system feel their security shaken, the victims of the system face the much more serious threat of death and destruction. The hungry, the poor, other victims of the current system and ordinary consumers now find themselves unable to meet their basic needs, suffering the loss of their jobs and the devaluation of their properties and assets. The crisis experienced by ordinary people is qualitatively different from that experienced by the managers and beneficiaries of the system. This is not a matter of recovering or normalizing the system, but a matter of life and death requiring radical transformation of the system into a life-giving economy.

What is the nature of the current economic system?

The present capitalist system, protected by the dominant imperial power and its allies, is like a cancer. It kills people and nature because it subjects all life to the global market, geared at capital growth for the few owners of property and financial capital, instead of satisfying the needs of all people and living beings.

It is a system aimed at unlimited growth and maximum profits. Under this system, now in crisis, the survival of life itself is threatened; but the managers of the system continue to seek only their own profits. The name of this reality is greed. And greed begets evil, and evil leads humans and other living beings to destruction and death. Human greed has continued to grow, uncontrolled and unlimited.

Our first theological affirmation is that God and greed are incompatible! They have a *Sangkeuk* relation; that is, God and greed are at opposite poles. Human greed, focused in the greed of corporate agencies, is now on the borderline, challenging God as the ultimate source and ultimate protector of life. To affirm the incompatibility between God and greed is an ethical and theological act. Universally and explicitly, in all religions and cultures, greed is regarded as unethical, immoral and evil.

The recent financial crisis, originating in the United States and spreading throughout the world, raises these deeper theological questions because we analyze the crisis as the manifestation of greed in the system. Greed has brought about the crisis, and greed is the salient symptom of the global economic breakdown that now threatens life on earth.[1] Some see this as a crisis of life and civilization as a whole, a profound philosophical and religious crisis that goes beyond moral or social-scientific policy questions. Is faith in God compatible with an economic regime that has produced such a devastating crisis?

Questions
Is a global economic system based on unlimited industrial growth, financial speculation and land mortgage speculation, sustainable?[2]
Why is the current financial crisis – that is, capitalism - so threatening to the life of humans and other living beings?

---

[1] The context is the global symbiotic power-nexus of capitalist market, world empire and global technocracy. It is a complex regime of imperial hegemonic domination, a global economy based on speculation, uncontrollable greed and "almighty" technocracy—that is, a convergent, symbiotic power dynamic.

[2] Do the "signs of the times" indicate an eschatological Omega point toward a new, convivial life order under a "new heaven and new earth"?

Does the current economic regime beg the question of faith in God? What are the theological implications of the financial crisis and its economic system?

What is the direction of scripture and faith(s) for the economy of life for all living beings? What can we discern for a new order of life?

Structural greed and universal suffering: Oikonomia of life destroyed by the power of greed

The capitalist economy is destroying the order of God's creation for all living beings. Nature's resources are being depleted by the policy of unlimited economic growth. Life in all dimensions – its genesis, growth and nurture, its health and healing, and its fulfilment in economic and cultural terms – is dominated and manipulated by the market regime. We affirm that the crisis of capitalism is integrally interconnected with the ecological crisis of Planet Earth.

The biblical witness tells us that God graciously bestowed the earth with plenty of resources so that all living beings may live together in fullness. The essence of the capitalist economy, however, is designed not to satisfy the needs of all people and other living beings, but to create wealth for the greedy owners. The power and reality of greed in its systemic regime are destroying the oikonomia of life given by God.

What is the fundamental nature of capitalism from a theological perspective? Is the Christian faith incompatible with modern capitalism? If capitalism has deteriorated into a system of greed, then this question must be asked.

Both the intense suffering of humanity and the wanton destruction of nature are caused by an economy based on structural greed. Capital is characterized as having to grow through investment in order to be reinvested to be reinvested, *ad infinitum*. As the highest returns can be secured through speculative financial transactions, most of the money goes there and not into the production and distribution of necessary goods and services. Financial speculation can involve the buying, holding, selling, and short-selling of stocks, bonds, commodities, currencies, collectibles, real estate, derivatives, or any valuable financial instrument to profit from fluctuations in its price, irrespective of its underlying value.

Finance capital rushes into a mania of investing in the popular business of the day where there is an expectation of high profits. At the start the bubble will grow bigger and bigger, seeming as if the sky is the limit. But the bubble will burst the moment it becomes clear that the prospect of high profits is all hot air. Speculative ventures, or bubbles, can only end in a crash since no new wealth is created in this world. The core of the present economy is that capital owners invest their money where it can grow quickest. The result is unemployment and the destruction of the earth, instead of using the increase in productivity to reduce work hours and deal carefully with nature.

All elements of life are being commoditized, privatized and subjected to the accumulation of capital: seeds, animals and even the genes of human beings. The result is wealth for the few on the one side, and hunger, exclusion, mass misery, despair, violence, death and ecological destruction on the other. As long as global capitalist economic system is maintained, all life is unsustainable and in jeopardy. We need to see the whole picture. At the root is speculative activity. We are living in an economic system that is driven by the greed of usury and speculation.[3]

Capitalism today is a financial system that can expand the muscle of its credit so swiftly that its clothing of real world assets cannot stretch fast enough to contain it. The inevitable result is a risky, unregulated expansion into sub prime mortgage markets followed by financial explosion and credit-crunch collapse, threatening life. How is it possible to argue for the relative good of capitalism today? The fact that we live under the system implicates us as participants in greed and speculation. Consider the investment of church assets, and banking life. Is it merely a question of ethical behaviour in current financial life? Does the system of greed subvert our very faith in the God of life?

The hunger of the poor

The systematic denial of food to living beings can be regarded as "genocidal". But food, water, shelter and basic healthcare are in fact being denied. The supreme command of God, in the mandate of love, is to feed the hungry and to sustain God-given life – to love life.

We have all heard the claim made by the global economic regime – the UN, IMF, WTO, World Bank, G7, developing nations and their advocates and leaders – that hunger can be eliminated. Are these claims tenable under the existing system? The need for sustenance is a key factor in any economic system. But under the current capitalist system, the supply of sustenance for life has been subjugated to the system of greed.

---

[3] It is just paper money. It turns into debt, since it no longer has the backing of gold, silver or commodities. How can such a system be permitted, when the **stock exchange wipes out almost 25 trillion US dollars in corporate values** – almost twice the US GDP – in less than a month? Speculation leads to billions of dollars in profit for the rich and powerful; ExxonMobile 3rd Q records profits over 14.8 billion US dollars – 15% above previous record profit; and yet Government gives it further tax breaks.

The current financial crisis comes on the heels of a major worldwide food-price crisis, which pushed millions of people deeper into hunger and poverty. According to the World Bank, the food crisis set back progress on meeting the Millennium Development Goal on poverty by seven years.[4] Von Braun said,

> Recent estimates from the Food and Agriculture Organization of the United Nations show that the number of undernourished people increased from 848 million to 923 million from 2003–2005 to 2007, largely owing to the food price crisis … The number of undernourished likely increased even further in 2008 as prices continued to rise and the financial crisis hit.[5]

Such high levels of undernourishment have huge long-term consequences. For example, the physical and cognitive development of babies and children is negatively affected when they do not get enough calories and micronutrients in their diets. The World Bank predicts that high food and fuel prices will increase the number of malnourished people in the world by 44 million this year, to reach a total of 967 million. Pope Benedict said the blame for hunger could be directed at "boundless speculation" in markets. According to Oxfam, the British-based aid and development charity,

> Nearly 1 billion people went hungry on Thursday as the world marked World Food Day. The global financial crisis has sent food prices soaring and pushed an extra 119 million people into hunger, meaning 967 million people are now living below the hunger line.[6]

This reality of hunger is against the God of life. Hunger can be overcome economically, but does the regime of greed allow this possibility and necessity? We don't need a mediation of the system of greed to deal with the lack of the food and basic resources of life; that system is only interested in making profits, not in feeding the hungry.

Poverty and the gospel for the poor
The Christian gospel is incompatible with poverty. The Bible says that the gospel is for the poor. If it is not for the poor, it is not the gospel. The global economic regime claims that it can eliminate poverty. It has replaced the gospel. Is this credible?

---

[4] World Bank 2008.

[5] Joachim van Braun, "Food and Financial Crises: Implications for Agriculture and the Poor", International Food Policy Research Institute, December 2008 http://beta.irri.org/solutions/images/publications/papers/ifpri_food_financial_crisis_dec2008.pdf

[6] "World food crisis worsens amidst global financial crisis," Oxfam, 17 October 2008.

A UNESCO report documents the potential impact of the current worldwide economic meltdown on the millennium development goals (MDGs) – internationally agreed targets to eradicate poverty and reduce child mortality, among other human development objectives. The report highlighted the prospect of an increase of between 200,000 and 400,000 in infant mortality and stated that child malnutrition, already rising, will be one of the main drivers of higher child death rates. "Millions of children face the prospect of long-term irreversible cognitive damage as a result of the financial crisis," said Patrick Montjourides, one of the authors. The world's poorest countries are unable to insulate their citizens from the crisis, with an estimated 43 out of 48 low-income countries incapable of providing a pro-poor government stimulus.

Work (and employment) as care for life

Work under the greedy capitalist system has been distorted into toil under systematic exploitation. Employment is not now the right to livelihood, but bondage and slavery to the system of greed. Now workers are losing their employment even under the system of greed, in its search for higher profits. Can this be a liberation of workers for their new life?

Work is the God-given vocation to care for life and the garden of life. Workers today, however, are denied their vocation to care for their families and for the lives of all living things. Work is not a commodity but a vocation of service to the fullness of life for all, a social and ecological vocation.

As the financial crisis hits the real economy, workers are being laid off through structural adjustment programs in the name of "flexibility of labour", with migrant workers most severely affected. Reductions in workforces and workdays are being implemented in export zones and industrial estates in proportion to the reduction of orders from abroad. Permanent closures, temporary shutdowns and work rotations have become common in the last three months, affecting thousands of garment, electronics and furniture workers. These retrenchments and rotations herald a graver unemployment that will result when the global recession reaches maturity and fully impacts the countries.

Unemployment is the modern version of human sacrifice on the altar of Mammon. The theory of "disaster capitalism" demonstrates that in case after case, capitalist governments – particularly in the third world – exploit disaster to intensify their attacks on workers and poor farmers.[7] Denying people work robs them of their vocation to care for the life of the community. The exploitation of workers drains them of their essential livelihood.

---

[7] Naomi Klein, *The Shock Doctrine: the Rise of Disaster Capitalism, Random House of Canada, Ltd. 2008.*

the targets of the market. The resultant "imperial hegemony" over culture is a symbiosis of Cartesian epistemology, the modern natural scientific method, and its technological and cybernetic manifestations, along with hi-tech multi-media technology. The media, owned by big capital, influence people to follow the "laws of the market", to be driven by market forces. The market's objective is to dominate the minds, consciousness and perception of all human beings. This is manifested in advertising that causes cultural homogenization and the erosion of cultural and religious identity, the colonization of consciousness and perceptions, the commodification of cultural products, and the promotion of consumerism and the infinite desire to buy and consume. Epistemological objectification, fragmentation and reductionism in modern science are underlying factors in this process of technological domination and control.

Science is the criterion for truth and the epistemological master; and technology is the chief of efficiency and control. Science and technology seek domination over all other powers on earth. This has penetrated many theological discourses, and it dominates bio-ethics in the biotech industry.

War and economy
The financial crisis is also related to the war industry. The military-industrial complex is deeply implicated in the current economic regime. War is waged on economic grounds, whether energy-related or to benefit the war industry itself.

Throughout the entire Cold War period, US capitalism was dependent on military spending to keep the economy going. The growth of the military-industrial complex, with its web of prime contractors and tens of thousands of subcontractors thriving on Pentagon appropriations for war and for arms exports, was the principal means of keeping the capitalist economy from sinking into stagnation and depression. This history illustrates that capitalism has had to resort to artificial measures that bring in their wake disaster in the form of war, depression or both in order to sustain it. The new wars (the military doctrines such as the "war on terror") will have devastating consequences, as illustrated by the Iraq and Afghanistan wars. Arms production for the military and consumption in war, military research and development in the name of national security, the arms trade, and small-arms sales for profit are some of the manifestations of the military-industrial-financial complex. Nuclear warfare and cyber and space wars and their implications are disastrous to the whole of life.

Authorities should be denied any right to work for security and peace for the life of living beings. The life of living beings has its own way and wisdom of security and wellbeing. The security doctrine is an ideology of violent, military domination by the powerful. Let the community of life take care of its sustainability. War should be banned, for it is omnicidal. Jesus the Galilean is against the Roman Empire. His peace is not the peace of this world.

Is the "genocidal" nature of life an integral dimension of the global regime?

Doesn't this reality of suffering constitute a partial genocide of all living beings in economic, ecological, biological, social, political, geopolitical, cultural and religious terms, as well as in ecological terms? The futurologist laments the increase of human population. The historical view, grounded on the logic of survival of the fittest, spells the apocalyptic doom of the earth as a community of living beings. Given the neo-Darwinist logic, violence and destruction of life and living beings are the inevitable consequence. Likewise, the market is an agent of exclusion, exploitation and destruction because it only meets the demands of those with money. According to Goodchild, the sovereign force associated with a market society must necessarily be in a state of total war against all other social forces that resist its expansionary claims.[10]

These realities of death and destruction are integrally and systematically related under the global system of greedy capitalism. The convergence of suffering and destruction in this situation are the death of justice, peace and compassion in the community of life. The survival of the fittest is the ideology used to justify genocidal trends in many dimensions of life.

Does this not deny the God of life?

So how does real-world economics develop into a totally faith-based pseudo-religion that promises great financial rewards for the elite few, but delivers fiscal chaos, staggering government bail outs and ever-increasing amounts of debt and hardship for honest, hard-working taxpayers? The bailing out of the financial giants is sold as the so-called recovery of the financial system so that capitalism can function "normally". It imposes immense suffering on the people and continues the ecological destruction. The sacrifice of people and other living beings is the price to be paid. This represents the Mammonic ideology of capitalist market.

In the Bible, *mammon* is not a demon but simply an Aramaic word meaning "wealth" or "property". Matthew states, "No one can serve two masters; for a slave will either hate the one and love the other, or be devoted to the one and despise the other. You cannot serve God and wealth [mammon]" (Matt. 6:24). Obviously the mammonic nature of global capitalism is not compatible with faith in God. What are the key points in mammonic ideology? It affirms God's sovereignty over life and the earth, by affirming private ownership of land and property as absolute. It also provides unlimited freedom for the corporate agency of the market

---

[10] Philip Goodchild, *Capitalism and religion: the price of piety*, 2002, p. 25.

to override regulations of any kind. This means that its freedom is absolute. It also allows the use of any means, including speculation to maximize profit and satisfy unlimited greed.

The global capitalist market has operated under the ideology of neoliberalism, which served as the foundation of the finance economy. Under this ideology the greedy pursuit of riches through the maximization of profit is permitted, as is the consequent victimization of life of people and living beings. This ideology is indeed Mammonic. Webster's dictionary defines Mammon as,1) the false god of riches and avarice; 2) riches regarded as an object of worship and greedy pursuit. Those who worship mammon are greedy people who value money too highly.

Usury is a very big sin in Islam. One verse in the Qur'an forbids it and another says that God will declare war on those who undertake it. "The rich rule over the poor, and the borrower is the slave of the lender." (Proverbs 22:7). The borrower is servant to the lender, and the method used by the lender is the insidious system of usury.

Today's society worships the greed of corporate power in the form of the transnational corporations. The free market acts as a haven for corporate powers. Financial capital thrives in this free market, manifested in the form of speculative capital. It is widely known that more than 98 percent of all global transactions today are those made by speculative financial capital. The World Trade Organization (WTO) is a global regime of free trade, or the global free market. Here, money has absolute power and cannot be controlled. The corporate powers seek to maximize their profit through the sacrifice and victimization of peoples, including the peoples of Asian countries who have been subjected to this financial capital regime justifying itself by the ideology of the free market. We name this kind of money power Mammon. We are not concerned merely with some misdeeds of the capitalist market, but with its resistance to God, which is the love of life. The absolute regime of private property rights denies sharing as the fundamental order of life.

A theological and ethical critique

Mammonism is an economic ideology that justifies the victimization of all living beings in resistance to God, and further the "ecological genocide" of all living beings. The power of mammonic greed in the global capitalist economy should be rejected.

Any affirmation of power and its ideological and messianic claims is a rejection of the faith and spiritual foundation of *economia* as the management of life of all living beings. "Soft" greed is justified in the name of the sinfulness of humanity. Although any excess of self-interest is tolerated as an ethical misdeed in the name of realism, unlimited greed is not tolerated. But greed and self-interest in the system of profit maximization are no different from one another. Thus, so-called theological realism and its ethical consequences cannot be accepted. Theological realism accepting human nature as sinful provides a loophole for capitalism as a mere expression of human nature and its shortcomings. Greed is individualized so that a greedy individual may be tamed through education and control. Competition brings about efficiency and opens the loophole to unlimited competition and the ideology of social Darwinism. In the name of efficiency, unlimited productivity is promised for unlimited growth.[11]

This means the erosion of morality and ethics. It is not merely the secularization of Western culture that has eroded the foundation of ethics and morality; it is greed – collective and individual, carnal and spiritual, political and ideological – in symbiosis with power that is self-centred and dominating. Utilitarian principles open up serious ethical loopholes, leading to the formation of ethical agencies, individual and collective, devoted to the pursuit of happiness and self-interest by all means possible. This is manifested in the current trend of bioethics development for the biotech industry (playing God). The argument of enlightened self-interest can easily creep into this strand of ethical thought.

A critique of imperative ethics is in order due to the dogmatic, negative nature of its ethical discourse. I do not have scope here to address the topic, but I would argue for an ethics of compassion and care for all living beings. While imperative ethics are founded on principles derived from religious or philosophical beliefs, the ethics of compassion and care are based upon faith(s) and may be regarded as faith-based and wisdom-based ethics.

Biblical faith-based *oikonomia* for all living beings

God is sovereign over all creation. "The earth is the Lord's, and all that is in it" (Ps. 24:1). We are called to share with our neighbours out of the abundance that God gives to the world. God's economy is a gift of grace that is not for sale in the marketplace (Matt 14:13-21; 15:32-38). God's economy of life provides abundantly for all God's people and all living beings. The poor and marginalized are special members of God's community and we are

---

[11] "The European Protestant work ethic has been praised much even in connection with capitalist development and scientific advancement. Economic activity 'is part of the *telos* or benevolent purposes of God in creating a just and genuinely human society. This natural benevolent order, however, could be disrupted and disturbed, particularly when certain elements within the commercial classes developed an excessive interest and pleasure in their own personal wealth and property!' we arrive at the modern notion of the economy but viewed as the work of collective agencies or an '*interlocking set of activities of production, exchange and consumption, which form a system with its own laws and its own dynamic.*'"

called to put justice for "the least of these" at the centre of the community of life and the mission of the church (Matt. 25:40). God's vision for the earth is of justice and peace. God calls the church to "loose the bonds of injustice, to undo the thongs of the yoke, to let the oppressed go free, and to break every yoke" (Is. 58:6)

Rules devised to benefit some segments of society should not stand if they also disadvantage or harm the poor.

> Hear this, you that trample on the needy, and bring to ruin the poor of the land, saying, ... "We will make the ephah small and the shekel great, and practice deceit with false balances, buying the poor for silver and the needy for a pair of sandals, and selling the sweepings of the wheat" (Amos 8:4-6)

The oikonomia of sabbath and jubilee

All living beings enjoy the sabbath, in which here we see the integral wholeness of economy and ecology. This is exemplified by the sabbath day, particularly during the journey through the wilderness as described in Exodus 15-17; the sabbath year, described in Exodus 23, where the land was not cultivated, and slaves were released every seventh year; the year of jubilee, every 50th year – the "sabbath of sabbaths" – when all debts were cancelled, and all property returned to the original owners.

The oikonomia of sabbath and jubilee is not merely a release from the bondage of the ancient economy in Old Testament times. It is a precursor of a new economy of life of all living beings, not merely the antithesis of the imperial and royal economy; it opens a new horizon for the oikonomia of life. Economy of tithing, *koinonia* as justice and compassion, economy of community of life sharing, oikonomia as *diakonia*, and economy serving the life of all living beings: these are some of the dimensions of the biblical oikonomia of life.

Convergent vision of oikonomia for the full life of all living beings

Macro-ecumenically speaking, a convergent vision of "economy of life" is emerging from Buddhist thought for the oikonomia of compassion against greed (ontological corruption), from the Confucian economy of benevolence and virtue against self-interest (oikonomia of KyeongSeJemin [經世濟民]), which is the oikonomia of SangSaeing (conviviality), from the Tonghak oikonomia, which is a convergence of Seon, Yu, Bul, Mu and Ki.[12]

---

[12] Political Economy of 輔國安民 and religious teaching of 侍天主, 人乃天.

A SangSaeing/Ubuntu economy of the communities of living beings and a convergent vision of oikonomia of life were proposed at the Changsung Consultation in Korea. Convergent visions of the oikonomia of life can be found in the meeting of visions among faith traditions and theologies, among cultural traditions and philosophies, among diverse ecological, economic, political and geographical communities.

Economic repentance

Transparency of the finance of the church and its financial investments; its transactions through private banks; usury practices.

Christianity-capitalism symbiosis.

God and new oikonomia of life.

Macro-ecumenical view of oikonomia of life.

A time for *status confessionis*?

Milan Opocensky is with us spiritually! Milan called us to this prophetic stance. To declare a *status confessionis* is to say that time has run out, that tolerance has reached its limits and that a line must be drawn. Our faith in God is fundamentally challenged. It is to say that the time is "an evil time" (Amos 5:13), but one in which we may no longer keep a prudent silence. It is to acknowledge that scandals must come, but to declare woe to those through whom they come (Matt. 18:7). It is to say that a state of emergency has been imposed upon the church by others, and that faith requires a response. It is by its very character a risky judgment, for it deals with historical contingencies, saying that what would remain acceptable under other circumstances is no longer so. Our words are, let us get utterly serious as a people of faith in God!

THE ROLE OF THE ECUMENICAL MOVEMENT IN ADVOCATING FOR ETHICAL PRINCIPLES

Rev. Dr Rienzie Perera

At this critical time in history the majority of the human race, who are the victims of this crisis, are looking for signs of hope and waiting for the moment of deliverance. It is at times like this we hear the voices of both false and true prophets. As people are confused and swept away by this man-made crisis – which has made inroads into economics, ecology, food, shelter, energy, security and their survival – they are also faced with the dilemma of distinguishing between false and true prophets. I believe one of the tasks of the ecumenical movement is to equip the victims of this crisis to discern truth from falsehood and to name and unmask the powers that try to pretend to be the saviors of this world.

I am grateful for the opportunity to provide some guidelines about how we who represent the ecumenical movement can work with God to speak the truth in love and join forces with people of diverse religions and no religion, ideology, colour, ethnicity, gender, class and caste to reshape and transform this world.

The call to repent

As stated, we live at a critical moment in history and we human beings, created in God's own image, are responsible for the mess we have created. Although the mess was created by the rich and the powerful of this world, the victims are the poor, who have always been trapped and condemned. They are the "wretched of the earth" or the "sinned against". In one of the WCC statements this idea is expressed in the following manner:

> The WCC is particularly concerned about the crises' unfolding impacts on the lives and livelihoods of the economically weak and vulnerable. While they had little or no part in the creation of these crises, poor countries and people in poverty – already struggling to make daily ends meet – are paying the highest price for reckless economic liberalization and deregulation.[1]

Although we are quick to blame the "other", be it capitalism or G20 nations, we cannot escape from the guilt of benefiting from the system which has condemned millions to perish.

[1] World Council of Churches, Statement on the Doha Outcome Document, Doha, Qatar Forum, 29 November – 2 December 2008.

When I say we, I mean the institutionalized religions, be it Christianity or any other that enjoys the patronage of the principalities and powers.

The sins of capitalism are spelt out in many of the chapters of this book and therefore I will not elaborate on that issue at this point. However, it must be said that at the heart of capitalism lies the desire to make more and more profit, even at the expense of the other. It is a system with the power to create individuals at the expense of community, to enslave one to greed and accumulation rather then to share and care. It is a system that creates in people a craving for more and more and, in the end, people become dehumanized by worshipping money, power, privilege and pleasure. It is a system that replaces the worship of the true, living and life-giving God. Therefore, this system called capitalism is anti-God and anti-people. It is evil and promotes idol-worship. That is the reason Jesus said that, "You cannot serve God and wealth" (Matt. 6:24). We have being living amidst this idol for many years and yet failed to recognize, identify, expose and condemn it as anti-God.

The sin of the established or institutionalized religion is not simply an inability to see, hear and denounce, but its refusal to see, hear and speak. Established religions, including Christianity, have often refused or failed to denounce and expose the idol as anti-God. In other words, established religions have failed to unmask the golden calf in their midst.

This sin has been part and parcel of the church since it became a religion protected and promoted by the state. When we become beneficiaries of the state we distort the truth and deform Jesus the Christ and distort the values of the kingdom of God. The Jesus of the empire is a "golden crown Jesus", or a Jesus devoid of the cross. When a religion, especially Christianity, ceases to be the authentic body of Christ, it ceases to be the church of the living God that is called to be a fountain of life amidst a valley of dry bones. This is the sin of the church; that it is no longer God's messenger of hope for the world.

Therefore, we have to share in the collective guilt of what has caused this world to become what it is. When I say this, I am aware of the radical stances we have taken as individuals and the statements made by the World Council of Churches and the denominations we represent, on various issues, which are contrary to gospel values. Although we have made statements and taken steps to condemn many of the issues, the power of sin has triumphed and still people in our midst cry the words of the Psalmist, "How long, O Lord, will you look on?" (Ps. 35:17a).

The question is, have we failed to make this world a place of *shalom* for everyone? And if so, why? My understanding is that the Christian community as a whole is divided and as a result our voices are often voices in the wilderness. Therefore, we have to recognize that the sin that is in the world is also in the church.

The call to a new commitment

As in biblical times, God's voice is heeded only by a small minority. They are the "remnant" community, and it is through that community that the voice of prophesy will be heard. The task of the prophetic community is to help people to imagine that another world is possible. That is what the prophets of old did. They denounced the world of injustice, inequality and oppression, and announced a world where,

> ... [t]hey shall beat their swords into plowshares, and their spears into pruning hooks; nation shall not lift up sword against nation neither shall they learn war any more; but they shall all sit under their own vies and under their own fig trees, and no on shall make them afraid (Micah 4:3-4).

In order to bond with God to create a world free of competition, war and greed, we must have a new understanding of *ecclesia* or a new understanding of who God's people are. A new understanding of God's people may require us to take a theological leap, to embrace those who are committed and take risks to do God's work irrespective of their religious beliefs, rather than confining our understanding to baptized Christians or the institutional church, which make the claim to represent God's people. This thought should accompany Jesus' saying, "Not everyone who calls me 'Lord, Lord' will enter the kingdom of Heaven, but only the one who does the will of my Father in heaven" (Matt. 7:21).

If we accept this theological premise then the ecumenical movement should have the humility

- To forge alliances and work in partnership with people of diverse faith communities and with civil society groups to work out ethical principles and methods to engage in advocacy;
- To bring together from time to time diverse religious and community-based groups to reflect on issues related to humanizing the world, and draw from diverse spiritual reservoirs to empower people to take risks to mend the broken creation;
- To go beyond the "churchy mentality" to recognize the God who transcends all barriers, institutions and ideologies, and accompany those already engaged in the work of transformation;
- To encourage and support communities and movements in nations and regions already committed to change, and provide resources to build bridges so that they

can become a movement for justice, peace and reconciliation;

- To encourage national churches and local congregations to work in partnership with people of diverse and even no faiths, to work for justice, peace and reconciliation rather than compete with one another; and
- To encourage religious communities to draw from their spiritual resources a common ethical code which can become the norm for everyone

These are some of the ways we can work in multi-religious communities where Christianity is no longer the faith of the majority. Even in countries where Christianity is the majority faith, it must have the humility or the mind of Christ to work in partnership with others.

The world in which we live is part of God's creation. However, we are aware that all creation is groaning in pain. Therefore, our calling is to be a healing and a reconciling community. This involves being the church in a new way, which in turn involves imitating Jesus the Christ, so that the world will experience and know the compassion, mercy, peace and justice of God.

CENTRAL COMMITTEE STATEMENT ON JUST FINANCE AND THE ECONOMY OF LIFE

And Jesus said to them, "Take care! Be on your guard against all kinds of greed; for one's life does not consist in the abundance of possessions." (Luke 12:15)

1. The World Council of Churches (WCC) first articulated its concerns about finance and economics in 1984 when it issued a call for a new international order based on ethical principles and social justice. In 1998, the WCC assembly in Harare mandated a study on economic globalization together with member churches. WCC worked closely with the World Alliance of Reformed Churches, the Lutheran World Federation, Aprodev and other specialized ministries. Out of this, the Alternative Globalization Addressing People and Earth (AGAPE) process, which was set up to further study the topics of poverty, wealth and ecology, was born. During the course of this process, several issues relating to various crises were identified: climate change and the food, social and financial crises. In May 2009, the WCC convened a meeting of the Advisory Group on Economic Matters (AGEM) to (1) discern what is at stake in the current financial architecture, (2) propose a process that could lead to a new financial architecture and (3) outline the theological and ethical basis for such a new architecture.

2. Jesus warns that, "You cannot serve both God and wealth" (Luke 16:13). We, however, witness greed manifested dramatically in the financial and economic systems of our times. The current financial crisis presents an opportunity to re-examine our engagement and action. It is an opportunity for us to discern together how to devise a system that is not only sustainable but that is just and moral. Economics is a matter of faith and has an impact on human existence and all of creation.

3. The financial system of recent times has shaped the world more than ever before. However, by becoming the engine of virtual growth and wealth, it has enriched some people but has harmed many more, creating poverty, unemployment, hunger and death; widening the gap between rich and poor; marginalizing certain groups of people; eroding the whole meaning of human life; and destroying ecosystems. There is a growing and sobering awareness of our common vulnerability and of the limits of our current way of life. Today's global financial crisis, which originated in the richest parts of our world, points to the immorality of a system that glorifies money and has a dehumanizing effect by encouraging acquisitive individualism. The resulting greed-based culture impoverishes human life, erodes the moral and ecol fabric of human civilization, and intoxicates our psyche with materialism. The cris is, at the same time, both systemic and moral. Those most affected are wom

disproportionate share of the burden; young people and children, as doubts are raised and their sense of security for the future is eroded; and those living in poverty, whose suffering deepens.

4. In an era of financial globalization, economic expansion has been increasingly driven by greed. This greed, a hallmark of the current financial system, causes and intensifies the sacrifice and suffering of impoverished human beings, while the wealthy classes multiply their riches. Finance is, at best, the lubricant of real economic activities. However, we note that money is not wealth; it has no inherent value outside the human mind. When it is turned into a series of fictitious instruments to create ever more financial wealth it is increasingly divorcing itself from the real economy, thereby creating only virtual or phantom wealth that does not produce anything to meet real human needs.

5. The abuse of global finance and trade by international businesses costs developing countries more than 160 billion US dollars a year in lost tax revenues – undermining desperately-needed public expenditures. Developing countries are lending their reserves to industrial countries at very low interest rates and are borrowing back at higher rates. This results in a net transfer of resources to reserve currency countries that exceed more than ten times the value of foreign assistance, according to the United Nations Development Programme (UNDP). This global financial crisis is proving the bankruptcy of the neoliberal doctrine, as promoted by the International Financial Institutions through the "Washington Consensus". The leaders of the rich countries that promoted the consensus so emphatically declared it "over" at the G20 meeting in April 2009. And yet much of the G20's agenda reflects misguided efforts to restore the same system of overexploitation of resources and unlimited growth. Furthermore, resources are channelled through the militarization of some societies, due to a perverse understanding of human security through military power.

6. Unfortunately, churches have also been complicit in this system, relying on popular models of finance and economics that prioritize generating money over the progress and wellbeing of humanity. These models are largely oblivious to the social and ecological costs of financial and economic decisions, and often lack moral direction. The challenge for churches today is to not retr͏͏ eir prophetic role. They are also challenged by their complicity with this system and its embedded greed.

ural elements of the current paradigm which must be changed ͏ surplus value, unlimited growth and the irresponsible cons urces contradict biblical values and make it impossible for ͏mpassion and love. Secondly, the system that privatizes pr ͏nnecting them from people's work and needs and denyir access to and use of them is a structural obstacle to an economy of cooperation, sharing, love and dynamic harmony with nature. Alternative morality for economic activity is service/ *koinonia* (fellowship) to human needs; human/social self-development; and people's wellbeing and happiness. An alternative to the current property system is connected to need, use and work invested in the production and distribution process. In order to achieve this goal, the existing organizing principles of production and claims settlements (i.e., distribution) must change. This also warrants a situation where an ethical, just and democratic global financial architecture emerges and is grounded on a framework of common values: honesty, social justice, human dignity, mutual accountability and ecological sustainability. It should also account for social and ecological risks in financial and economic calculation; reconnect finance to the real economy; and set clear limits to, as well as penalize, excessive and irresponsible actions based on greed.

8. It is in this context that the central committee of the WCC acknowledges that a new ethos and culture which reflects the values of solidarity, common good and inclusion must, at this time of crisis, emerge to replace the anti-values of greed, individualism and exclusion. New indicators of progress other than Gross Domestic Product, such as the Human Development Index, the Gross National Happiness (GNH) index, ecological footprints and other corresponding systems of accounting need to be evolved. For example, a GNH index that reflects the following values: 1) Quality and pattern of life; 2) Good governance (true democracy); 3) Education; 4) Health; 5) Ecological resilience; 6) Cultural diversity; 7) Community vitality; 8) Balanced use of time; and 9) Psychological and spiritual wellbeing.

9. The central committee of the WCC also emphasizes the need for a new paradigm of economic development and a reconceptualization of wealth to include relationships, care and compassion, solidarity and love, aesthetics and the ethics of life, participation and celebration, cultural diversity and community vitality. This will involve responsible growth that recognizes human responsibility for creation and for future generations – an economy glorifying life.

In view of the need to support international organizations that are democratic, to represent all member nations of the United Nations (UN) and to affirm common values, the central committee of the WCC, meeting in Geneva, Switzerland, 26 August – 2 September 2009, calls upon governments to take the following necessary actions:

A. *Adopt* new and more balanced indicators, such as the Gross National Happiness (GNH) index, to monitor global socio-environmental/ecological-economic progress.
B. *Ensure* that resources are not diverted from basic education, public health, and poor countries.

C.   *Uphold* their commitments to and assistance for meeting the Millennium Development Goals (MDGs), particularly the goal number 8 on cooperation worldwide.

D.   *Implement* gender-just social protection programs as an important part of national fiscal stimulus packages in response to the current financial crisis.

E.   *Emphasize* the participation of people and civil society organizations in policy-making processes, including the promotion of decentralized governance structures and participatory democracy.

F.   *Treat* finance as a public service by making loans available to small and medium enterprises, farmers and particularly poor people through, for example, microfinancing in support of not-for-profit enterprises and the social economy.

G.   *Support* regional initiatives that decentralize finance and empower people in the global South to exercise control over their own development through such proposed bodies as the Bank of the South, the Asian Monetary Fund and the Bank of ALBA.

H.   *Revise* taxation systems, recognizing that tax revenues are ultimately the only sustainable source of development finances, by establishing an international accounting standard requiring country-by-country reporting of transnational companies' economic activities and taxes paid and by forging a multilateral agreement to set a mandatory requirement for the automatic exchange of tax information between all jurisdictions to prevent tax avoidance.

I.   *Explore* the possibility of establishing a new global reserve system based on a supranational global reserve currency and regional and local currencies.

J.   *Achieve* stronger democratic oversight of international financial institutions by making them subject to a UN Global Economic Council with the same status as the UN Security Council.

K.   *Explore* the possibility of setting up a new international credit agency with greater democratic governance than currently exists under the Bretton Woods institutions

L.   *Set up* an international bankruptcy court with the authority to cancel odious and other kinds of illegitimate debts and to arbitrate other debt issues.

M.   *Regulate* and *reform* the credit agency industry into proper independent supervision institution(s), based on more transparency about ratings and strict regulation on the management of conflict of interest.

N.   *Use* innovative sources of finance, including carbon and financial transaction taxes, to pay for global public goods and poverty eradication.

Approved by unanimous consensus by the Central Committee of the World Council of Churches, 2 September 2009

OTHER WCC PUBLICATIONS ON ECONOMY SINCE 2000

Poverty, Wealth and Ecology in Asia and the Pacific: Ecumenical Perspectives, World Council of Churches and Christian Conference of Asia, WCC Publications, 2010.

Poverty, Wealth and Ecology: The Impact of Economic Globalization. A Background to the Study Process, Rogate R. Mshana (ed), Geneva: WCC Publications, 2008.

Alternative Globalization Addressing People and Earth (AGAPE), A Background Document, Rogate R. Mshana (ed.), Geneva: WCC Publications, 2006, (translated from English into, German, Italian, Hungarian, Norwegian, Indonesian and Korean.).

Ecological Debt: The Peoples of the South and Creditors- Cases from Ecuador, Mozambique, Brazil and India, Athena Peralta (ed.), Geneva: WCC Publications, 2006.

Poverty Eradication and Injustice: Differences and Common Ground: The WCC encounters with the World Bank and the IMF, Rogate R. Mshana (ed.), Geneva: WCC Publications, 2004.

The Debt Problem for Poor Countries: Where Are We? A Report on Illegitimate Debt and Arbitration, Rogate R. Mshana (ed.), Geneva: WCC Publications, 2004.

In Search of a Just Economy: Common Goals, Separate Journeys, Rogate R. Mshana (ed.), Geneva: WCC Publications, 2003.

Wealth Creation and Justice, Rogate R. Mshana (ed.), Geneva: WCC Publications, 2003.

Passion for Another World: Building Just and Participatory Communities, Rogate R. Mshana (ed.) , Geneva: WCC Publications, 2003.

"The Impact of Globalization on Eastern/ Central Europe", *The Ecumenical Review*, World Council of Churches, Volume 53, Number 4, October 2001.

Unpublished documents on economy and ecology

"Climate Change and World Council of Churches: Background Information and Recent Statements", November 2009. http://www.oikoumene.org/climatechange

"Alternative Globalization Addressing People and Earth (AGAPE, Consultation Report on "Linking Poverty, Wealth and Ecology: African Perspectives", WCC, 2007). Available in French and English.

Poverty, Wealth and Ecology: Ecumenical Perspectives from Latin America and the Caribbean, edited by Rogate R. Mshana, Spanish version by Council of Churches in Latin America (CLAI) and English Version by WCC, Geneva, 2009.

A Study on Wealth Creation, Poverty and Ecology in Africa, Clement Kwayu, WCC 2007. Available in English and French.

"Semillas de Alternativas a la Globalizacion", Dossier por José Cuauhtémoc Lopez Vazquez, WCC 2006.

"Life-Giving Agriculture Global Forum April, 2005", Ecumenical Coalition on Alternatives to Globalization (The Lutheran World Federation, World Council of Churches, World Alliance on Reformed Churches, World YWCA

"Economic Globalization: A Critical View and an Alternative Vision". Programme Implementation ed. by Rogate R. Mshana, WCC, Justice Peace and Creation, Geneva 2002.

"Lead us not into temptation: Churches' response to the policies of International Financial Institutions. A background document", WCC, October, 2001, Translated into German, Spanish, French and Russian.

"Island of Hope: A Pacific Alternative to Economic Globalization", Report of the Churches' Conference on Economic Globalization – Island of Hope, Nadi, Fiji 2001, WCC Publications.

"Linking Trade and Trafficking in Women in Asia to Neo Liberal Economic Globalization", Athena Peralta.

Related books and documents by churches

Michael Taylor, *Christianity, Poverty and Wealth: the findings of "Project 21"*, Geneva: WCC Publications, APRODEV, 2003.

"The Church and Economic Globalization", by The Commission on International Affairs, Church of Norway Council of Churches on Ecumenical and International Relations, Oslo, 2007 (Responding to the WCC AGAPE document).

"Globalization: a Call to Listen, a Challenge to Respond: Church and Society", Presbyterian Church (U.S.A), March/April 2006 (Addressing the AGAPE call).

"European Churches Living their Faith in the Context of Globalization, Church and Society Commission on the Conference of European Churches", CEC, Brussels, 2006 (responding to the WCC AGAPE background document).

"Globalisierung, Wirtschaft im Dienst des Lebens-Stellungnahme der Evangelischen Kirche von Westfalen zum Soesterberg-Brief", Evangelischer Presseverband fèr Westfalen und Lippe, Bielefeld, 2005.

"The Accra Confession: Covenanting for Justice in the Economy and the Earth", World Alliance of Reformed Churches, Geneva 2005.